The Veganopolis Cookbook

A Manual for Great Vegan Cooking

By David Stowell and George Black

Surrey Books

An Agate Imprint

Chicago

Surrey Books is an imprint of Agate Publishing, Inc.

All photography copyright © 2010 Michael Pocius

Printed in the United States of America.

Library of Congress Cataloging-in-Publication Data

Stowell, David.
 The Veganopolis cookbook : a manual for great vegan cooking / David Stowell and George Black.
     p. cm.
 Includes index.
 ISBN-13: 978-1-57284-110-9 (pbk.)
 ISBN-10: 1-57284-110-9 (pbk.)
 1. Vegetarian cooking.   2. Vegan cooking.   3. Veganopolis (Restaurant)
 I. Black, George. II. Title.
 TX837.S777 2010
 641.5'636--dc22

                                                           2010028123

14 13 12 11 10   10 9 8 7 6 5 4 3 2 1

Agate and Surrey books are available in bulk at discount prices. For more information, go to agatepublishing.com.

Dedication

We would like to dedicate this volume to those people who have taught, encouraged, and helped us in our development, both as chefs and as lovers of the millions of beautiful creatures with whom we share this amazing and interesting world:

Alysin, Andrew, Isabel, Santos, Lindsay, Luis, Bernard, Rhoda, Mimi, Dennis, Sara, Todd, Angel, Tammy, Michael VP, Mickey, and, of course, our families. Thanks for your support as test-recipe-result consultants in one way or another.

Contents

Introduction

George's Introduction

Welcome to the Veganopolis kitchen. Everyone is welcome! You need not be a culinary program graduate, nor must your pantry contain a long list of specialty ingredients to achieve success with the recipes in this book. We encourage you to use them as a starting point, and by all means create your own variations and add your own flair.

The recipes in this book are not difficult. They produce dishes that might be termed casual gourmet cuisine or, perhaps, vegan comfort food. You will find soups; sauces; vegan proteins; baked goods; and breakfast, lunch, brunch, and dinner items. The bulk of the recipes are identical to the ones we use in our restaurant, and the dishes have been prepared and served the same way many hundreds of times with dependable results.

Operating in the fast-paced environment of a busy restaurant kitchen, we learned to keep a tight inventory, to find the quickest techniques for preparing ingredients, and to streamline the recipes so that they could be faithfully reproduced day after day. Think of prepping, seasoning, cooking, and serving about ten thousand pounds of potatoes a year. Then multiply that work by 50 menu items, and you may begin to understand the need for speed in a restaurant kitchen.

We also learned to continually develop and offer new menu items to keep our customers enticed and excited, as well as to keep ourselves and our staff sharp and involved. We encourage you to do the same and to keep your kitchen moving forward with new ideas and new items.

All the recipes in this book are made using vegan, animal-free ingredients. We have done a great deal of study in this area and have tried to pass on what we have learned.

White sugar manufactured and sold in the United States is filtered through bone char, a byproduct of the slaughterhouse industry. The Veganopolis kitchen uses evaporated cane juice, or turbinado sugar as a healthier, cruelty-free alternative. Agave syrup also makes a great sweetener. We have replaced animal fats with vegetable oils and shortenings in all our recipes. We have also replaced gelatin, which is made from animal bones. To substitute dairy ingredients, we use rice, soy, or almond beverage and vegan margarines.

Let's Get Started!

First, prepare your deck. We refer to your prep area as your deck because it is the place where the culinary journey begins. At the restaurant, the deck is where we perform the early morning tasks that set the stage and guide each day through its twists and turns and often to a surprise or a happy accident that might result in a new dish.

Our top kitchen staff members—Isabel, Santos, and Angel—enter first to wash and sanitize the tables and cutting boards. A spray bottle containing a mixture of 1 part nonchlorine bleach to 10 parts water makes kitchen resets a breeze.

Read the Recipe

Before you start, read the recipe through once to familiarize yourself with what you will need. Then read it again. This will help you get organized and ready to create something fabulous! Look for cooking tips and ingredient substitutions in many recipes in the book.

Mise en Place

Gather all your ingredients before you begin a recipe. You can use small bowls and cups to hold prepared vegetables, oils, and measured flours and other dry ingredients. Then, when the recipe calls for the addition of an ingredient, you will have it at hand and ready to use.

Pots, Pans, and Plans

Things move fast while you are cooking, so be sure to have two or more clean kitchen towels at hand and your pots, pans, and baking sheets all ready to go. A roll of parchment paper is great to have handy—in addition to providing a nonstick surface, it makes cleaning up your baking sheets much easier.

You can also use a lipped serving tray measuring approximately 20 × 14 inches (50 × 35 cm) on your countertop as a surface to prepare and knead dough. You may find the tray more convenient to clean than a large area of your counter space.

A Vegan Pantry Inventory

This is a complete list of the items you may need to prepare almost all of the recipes in the book. Of course, you need not purchase all of them to begin cooking. Some of these ingredients may require a trip to a specialty store or a natural foods store.

Spices

Achiote paste

Asafetida

Brown mustard seed

Cayenne pepper

Chia seeds

Chili powder

Chipotle chile powder

Freshly ground black pepper

Garlic powder

Ground cardamom

Ground cinnamon

Ground cumin

Ground nutmeg

Ground turmeric

Ground white pepper

Italian seasoning

Onion powder

Oregano

Paprika

Poppy seeds

Red chile flakes

Saffron

Sea salt

Smoked paprika

Whole fennel seed

Flours

Garbanzo bean flour

Quinoa flour

Rice flour (for kneading)

Unbleached white spelt flour

Vital wheat gluten

Raw Nuts and Seeds

Almonds

Cashews

Pine nuts

Pumpkin seeds

Sunflower seeds

Hazelnuts

Flavorings and Extracts

Almond extract

Cocoa powder (good-quality, Dutch-process recommended)

Natural lemon flavoring or lemon oil

Natural orange flavoring or orange oil

Pure vanilla extract

Oils

Canola oil (a great all-purpose oil)

Grapeseed oil (for sauces, dressings, vegan mayo, or sautéing)

Olive oil (for sauces, dressings, baking, or sautéing)

Safflower oil (as all-purpose vegetable oil, or for sautéing)

Vegan margarine (contains no casein, caseinate, whey, or fish oils)

Vinegars

Apple cider vinegar

Balsamic vinegar

Champagne vinegar

Distilled white vinegar

Red wine vinegar

Seasoned rice vinegar

Sherry vinegar

White wine vinegar

Sweeteners

Pure maple syrup

Raw agave syrup

Turbinado sugar (evaporated cane juice)

Thickeners

Agar powder or flakes

Arrowroot powder

Cornstarch

Stocks

Vegetable broth bouillon cubes

Vegetable broth powder

Rices and Grains

Barley

Basmati rice

Pale quinoa

Organic wild rice

Quick-cooking oats

Whole-grain wheat berries

A Note about Pastas

Spelt, quinoa, and amaranth have the highest nutritional values among pastas. Jerusalem artichoke pastas also have high nutritional value and produce good results. Semolina pastas are abundant and available in many varieties.

A Note about Tofu

The quality of packaged tofu depends almost entirely on one step in the processing of the soybeans: washing and rinsing them thoroughly before cooking. Manufacturers who skip this step produce tofu that is loaded with indigestible elements, creating a tofu that, while it appears the same as other brands, is really unpleasant to digest. Take the time to find the finest tofu you can. A few pennies more per pound is really worth the difference it will make to your finished dishes. Look for organic and/or non-GMO indications on the label, which usually indicates a superior product.

Some Cooking Suggestions

- When working with rye dough and other dense doughs, divide the dough and place each half in a separate rising bowl to speed the process.

- Instead of oil, you may use vegetable stock or a combination of oil and vegetable stock to sauté vegetables for lower oil content in the finished dish.

- A little fresh lemon juice will prevent apples and pears from discoloring as they sit in cold water waiting to be used in a recipe. The same applies to root vegetables such as parsnips, turnips, and rutabagas.

- After roasting peppers, immediately place them in a bowl and cover with an inverted plate. As they cool to room temperature, the contained steam will loosen their skins and make them easier to peel.

- To make larger portions of tofu scrambles, you may heat the crumbled and seasoned tofu in a covered dish in the oven while you sauté the vegetables on the stovetop. When the tofu is hot, simply add the sautéed vegetables from the pan to the tofu, stir, check for seasonings, and serve.

- To replace buttermilk in biscuits, add a tablespoon of fresh lemon juice to your vegan soy or rice beverage and let stand while you prepare the dry ingredients. The lemon juice will clabber the milk substitute and provide that slightly sour flavor that will make your biscuits irresistible.

- Flax meal may be added to crusts, rolls, biscuits, or breads for a nutrition boost. Flax meal or flaxseed allowed to stand in warm water for thirty minutes produces a gel that may be used as a binder or as a syrup if sweetened with sugar or agave.

- Try using cardamom pods, cinnamon sticks, or a vanilla bean to create different flavored syrups. Boil the whole spice in a simple syrup made from 1 cup (236 mL) water and 8 tablespoons (120 mL) turbinado sugar, and then strain the liquid.

- Lemons stored in water in the refrigerator will release more juice when squeezed.

- Tomatoes that look as though they are about to spoil can be brought back by dipping them in very cold water, toweling them dry, and placing them in a container in which a layer of salt has been spread over the bottom. Fresh tomatoes can be saved by blanching, peeling, seeding, and chopping or puréeing them. Frozen tomatoes can be used in sauces and soups.

- To dice an onion without tearing up, try chilling the onion in the freezer for a few minutes to subdue the irritants. Be sure to use a very sharp knife for dicing.

- Fresh basil is best stored outside the refrigerator, stems downward, in a glass of water.

- Freshly made vinaigrettes will improve if they are allowed to stand for thirty minutes or longer before serving. When tossing salad greens in vinaigrettes, coat the sides of the bowl with the vinaigrette first, and then add the greens to toss. A wooden or ceramic bowl is best for salads, as metal bowls may react with the acids in the vinegars and affect the flavor.

- White rice can be brightened in tone by adding a quarter lemon to the water during cooking.

- When boiling pastas of any kind, salt the water and add a few tablespoons of inexpensive vegetable oil before adding the pasta.

David and I hope that you enjoy preparing the recipes in this book and that the book earns a permanent place in your kitchen.

David's Introduction

"A bellyfull is a bellyfull." —Rabelais, *Gargantua and Pantagruel*

George and I met in 1979 and formed a rock-and-roll band. At our first rehearsal, I served the band some chili I had made that day, so cooking and making music began at the same time for us. At that time, I was working in catering businesses and restaurants, learning everything I could from professional chefs such as Bob Gianetti, Didier Durand, and my pastry chef from school, Bernard Neveu. Over the years, we experimented in the kitchen and developed our skills.

One day in 1985, George came home from a farmer's market with some literature about factory farming. He became a vegetarian that very day. It took me another year to become a vegetarian, and several years later I became a vegan. In 1991, we went to Paris, where I attended the Ritz-Escoffier School of French Gastronomy at the Hôtel Ritz at the Place Vendôme. I wanted to learn the classic techniques of cooking from the top chefs, and the Escoffier School gave me that opportunity.

The two most important things I learned at the Escoffier School had nothing to do with dicing vegetables or rolling out perfectly prepared croissant dough. First, there were the encouraging words of my chef de cuisine, Jean Louis Thibaux. He saw me struggling with a dish and, in his deeply French-inflected English, kept saying "No paneek, no paneek." I took this advice to heart, and I try to remember to never panic in the kitchen. The kitchen is a place where order, grace, and harmony should reign and panic should be banished.

The second thing that I learned was from the maître d'hôtel at the Ritz, who told us that two subjects of conversation are taboo in the kitchen and dining room—religion and politics. After delivering this gem of wisdom, the graceful maître d' waited a moment for his words to sink in and then grinned. "It's bad for the digestion," he said. This maxim has shaped not only my thinking about preparing and serving food, but also my attitude toward society.

We have been promising this cookbook for years to customers, friends, and family, and we are happy to have the opportunity to assemble it. We have made every attempt to provide clear instructions and to share the tips and procedures we have learned over the years in professional kitchens.

Our goal is to apply the classic techniques of professional chefs to the vegan environment and to bring cruelty-free cuisine into the domain of the gourmet.

George and I hope that you enjoy the recipes in this book.

CHAPTER 1

Stocks and Soups

A Note about Stocks

Auguste Escoffier believed that stocks were the single most important element in one's kitchen, and we agree. Many of the recipes in this book are best produced by adding good-quality vegetable stock. You can make your own, and it is quite rewarding to do so. It is also much more economical, in that you can use vegetable scraps that may otherwise be discarded.

However, commercially produced stocks can be more convenient, and I often use these. Try to find the best vegetable base you can. Gel bases are usually superior to the powdered variety. Some markets sell canned or boxed liquid vegetable broths, some of which are of good quality, but I prefer gel bases because I can control the richness of the stock by adding more or less of the base to water. A nondiluted gel base can also be used right out of the container as a glaze for a lentil loaf.

The production of a rich vegetable stock depends on cooking the stock correctly and for a long time. Be patient and let your stock simmer all day if possible. If you are going to the trouble of making stock, make a large quantity and freeze some of it for future use. To do this, let the finished, strained stock cool to room temperature. Then measure it into sealable, plastic 1-quart (.95-L) containers and place them in the freezer for later use.

Rich Vegetable Stock

YIELD: 4 QUARTS (3.8 L)

> 6 stalks celery
>
> 6 carrots
>
> 4 tomatoes
>
> 3½ medium onions, any kind, peeled
>
> 2 leeks
>
> 1 bunch parsley
>
> ¼ cup (59 mL) canola oil
>
> ½ onion, blackened over a gas flame or under a broiler
>
> 3 bay leaves
>
> 2 tablespoons (30 mL) black peppercorns

1. Rinse and chop the celery, carrots, tomatoes, onions, leeks, and parsley roughly (you do not need to peel them).

2. Put the canola oil in your largest stockpot and heat over medium-high heat until it is bubbling hot.

3. Add the chopped vegetables, blackened onion, bay leaves, and peppercorns.

4. Cook thoroughly over medium heat, stirring frequently, until the vegetables are fully browned, about 30 minutes.

5. Add enough water to cover the vegetables by about 4 inches (10 cm). Bring to a full rolling boil and then reduce to a low simmer and cook for 3 to 4 hours, skimming the stock every 30 minutes to remove any scum on the surface. Discard the scum.

6. When the stock is finished, it will be golden brown and fragrant. Strain it through a large fine-mesh strainer into a clean pot. If you wish your stock to be absolutely clear, you may strain it again through cheesecloth.

7. At this point, you may continue to cook the stock down into a more concentrated reduction. This reduction can be stored and/or frozen for later use.

Cooks' Note

This recipe is produced without salt, so you will need to add salt to your recipe to bring out the flavor of your stock. Commercial vegetable stocks and bases often have a high concentration of salt, so you may need to add quite a bit to make your home stock taste like the commercial varieties.

You can add shallots, scallions, fresh herbs, and other vegetable scraps (such as mushroom stems, etc.) to a vegetable stock. The addition of starchy vegetables such as potatoes, however, will produce a cloudy stock that may be undesirable in a soup with a clear broth base. Avoid highly acidic vegetables such as bell peppers, as they tend to dominate the flavor of any dish.

Soups, Soups, Soups

I love making soups. At the restaurant, I usually make the soup of the day before anything else, starting early in the morning when my mind is relaxed and my palate is clean. If the soup comes out well, I sense that the whole day will go in a positive direction—and it usually does.

When using dry spices in a soup or sauce, add them at the beginning of the cooking process, not at the end. For example, when you begin a soup by cooking onions in oil, add the dry spices at the same time. The aromatic elements in the spices will be released into the hot oil and will permeate the entire soup or sauce. If you wait until the end of the cooking procedure to add dried thyme, for example, the thyme will simply float around without imparting much flavor at all.

I cannot overemphasize the importance of *tasting* while you cook, and this is especially true when it comes to soups. The flavor of the soup will most likely be your guests' first impression of your kitchen.

So please taste your soup before serving it. Is there enough salt? Can you taste the seasonings? Is there enough acidity to the soup? Have your salt and vinegars at hand as you finish your soup, and trust yourself. If you have made a certain soup numerous times, you will know precisely how it should taste. If you are working on something new, trust your nose and your tongue.

Many of the soups in this cookbook need to be blended before they are served. I use an immersion blender to blend soups right in the pot they were cooked in. You can get a professional-quality immersion blender, and if you do a lot of cooking, you should consider getting one. They are simple to use, safe, and easy to clean. Otherwise, you'll need to blend your puréed soups in small batches in a blender or a food processor and return them to the pot for reheating.

Bouillabaisse with Rouille

This classic is traditionally made with six different kinds of fish. The flavor and texture of this vegan version will delight you and your guests; this makes a wonderful special occasion soup. Don't skimp on the saffron. Though it is expensive, this spice is essential to the remarkable flavor of this soup.

This recipe involves a bit of vegetable trimming for an elegant effect. You can cut your vegetables roughly for a more country-style soup if you prefer or if you don't have time to make all of those neat little bâtonnets. Either way, this soup is marvelous. Rouille means "rust" in French, which is just the color you are looking for.

YIELD: 3 QUARTS (2.85 L)

¼ cup (59 mL) extra virgin olive oil, plus more as needed

3 leeks, thoroughly washed and sliced into ⅛-inch (¼-cm) rounds

2 medium yellow onions, peeled and thinly sliced

4 large, ripe tomatoes, peeled, seeded, and diced, or 1 (12-ounce [336-g]) can diced tomatoes with their juice

10 cloves garlic, peeled and crushed

1½ cups (375 mL) very dry white wine or dry white vermouth

2 quarts (1.9 L) good-quality vegetable stock

1 bunch Italian parsley, thoroughly washed, dried, stemmed, and finely chopped

2 pinches saffron

1 orange peel, stripped off carefully into long pieces, avoiding the pith*

1 lemon peel, prepared as the orange peel

1 bay leaf

2 teaspoons (10 mL) dried thyme

1 large, firm, waxy potato, whole and unpeeled

2 large, firm, waxy potatoes, peeled and diced into ¼-inch (.5-cm) bâtonnets about 1 inch (2.5 cm) long

3 large carrots, peeled and sliced into bâtonnets

3 medium parsnips, peeled and sliced into bâtonnets

1 fennel bulb, outer parts removed, sliced into bâtonnets

2 medium turnips, peeled and sliced into bâtonnets

1 teaspoon (5 mL) salt

1 teaspoon (5 mL) cayenne pepper

Freshly ground black pepper, for seasoning

1 baguette, sliced into ½-inch (1-cm) rounds, brushed with olive oil, and toasted

1. Warm the olive oil in a large, heavy-bottomed soup pot over medium heat. Add the leeks and onions, and cook until the onions are soft and transparent.

2. Stir in the tomatoes and 3 tablespoons (45 mL) of the crushed garlic, and cook for 5 minutes.

3. Add the wine or vermouth and cook until the mixture is reduced by half—about 10 minutes. Add the stock, 4 tablespoons (60 mL) of the chopped parsley, 1 pinch of the saffron, the orange peel, the lemon peel, the bay leaf, and the thyme. Bring to a boil.

4. Add the whole potato to the boiling pot.

5. Add the chopped potatoes, carrots, parsnips, fennel, and turnips, and cook until all the vegetables are tender, about 40 minutes. Near the end of the cooking time, skim the surface well.

6. To make the rouille, remove the whole potato from the soup when it is fully cooked and slice it in half. Carefully scoop the flesh out of the peel with a spoon and place the pulp in a food processor. Add the remaining crushed garlic, the other pinch of saffron, the salt, and the cayenne pepper.

7. With the food processor running, add about ½ to ¾ cup (125 to 177.5 mL) of the soup liquid to the potato garlic mixture and process until you achieve a creamy but thick consistency. With the food processor still running, add the olive oil until you get a thick, rust-colored sauce that stands in a mound by itself. Taste for seasonings and add salt as needed.

8. When all of the vegetables in the soup are tender, remove the bay leaf and the orange and lemon peels and discard. Taste the soup and add salt as needed.

Cooks' Note

To serve, fill large soup bowls with the soup. Take one of the toasted baguette slices, place a large dollop of rouille in the center of it, and float it in each serving of soup. Sprinkle the entire bowl with parsley and serve immediately.

Serve the rouille at the table in a small bowl surrounded by the remaining baguette slices. I would recommend a full-flavored white wine, such as a white Burgundy, with this meal. If you want a more traditional bouillabaisse, try adding chunks of vegan tuna substitute that have been marinated for an hour or two in olive oil, garlic, and saffron.

*To easily strip the peel from an orange or lemon, take a very sharp vegetable peeler and, starting at the stem end, cut away from the surface of the fruit the thinnest layer that you can in a downward descending spiral pattern. Try to avoid the white pith inside, as it may impart a bitter flavor to the dish. With a little practice, you should be able to strip most of the peel from the fruit in one long strip.

Cream of Broccoli Soup

A simple roux thickens this soup, and a hint of lemon sparkles up the flavor.

YIELD: 3 QUARTS (2.85 L)

2 quarts (1.9 L) rice or soy beverage

2 or 3 heads fresh broccoli, cut into florets

¼ cup (59 mL) olive oil

⅓ cup (79 mL) white spelt flour

3 shallots, peeled and very finely diced

Zest and juice of 1 lemon

2 teaspoons (10 mL) white pepper

½ teaspoon (2.5 mL) grated nutmeg

½ teaspoon (2.5 mL) cayenne pepper

Salt and freshly ground black pepper, to taste

1. Fill a large pot with water and bring to a boil.

2. Fill a second large pot with the rice or soy beverage and place it over medium heat.

3. Salt the boiling water liberally. Add the broccoli florets and blanch for about 8 minutes. Drain the florets in a colander and cool them down under cold running water. Alternatively, you can place the florets in a microwave-safe bowl with a cup of water, cover the bowl, and microwave it on high for about 10 minutes.

4. In a large, heavy-bottomed soup pot (you may use the same one that you have just blanched the broccoli florets in), heat the olive oil over medium-high heat. When it is hot (but not smoking), add the flour and use a long-handled whisk to combine the flour and oil into a paste. Continue whisking the roux until it is cooked and just starting to darken, about 4 minutes.

5. Whisk in the shallots and lemon zest, followed by the white pepper, nutmeg, cayenne pepper, and salt to taste.

6. Cook the roux, shallot, and spice mixture for another 2 minutes to incorporate the flavors. Add the hot soy or rice beverage 2 cups (473 mL) at a time, whisking between each addition to produce a smooth, creamy soup base.

7. Add most of the blanched broccoli florets, reserving 10 or 15 of the smallest ones to use as garnish.

8. Simmer for about 15 minutes, and then either blend the soup smooth with an immersion blender or blend it in batches in a food processor, returning it to the pot and heating it to serving temperature.

9. Add the reserved florets.

10. Stir in the lemon juice and adjust for salt. Serve in bowls garnished with a grinding of black pepper, if desired.

Variation

Add 2 cups (473 mL) fresh or frozen corn kernels after blending for Cream of Broccoli Soup. Cook the soup after adding the corn kernels for an additional 10 minutes over medium heat, stirring frequently.

Creamy Potato Leek Soup with Roasted Garlic

Potato leek soup is a standard of French cuisine. Served cold, it is called vichyssoise and makes a lovely, light, summertime soup. The addition of oven-roasted garlic to this version gives it a delicious flavor. Roasting garlic reduces its acidity and brings the sugars out, making it mild and sweet. Toasted pumpernickel bread makes a nice visual contrast for this pale soup.

YIELD: 3 QUARTS (2.85 L)

> 15 cloves garlic, peeled
>
> ¾ cup (177 mL) water
>
> ¼ cup (59 mL) plus 4 tablespoons (60 mL) olive oil, divided
>
> 3 leeks, thoroughly washed and sliced into ⅛-inch (¼-cm) rounds
>
> 1 tablespoon (15 mL) salt, plus more for roasting garlic
>
> 10–12 small to medium potatoes, peeled and diced, about 3 pounds (1.36 kg)
>
> 2 teaspoons (10 mL) white pepper
>
> 1 teaspoon (5 mL) grated nutmeg
>
> 2 quarts (1.9 L) rice or soy beverage
>
> 4 scallions, thinly sliced, for garnish
>
> Seasoned rice vinegar, to taste

1. Preheat the oven to 350°F (180°C).

2. Roast the garlic by placing the cloves in a small ovenproof pan with the water, 4 tablespoons of the olive oil, and 1 pinch salt. Cover the pan tightly with foil, and roast for about 40 minutes, or until the garlic cloves are brown and very soft.

3. In a large, heavy-bottomed soup pot, heat 4 tablespoons (60 mL) olive oil over medium heat and then add the sliced leeks and salt. Stir well and cook until the leeks are quite soft, about 10 to 12 minutes.

4. Stir in the diced potatoes, white pepper, and nutmeg.

5. Add the rice or soy beverage, enough to cover the potatoes by about 3 inches (7.5 cm). (If 1 quart [.95 L] of rice or soy beverage is not enough, add water until the liquid reaches the necessary level.) Bring the soup to a boil and then lower the heat to a simmer and cook until the potatoes are falling apart, about 1 hour and 10 minutes.

6. Mash the roasted garlic with a fork until you achieve a smooth paste. (You can use a blender or food processor for this step if you like.)

7. Break up the potato pieces in the soup with a whisk, pushing them up against the insides of the pot, until the mixture is fairly smooth. If the soup is too thick, you may add more soy or rice beverage or water until you get the consistency you desire.

8. Whisk the roasted garlic paste into the soup and combine thoroughly. If you desire an absolutely smooth and creamy soup, you may blend it at this point. Taste the soup for salt, and add as much as you like to bring out the flavors of the soup. Add a tablespoon or two (15 to 30 mL) of the seasoned rice vinegar and check the flavor again. Continue with additional salt and vinegar until you get the result you want. Ladle the soup into individual bowls, garnish with the scallions, and serve.

Cream of Ratatouille Soup

This is a quick soup, because most of the cooking is done in a hot oven before the soup is assembled, filling the kitchen with an irresistible aroma while you work. Made with vegetables from your garden or a local farmer's market, this is a great summer soup.

YIELD: 4 QUARTS (3.8 L)

10 cloves garlic, peeled

4 large, ripe tomatoes, sliced in half and stems removed

2 green zucchini, sliced into ¼-inch (.5-cm) rounds

2 red or yellow peppers, stems and seeds removed, diced into 1-inch (2.5-cm) cubes

2 red onions, peeled and quartered

1 large eggplant, peeled and diced into ½-inch (1-cm) cubes

½ cup (118 mL) olive oil

¼ cup (59 mL) balsamic vinegar, plus more to taste

2 tablespoons (30 mL) Italian seasoning

1 tablespoon (15 mL) salt

1 teaspoon (5 mL) red pepper flakes

1 quart (.95 L) rice or soy beverage

1 quart (.95 L) good-quality vegetable stock

1 bunch fresh basil, for garnish

1. Preheat the oven to 500°F (260°C). Line a roasting pan with parchment paper.

2. Combine the first 11 ingredients (up to the red pepper flakes) in the roasting pan, and mix well with your hands. Make sure all the vegetables are coated with the olive oil and seasoning mixture. Roast the vegetables uncovered for 30 to 40 minutes or until the edges are well browned but not blackened. Remove the pan from the oven halfway through the roasting procedure and stir the vegetables, turning them over to expose the undersides to the heat.

3. After the vegetables have roasted for 20 minutes, heat the rice beverage and stock together in a large soup pot. When the vegetables are done, add them to the rice beverage and stock mixture and return it to a boil. Blend the soup with an immersion blender or in a food processor and return the soup to serving temperature. Taste for seasonings and add salt as needed. A bit more balsamic vinegar may also be desired at this point.

4. Stack 6 large leaves of basil and roll them up into a cylinder. Slice across the cylinder very thinly to produce long strands of fresh basil. Use these as a garnish for your soup. Serve with a lighter Italian red wine, such as a Chianti.

Curried Roasted Cauliflower Soup with Green Peas

This is a lightly curried soup George created at Veganopolis. It became an instant favorite among our customers.

YIELD: 3 QUARTS (2.85 L)

> 2 heads fresh cauliflower, cut into florets
>
> 5 tablespoons (75 mL) garam masala*
>
> 2 teaspoons (10 mL) salt
>
> ¼ cup (60 mL) plus 4 tablespoons (60 mL) olive oil, divided
>
> 2 quarts (1.9 L) rice or soy beverage
>
> 6 tablespoons (90 mL) white spelt flour or other white flour
>
> 2 cups (473 mL) fresh or frozen green peas
>
> Fresh cilantro leaves, for garnish

1. Preheat the oven to 500°F (260°C).

2. Place the cauliflower florets in a large bowl and season them with garam masala, salt, and olive oil. Using your hands, rub the spices and oil into the surface of the florets until they are evenly coated. Transfer the florets to a baking sheet and roast until they are well browned but not blackened.

3. While the florets are roasting, heat the rice or soy beverage in a large pot over medium-high heat. In a large, heavy-bottomed soup pot heat 4 tablespoons (60 mL) of the oil over medium heat and add the flour. Whisk together to form a roux and continue whisking for 4 to 5 minutes, or until the flour is thoroughly cooked and the color has just begun to darken.

4. Add the hot rice or soy beverage in 2-cup (473-mL) batches, whisking well after each addition until the soup base reaches a creamy consistency. When the cauliflower is done roasting, add it to the soup base and blend everything together with an immersion blender or in a food processor.

5. Return the soup to a simmer and add the peas. Cook for an additional 10 to 12 minutes, or until the peas are tender. Taste the soup and add salt as needed. Serve in individual soup bowls, garnished with a few fresh cilantro leaves.

Cooks' Note

Warm naan or pita breads make a nice side for this soup.

*Garam masala is a mixture of ground spices used in Indian cuisine. Many varieties are available, but the mixture usually includes coriander, cumin, red pepper, and turmeric. You can also substitute other curry powders in this soup.

Madras-Style Sambar with Red Lentils and Vegetables

Sambar is usually more of a condiment than a soup, served alongside dosas and rice at South Indian restaurants. This version is thicker and richer than traditional sambar, and it makes a hearty meal by itself. The ingredient list is rather long and requires a trip to an Indian market, and the preparation is a bit complicated, but the finished dish is well worth the effort. The South Indian style of cooking is a natural for vegans.

YIELD: 4 QUARTS (3.8 L)

4 cups (.95 L) dried red lentils

6 tablespoons (90 mL) olive or canola oil

6 shallots, peeled

6 fresh green chilies, seeded and diced (the small slender green chilies available in Indian markets are preferable, but you can use serrano chilies instead)

4 curry leaves (sometimes available in Indian markets fresh or frozen; you may substitute bay leaves)

2 tablespoons (30 mL) black mustard seeds

1 tablespoon (15 mL) whole cumin seeds

1 teaspoon (5 mL) asafetida (sometimes called hing; this is a pale, very aromatic powder available in Indian markets)

3 cups (708 mL) assorted chopped vegetables (potato, carrot, cauliflower, eggplant, green peas, green beans, or whatever is available)

2 tablespoons (30 mL) ground turmeric

6 tablespoons (90 mL) tamarind paste

2 tablespoons (30 mL) sambar masala powder (available in some Indian markets; if unavailable, substitute a turmeric-based curry powder or garam masala)

Salt, to taste

Fresh lime juice, to taste

Fresh cilantro leaves, for garnish

1. Rinse the lentils well and break up any clumps that form. Place them in a large pot and cover with at least 4 inches (10 cm) of water. Bring the lentils to a boil, then reduce the heat to a simmer and cover the pot. Check them frequently and stir well, dragging the spoon across the bottom of the pot to prevent sticking or scorching. If you do scorch the lentils, immediately transfer the unscorched portion to a fresh pot and continue cooking them. Add water as necessary throughout the cooking process if the mixture becomes too thick.

2. Heat the oil in a large, heavy-bottomed soup pot over medium-high heat and add the shallots, chilies, curry leaves, mustard seeds, and cumin seeds. Cook until the shallots are soft, about 8 to 10 minutes.

3. Stir in the asafetida. This will give your kitchen a very pungent aroma for a few minutes, but it is essential to the finished dish.

4. Add the vegetables and the ground turmeric, and stir to coat the vegetables with the spices and oil.

5. Cook for 5 minutes and then add the tamarind paste and enough hot water to just cover the vegetables. Stir well to dissolve the tamarind paste. Cook until the vegetables are tender, about 30 minutes, adding more water if necessary.

6. Continue stirring the lentils as they cook. When they are ready, they will have broken down completely into a creamy base for your sambar. Add the cooked vegetables and 2 tablespoons (30 mL) of sambar masala powder to the lentils and stir well. Taste for seasonings and add salt and lime juice as needed. Remove and discard the curry or bay leaves. Ladle into soup bowls and garnish with fresh cilantro leaves.

Cooks' Note

This is brilliant when served with fresh naan on the side.

Mexican Tortilla Soup

Always popular, this soup is relatively easy to make and serve with a unique presentation. The finished soup is ladled over crumbled fresh corn-tortilla chips that have been placed at the bottom of each bowl. The chips soften in the hot soup but still retain a little of their texture.

YIELD: 4 QUARTS (3.8 L)

3 quarts (2.9 L) good-quality vegetable stock

3 tablespoons (45 mL) olive or canola oil

2 white onions, peeled and finely diced

6 cloves garlic, peeled and crushed

1 (8-ounce [224-g]) can diced hatch or other mild green chilies (optional)

2 jalapeño peppers, seeded and finely diced

2 teaspoons (10 mL) ground cumin

2 teaspoons (10 mL) dried oregano

2 teaspoons (10 mL) dark chili powder

4 carrots, peeled and diced

1 cup (226 mL) finely shredded green cabbage

2 cups (473 mL) chopped Cheitan Patties (page 163) or seitan, julienned

1 (12-ounce [336-g]) can diced tomatoes with its juice

Fresh lime juice, to taste

Hot pepper sauce, to taste

Salt, to taste

8 fresh corn tortillas, cut into wedges and fried crisp, or about 32 packaged corn tortilla chips (unsalted preferred)

Fresh cilantro leaves, for garnish

1. In a large saucepan, heat the vegetable stock.

2. In a large, heavy-bottomed soup pot, heat the olive or canola oil over medium-high heat. Add the onions, garlic, both peppers, and dry spices, and cook until the onions are softened.

3. Stir in the carrots, cabbage, Cheitan Patties or seitan, and tomatoes.

4. Add the hot stock and bring the soup to a boil. Lower the heat and simmer until the carrots are tender, about 30 minutes.

5. Taste the soup for seasonings and add salt, fresh lime juice, and hot pepper sauce as needed.

6. Break up the tortilla chips and place some in the bottom of each soup bowl. Ladle the hot soup over the chips and garnish each bowl with fresh cilantro leaves.

Moroccan Spinach Lentil Soup with Lemon

This soup is a staple at the restaurant and works well year round. Use French green lentils, if available, as they hold their shape nicely in the finished soup.

YIELD: 3 QUARTS (2.85 L)

3 tablespoons (45 mL) olive oil

1 large red onion, peeled and finely diced

Zest and juice of 1 lemon

1 tablespoon (15 mL) dry oregano

2 teaspoons (10 mL) paprika

2 teaspoons (10 mL) freshly ground black pepper

1 teaspoon (5 mL) ground cumin

½ teaspoon (2.5 mL) ground cinnamon

1 quart (.95 L) good-quality vegetable stock, heated

2 cups (473 mL) French green lentils (preferred) or brown lentils, well rinsed and drained

1 (20-ounce [560-g]) can diced tomatoes or about 5 medium, fresh tomatoes, peeled, seeded, and diced

1 pound (454 g) fresh spinach, stemmed and chopped

Salt, to taste

1. Warm the olive oil over medium heat in a heavy-bottomed soup pot. Add the onion, lemon zest, and dry spices.

2. When the mixture becomes fragrant, add the stock, lentils, and tomatoes. Bring to a boil and cook for about 30 minutes, or until the lentils are softened, stirring frequently.

3. Add the chopped spinach and cook until wilted, about 10 minutes. Taste for seasonings and add fresh lemon juice and salt as needed.

Poets' Allium Potage

I make this soup whenever I or one of my friends is stuck for a rhyme, literally or metaphysically. The allium family includes onions; shallots; garlic; leeks; and the strange, beautiful, and spherical purple allium flower. Try to find as many of these as you can to use in the soup, but don't add the flower. Instead, put it in a vase on the table. As the great Irish poet William Butler Yeats pointed out, "In nature, like follows like." This recipe just might inspire the poet in you—extra points for anyone who can come up with a rhyme for allium.

YIELD: 3 QUARTS (2.85 L)

> 4 tablespoons (60 mL) olive oil
>
> 6 cloves garlic, peeled and thinly sliced
>
> 4 shallots, peeled and very thinly sliced
>
> 2 leeks, thoroughly washed and thinly sliced
>
> 1 white onion, peeled and very thinly sliced
>
> 1 red onion, peeled and very thinly sliced
>
> 1 spanish onion, peeled and very thinly sliced
>
> 1 bunch scallions, trimmed and thinly sliced
>
> 2 tablespoons (30 mL) stemmed and chopped fresh rosemary
>
> 4 tablespoons (60 mL) seasoned rice vinegar, divided
>
> 1 tablespoon (15 mL) salt, plus more to taste
>
> 2 carrots, peeled and diced
>
> 1 large potato, peeled and diced
>
> 4 tablespoons (60 mL) tomato paste
>
> 2 quarts (1.9 L) rich vegetable stock
>
> Freshly ground black pepper, to taste

1. In a large, heavy-bottomed soup pot, heat the olive oil over medium-low heat and sauté the garlic, shallots, leeks, onions, scallions, and rosemary for about 30 minutes, or until the mixture begins to brown, stirring frequently.

2. Add 2 tablespoons (30 mL) of the seasoned rice vinegar and 1 tablespoon (15mL) of salt and stir well. Add the carrots, potato, tomato paste, and vegetable stock, and bring the soup to a boil. Reduce the heat to medium and simmer, covered, until the potatoes and carrots are cooked through. Skim as necessary.

3. Taste for seasonings and add salt and seasoned rice vinegar as needed. Serve with a liberal grinding of black pepper and warm, fresh, crusty bread.

Roman Vegetable Soup with Orzo Pasta

This delightful, authentic, Roman-style soup takes a little time to prepare because part of its charm lies in the finely diced vegetables.

YIELD: 4 QUARTS (3.8 L)

½ cup (118 mL) extra virgin olive oil

4 cloves garlic, peeled and crushed

1 red onion, peeled and finely diced

2 tablespoons (30 mL) Italian seasoning

¼ teaspoon (1.25 mL) red chili flakes

4 tablespoons (60 mL) tomato paste

2 green zucchinis, thoroughly washed, unpeeled, and finely diced

2 carrots, peeled and finely diced

2 stalks celery, finely diced

1 small eggplant, peeled and finely diced

1 red or yellow bell pepper, stemmed, seeded, and finely diced

1 turnip, peeled and finely diced

1 fennel bulb, stalks, fronds, and coarse outer leaves removed and finely diced

3 quarts (2.9 L) good-quality vegetable stock, heated

1 cup (226 mL) dry orzo pasta

Salt, to taste

Fresh basil leaves, finely sliced, for garnish

1. Heat the olive oil in a large, heavy-bottomed soup pot over medium heat. Add the garlic, onions, Italian seasoning, and red chili flakes, and sauté until the onions are softened.

2. Stir in the tomato paste and cook for about 2 minutes.

3. Add all of the diced vegetables and the heated stock. Bring the soup to a boil and then lower the heat to a steady simmer. Simmer the soup for about 30 minutes or until the vegetables are tender. Add the orzo and cook the soup for an additional 12 minutes, or until the pasta is cooked al dente. If, at this point, the soup is too thick you may add hot water to thin it. Taste the soup and add salt to taste. To serve, ladle the soup into bowls and garnish it with the basil.

Santa Fe–Style Pozole Soup

This feast-day soup originated in Mexico and is still prepared in certain regions there, but it really took hold in the New Mexico city of Santa Fe, where it is offered at many restaurants. Maize is another name for hominy: white corn that has been processed in lime, which bleaches it and expands it to the size and shape of popcorn. It is the core ingredient of pozole.

YIELD: 4 QUARTS (3.8 L)

> 4 tablespoons (60 mL) olive or canola oil
>
> ½ pound (226 g) seitan, sliced into ½-inch (1-cm) cubes
>
> 6 cloves garlic, peeled and crushed
>
> 2 white onions, peeled and diced
>
> 2 tablespoons (30 mL) finely chopped chipotle in adobo sauce
>
> 1 tablespoon (15 mL) dried oregano (Mexican oregano preferred)
>
> 1 tablespoon (15 mL) ground cumin
>
> 1 tablespoon (15 mL) dark chili powder, plus more for garnish
>
> 2 quarts (1.9 L) good-quality vegetable stock
>
> 2 cups (473 mL) canned diced tomatoes with their juice
>
> 1 (20-ounce [560-g]) can hominy/maize, drained and rinsed well in cold water
>
> 2 cups (473 mL) shredded white cabbage
>
> ⅓ cup (75 mL) finely chopped fresh cilantro leaves
>
> 4 limes
>
> Salt, to taste
>
> Hot sauce, to taste (optional)
>
> ¼ head green cabbage, root left on, sliced into thin fans, for garnish

1. Heat the oil in a large, heavy-bottomed soup pot over medium-high heat. Add the seitan and sauté until the edges begin to brown.

2. Add the garlic, onions, chipotle, and dry spices and sauté until the onions are softened.

3. Add the stock and tomatoes, and bring to a boil.

4. Add the hominy/maize and cabbage and cook until the hominy/maize is tender and a little bit expanded, about 1 hour.

5. Add the cilantro, juice from 3 of the limes, and salt to taste. If you want a spicier pozole, add hot sauce to taste. Better yet, have a few different hot sauces available on the table and let your guests decide. Cut the remaining lime into 6 wedges. Serve in a large bowl garnished with a fan of cabbage, lime wedges, and a sprinkling of chili powder.

Cooks' Note

Warmed, fresh corn tortillas on the side are a grand touch. This recipe is great in the summertime, served with a cold beer.

Spanish Roasted Red Pepper Soup with Chickpeas

Roasted red peppers and garlic are key ingredients in Spanish cuisine. It was the prevalence of these ingredients that caused Frédéric Chopin to detest Spanish cuisine.* I, on the other hand, adore red peppers and garlic and Spanish cuisine in general. I cannot, on the other hand, successfully compose complicated piano pieces. The addition of chickpeas makes this soup a good source of protein. The finished soup is a brilliant red-orange in color.

YIELD: 3 QUARTS (2.85 L)

> 6 large red bell peppers, or 1 (20-ounce [560-g]) jar roasted red peppers
>
> 1 quart (.95 L) good-quality vegetable stock
>
> 1 quart (.95 L) rice or soy beverage
>
> 4 tablespoons (60 mL) extra virgin olive oil
>
> 4 tablespoons (60 mL) white spelt flour
>
> 10 cloves garlic, peeled and crushed
>
> 2 teaspoons (10 mL) ground cumin
>
> 1 tablespoon (15 mL) paprika
>
> 1 teaspoon (5 mL) cayenne pepper
>
> 1 (12-ounce [336-g]) can chickpeas or 1½ cups (354 mL) dried chickpeas, soaked overnight and drained
>
> 1 bunch Italian parsley, thoroughly washed, stemmed, and finely chopped
>
> Salt, to taste
>
> Red wine or sherry vinegar, to taste

1. To roast the peppers, coat each with olive oil and place them on a sheet pan or pizza pan covered with parchment paper. Place the pan under the broiler or in the oven preheated to 450°F (240°C). Roast the peppers until they are about 75 percent blackened on the outside, turning once during the process. Remove them from the oven, place them in a bowl, and cover the bowl tightly with aluminum foil or an inverted plate. Set aside. When they are cool enough to handle, peel and discard the skin. Open each pepper and remove and discard as many of the seeds as you can. Remove and discard the stems. If you are using canned peppers, drain them well and remove any bits of stems, seeds, or skin you find. Chop the roasted peppers into 1-inch (2.5-cm) dice.

2. Combine the stock and soy or rice beverage in a saucepan and bring to a boil. Lower the heat to a simmer.

3. Heat the olive oil over medium-high heat in a large, heavy-bottomed soup pot. Add the flour and whisk together until a roux is formed.

*See *Winter in Majorca* by George Sand.

CONTINUED ON PAGE 34

CONTINUED FROM PAGE 33

4. Add the garlic and dry spices and whisk constantly, about 5 minutes or until the mixture is fragrant and just beginning to darken. Add the stock and soy or rice beverage mixture to the roux in 2-cup (473-mL) batches, whisking after each addition to create a creamy, smooth soup base.

5. Add the roasted red peppers and stir. Blend the soup thoroughly with an immersion blender, or blend in a food processor and return to the pot.

6. Add the chickpeas and cook for approximately 20 minutes.

7. Add the parsley and check the soup's consistency. If it is too thick, you may add a little more stock to thin it. Taste for seasonings, add salt and red wine or sherry vinegar as needed, and serve.

Cooks' Note

Enjoy this dish with a fresh loaf of rustic bread and a Spanish white wine. Fresh tangerines make an excellent dessert.

Split-Pea Soup with Oven-Roasted Shallots and Baby Croutons

This is a great choice for a cold winter night when you want something hearty and delicious to cheer you up. Roasting the shallots beforehand sweetens them so that they complement the flavors of the soup perfectly. The fresh horseradish adds another layer of interest.

YIELD: 3 QUARTS (2.85 L)

> 6 whole shallots
>
> ¼ cup (59 mL) plus 6 tablespoons (90 mL) olive oil, divided
>
> 2 leeks, thoroughly washed and sliced into ⅛-inch (¼-cm) rounds
>
> 2 stalks celery, diced
>
> 1 onion, peeled and diced
>
> 1 tablespoon (15 mL) salt
>
> 1 tablespoon (15 mL) freshly ground black pepper
>
> 1 teaspoon (5 mL) ground thyme
>
> 1 pound (454 g) dried green split peas, rinsed and soaked overnight in fresh water*
>
> 2 large potatoes, peeled and diced
>
> 2 quarts (1.9 L) good-quality vegetable stock
>
> 4 tablespoons (60 mL) freshly grated horseradish
>
> 6 thick baguette slices, cut into ⅛-inch (¼-cm) dice
>
> Fresh parsley, for garnish (optional)

1. Preheat the oven to 400°F (200°C).

2. Peel the shallots and place them in a small ovenproof dish. Add ¼ cup (59 mL) olive oil and ¾ cup (177.5 mL) water and cover tightly with foil. Roast the shallots for 40 to 50 minutes or until they are quite soft and a bit browned on the surface. Remove from the oven and set aside.

3. While the shallots are roasting, heat 3 tablespoons (45 mL) of the olive oil over medium heat in a large, heavy-bottomed soup pot. Add the leeks, celery, onions, and dry spices and sauté for about 10 minutes, or until the onions are transparent.

4. Drain the split peas and rinse them well under cold running water. Add them to the soup pot, along with the potatoes, and stir everything together, breaking up any clumps of split peas.

*Soaking the dried split peas overnight is essential. If the peas are old, you may even wish to soak them for 2 days, changing the water once. Insufficiently rehydrated peas will take a very long time to cook properly.

CONTINUED ON PAGE 36

CONTINUED FROM PAGE 35

5. Add the stock and bring to a boil. Reduce heat and simmer until the split peas are quite soft and easy to crush against the sides of the pot, about 2 hours.

6. Remove the foil from the roasted shallots and dump the entire contents of the roasting dish into the soup pot. Roughly blend the soup with an immersion blender or an electric mixer to break up the potatoes and shallots.

7. Add the horseradish and stir. Check for seasonings and add salt and pepper as needed. Sauté the diced baguette in olive oil until crisp, and season with salt and pepper. Serve the soup garnished with the baby croutons, perhaps a sprig of parsley, and an additional grinding of fresh black pepper.

Cooks' Note

This recipe is very nice with a glass of your favorite beer or a full-flavored white wine — perhaps a Sauvignon Blanc.

Summer Greens Soup with Roasted Shallots

This bright green soup has a high vitamin and mineral content and tastes absolutely fabulous. Start by roasting the shallots. This recipe calls for spinach and two different varieties of kale, but you can substitute any greens. You may actually feel the nutrients in this soup as your palate thanks you for treating it so nicely.

YIELD: 4 QUARTS (3.8 L)

> 6 whole shallots, peeled
>
> ½ cup (118 mL) plus 3 tablespoons (45 mL) olive oil, divided
>
> 2 quarts (1.9 L) good-quality vegetable stock
>
> 1 quart (.95 L) soy or rice beverage, heated
>
> 1 red onion, peeled and diced
>
> 1 teaspoon (5 mL) ground white pepper
>
> 1 teaspoon (5 mL) ground nutmeg
>
> 1 bunch green kale, stemmed and chopped
>
> 1 bunch lacinato kale, stemmed and chopped
>
> 1 bunch spinach, stemmed and chopped
>
> 2 cups (473 mL) fresh or frozen green peas
>
> Salt, to taste
>
> Seasoned rice vinegar, to taste

1. Preheat the oven to 400°F (200°C).

2. Place the shallots in a small roasting pan with ½ cup (118 mL) olive oil and ½ cup (118 mL) water. Cover tightly with aluminum foil and roast for 35 to 45 minutes, or until the shallots are very soft and slightly browned. Remove from the oven and set aside.

3. Bring the stock and soy beverage to a boil in a saucepan over medium-high heat. Reduce the heat to a simmer.

4. In a large, heavy-bottomed soup pot, heat the remaining 3 tablespoons (45 mL) of olive oil over medium heat. Add the red onion and dry spices, and cook until the onion is transparent.

5. Add the chopped greens and the peas and stir well, cooking until the greens are all wilted and begin to release their moisture.

6. Stir in the heated stock and the soy or rice beverage. Add the roasted shallots.

7. Blend everything together with an immersion blender or transfer to a blender in batches. Return the soup to the pot, and bring it up to serving temperature. Taste for seasonings and add salt and seasoned rice vinegar as needed. Serve immediately, perhaps with thick-sliced, toasted rye bread on the side.

Super Noodle Soup

This is your grandmother's chicken noodle soup—without the chicken and without the grandmother.

YIELD: 3 QUARTS (2.85 L)

> 2 quarts (1.9 L) good-quality vegetable stock
>
> 4 tablespoons (60 mL) olive oil
>
> 3 carrots, peeled and cut into ¼-inch (.5-cm) dice
>
> 3 stalks celery, cut into ¼-inch (.5-cm) dice
>
> 1 large onion, peeled and diced
>
> 2 cups (473 mL) diced Cheitan Patties (page 163) or other vegan chicken substitute
>
> 2 teaspoons (10 mL) ground white pepper
>
> 1 teaspoon (5 mL) dried thyme
>
> 8 ounces (224 g) eggless noodles (fettuccine works well), broken into 2-inch (5-cm) lengths
>
> Salt, to taste

1. Heat the stock in a saucepan.

2. In a large, heavy-bottomed soup pot, heat the olive oil over medium heat. Add the carrots, celery, onions, Cheitan Patties or vegan chicken substitute, and spices and cook until the onions are softened, about 8 minutes.

3. Add the hot stock and bring the soup to a boil. Cook until the carrots are tender, about 25 minutes. Add the noodles and cook for an additional 10 minutes or until they are tender. Taste for seasonings and add salt as required. Ladle into bowls and enjoy!

Tomato Bisque with Fried Basil Leaves

This soup can be made with canned tomatoes, but there is really no substitute for starting with fresh tomatoes. If fresh tomatoes are available, peel and seed them as follows: Using your sharpest knife, cut a shallow X in the skin of each tomato opposite the stem end. Plunge the tomatoes into rapidly boiling water a few at a time and blanch for about 3 minutes. Immediately plunge the hot tomatoes into a large container of iced water and let them cool down. Peel the skin off of each tomato and discard. Cut each tomato in half, lengthwise, and scoop out the seeds with your finger and discard. Dice all of the tomatoes roughly, saving as much juice from your cutting board as you can.

YIELD: 3 QUARTS (2.85 L)

4 tablespoons (60 mL) olive oil

6 tablespoons (90 mL) white spelt flour or other white flour

1 red onion, peeled and finely diced

1 cup (236 mL) strong-flavored red wine (a Spanish Tempranillo is great here)

1 quart (.95 L) good-quality vegetable stock, heated

1 quart (.95 L) soy or rice beverage, heated

2 (20-ounce [560-g]) cans diced tomatoes or 10 large tomatoes, peeled, seeded, and diced

1 bunch fresh basil, 20 large leaves reserved, the remainder stemmed and finely julienned

1½ cups (354 mL) canola oil

Salt and freshly ground black pepper, to taste

1. In a large, heavy-bottomed soup pot, heat the olive oil over medium-high heat. Whisk in the flour to form a roux. Cook the roux, whisking constantly, for 5 minutes.

2. Add the onions and cook until they are softened.

3. Add the red wine and cook for about 8 minutes, stirring constantly.

4. Add the hot stock and soy or rice beverage in 2-cup (473-mL) batches, whisking constantly until you have added it all.

5. Add the tomatoes and stir well. Cook for about 12 minutes, stirring frequently. The resulting soup should be fairly thick, just shy of a sauce consistency. Taste for seasonings and add salt and pepper as required.

6. Stir in the julienned basil.

7. Fry the reserved whole basil leaves in canola oil until they are shiny and dark green. They will spit some hot oil, so be careful. Drain the crisped basil leaves on a paper towel. To serve, ladle the soup into individual soup bowls and top with a few fried basil leaves and an extra grinding of black pepper. This soup is great with the rest of the red wine and some grilled baguette slices.

African Yam and Peanut Soup with Fresh Ginger

Delicious, nourishing, satisfying, and easy to make, this soup might be the kind you are served in Senegal, if you are fortunate enough to travel there. Bright orange, smooth, and velvety, it is sure to please you and your guests.

YIELD: 3 QUARTS (2.85 L)

> 4 tablespoons (60 mL) canola or olive oil
>
> 1 large red onion, peeled and diced
>
> 2 red or yellow bell peppers, stemmed, seeded, and diced
>
> ½ cup (118 mL) peeled fresh ginger, thinly sliced
>
> 1 tablespoon (15 mL) dried thyme
>
> 1 tablespoon (15 mL) paprika
>
> 1 teaspoon (5 mL) cayenne pepper
>
> 1 teaspoon (5 mL) nutmeg
>
> ½ teaspoon (2.5 mL) cinnamon
>
> 5 large orange-flesh yams or sweet potatoes, peeled and diced into ½-inch (1-cm) cubes
>
> 2 large tomatoes, peeled, seeded, and diced or 1 (12-ounce [360-mL]) can diced tomatoes with their juice
>
> 2 large carrots, peeled and diced
>
> 2 quarts (1.9 L) hot water or vegetable stock
>
> 1 tablespoon (15 mL) salt, or more to taste
>
> 1 cup (236 mL) peanut butter, or more to taste
>
> Seasoned rice vinegar, to taste
>
> Fresh cilantro leaves, for garnish

1. Heat the oil in a large, heavy-bottomed soup pot over medium heat and add the onions, peppers, fresh ginger, and dry spices. Sauté until the onions are softened.

2. Add the yams, tomatoes, carrots, water or stock, and salt. Bring to a boil.

3. Reduce the heat to medium and simmer the soup until the yams are fork-tender. Add the peanut butter and stir until it is fully incorporated. Check for seasonings and add salt and a few tablespoons of rice vinegar as needed. You should be able to clearly taste the ginger and the peanut flavors of the soup.

4. Blend with an immersion blender or in a food processor until very smooth. Check for seasonings again and adjust with salt and vinegar.

5. Serve garnished with a few fresh cilantro leaves, if desired.

Cooks' Note

This filling soup works as either a meal in itself or a starter for a larger feast.

Black-Bean Soup with Jalapeño and Lime

This hearty, full-flavored soup is nourishing and easy to make. The sherry is optional, but it provides a fragrant undertone to the finished soup. A note about beans and salt: In general, it is wise to avoid salting any bean dish until the beans are tender enough to eat. Salting before this point will toughen the beans and slow the cooking process.

YIELD: 4 QUARTS (3.8 L)

> 1 pound (454 g) dried black beans, soaked overnight in cold water,* or 2 (20-ounce [600-mL]) cans of black beans, drained and well rinsed
>
> 4 tablespoons (60 mL) olive oil
>
> 2 red onions, peeled and finely diced
>
> 6 cloves garlic, peeled and crushed
>
> 2 fresh jalapeño peppers, stemmed, seeded, and finely diced
>
> 1 tablespoon (15 mL) dried oregano
>
> 1 tablespoon (15 mL) ground cumin
>
> 1 tablespoon (15 mL) dark chili powder
>
> ¾ cup (177 mL) sherry (optional)
>
> 4 quarts (3.8 L) water
>
> Salt, to taste
>
> Juice of 2 fresh limes
>
> Fresh cilantro leaves, for garnish
>
> Fresh lime wedges, for garnish
>
> Vegan sour cream, for garnish (optional)

1. Place the dried beans in a large pot and cover with fresh, cold water by 4 inches (10 cm). Soak overnight. The beans will expand as they soak up the water. Before using the soaked beans, drain them and discard the soaking water. Rinse the soaked beans in a large colander under cold running water.

2. Heat 4 tablespoons (60 mL) olive oil in a large, heavy-bottomed soup pot over medium-high heat. Add the onions, garlic, jalapeño chilies, and dry spices. Cook together, stirring frequently, until the onions are softened and the spices are fragrant.

*If you want to use dried beans—which are much more economical than canned beans—and you don't have time to soak them overnight, you can use the quick-soak method: Rinse the beans, place them in a large pot of unsalted water, and bring the water to a boil. Skim any foam off the top, then turn off the heat and cover the pot. Let stand for one hour. Drain and rinse the beans well before using.

3. If desired, add the sherry and cook for 5 to 7 minutes, or until ¾ of the alcohol is reduced.

4. Stir in the dry beans (or the drained, rinsed canned beans, if using).

5. Add the water and stir to combine. Bring the soup to a boil, and then lower the heat to a steady simmer.

6. Simmer for about 1½ hours, stirring occasionally and skimming any scum that appears on the surface as the beans cook. When the beans are tender, check the soup for seasonings and add salt as necessary to achieve the flavor you desire.

7. Stir in the lime juice. You may add 2 or 3 tablespoons (30 or 45 mL) more sherry at this point, if desired.

8. To serve, ladle the soup into individual bowls and garnish with fresh lime wedges, fresh cilantro leaves and, if desired, a dollop of vegan sour cream on top.

Cooks' Note

Warm, fresh corn tortillas or tortilla chips, or any sort of rustic bread, pair well with this soup.

Blended Mexican-Style Pinto Bean Soup

Recession got you on a tight budget? A bag of dried pinto beans is still pretty cheap. Back in the Reagan era, we lived on rice and beans in a little place on the wrong side of the tracks. We may have been poor, but we always ate well. Just remember to pay the gas bill, and you're golden.

YIELD: 3 QUARTS (2.85 L)

4 tablespoons (60 mL) olive or canola oil

1 white onion, peeled and diced

2 jalapeño peppers, seeded and finely diced

6 cloves garlic, peeled

2 tablespoons (30 mL) ground cumin

2 tablespoons (30 mL) dried oregano

2 tablespoons (30 mL) dark chili powder, plus more to taste

4 cups (.95 L) dried pinto beans, soaked overnight in fresh, cold water, drained, and rinsed

2 quarts (1.9 L) water

Salt, to taste

Hot sauce, to taste (optional)

Fresh cilantro leaves, for garnish

Lemon wedges, for garnish

1. Heat the oil in a large, heavy-bottomed soup pot over medium heat and add the onions, peppers, garlic, and dry spices. Cook until the onions are softened, but not browned.

2. Add the soaked pinto beans and water. The water should come about 2 inches (5 cm) above the level of the beans. Add more if needed. Stir well and bring the soup to a boil.

3. Reduce the heat and simmer until the beans are soft and beginning to break up. Skim the soup frequently and discard the foam. Add more water during the cooking process if necessary, and stir more frequently as the soup finishes.*

4. Blend the soup with an immersion blender or in a food processor, and return to the pot and bring back to serving temperature. Taste for seasonings and add salt and more chili powder as needed. If you like, add a few tablespoons of your favorite hot sauce.

5. Garnish with cilantro leaves and lemon wedges, and serve.

Cooks' Note

This soup is like a Mexican restaurant in a bowl! If you want to get fancy, add a dollop of vegan sour cream on top and serve with some fresh, warm corn tortillas.

*Be sure to drain and rinse the pinto beans well after soaking. Never cook the beans in the soaking water! Skim the soup frequently while cooking. The foam that gathers at the top of cooking beans is full of indigestible elements, so the more carefully you rinse and skim, the better the soup (and the happier your guests) will be.

Bresse Mushroom Soup with Rosemary and White Wine

This is a marvelous French-style soup thickened not with a roux but with day-old bread. It's a great way to use up those stale bits of leftover bread. This soup is one of my personal favorites, and it will not last long once your friends and family get a taste of it. It goes nicely with a green salad, crusty bread, and a glass of white wine.

YIELD: 3 QUARTS (2.85 L)

> 2 pounds (1 kg) fresh mushrooms—button, crimini, oyster, or whatever is at hand (my favorite mushrooms for this recipe are crimini, which have the perfect flavor and color)
>
> 4 tablespoons (60 mL) olive oil
>
> 4 shallots, finely diced
>
> ¼ cup (59 mL) fresh rosemary, stemmed and finely chopped
>
> Salt and freshly ground black pepper, to taste
>
> 4 tablespoons (60 mL) white wine vinegar or champagne vinegar
>
> 1 cup (236 mL) dry white wine
>
> 1 quart (95 L) soy or rice beverage, heated
>
> 1 quart (95 L) good-quality vegetable stock, heated
>
> 1 day-old baguette or other crusty bread, cut into 2-inch (5-cm) pieces

1. Remove any woody stems or other debris from the mushrooms, and chop any larger ones into 1-inch (2.5-cm) pieces. (Never wash mushrooms in water.)

2. Heat the olive oil in a large, heavy-bottomed soup pot over medium heat. Add the shallots and rosemary, and sauté until the shallots are softened.

3. Add the mushrooms and season liberally with salt and freshly ground black pepper and salt.

4. Stir the mixture from the bottom of the pan upward to distribute the shallots, rosemary, and oil evenly. Stir continuously so that all of the mushrooms spend some time on the bottom of the pot, where they will sear. After 7 to 9 minutes, the whole mixture should start to look soft.

5. Add the vinegar and cook for 3 to 5 minutes. Add the white wine and cook for an additional 3 to 5 minutes, stirring frequently.

6. Stir in the heated soy or rice beverage and stock.

7. Stir in the bread pieces and cook for 25 minutes.

8. Blend the soup thoroughly with an immersion blender or in a food processor. Return the blended soup to the pot and bring to a simmer. Check the soup for seasonings and add salt and pepper as needed. If the wine flavor is not strong enough for your liking, add a few more tablespoons of vinegar.

9. Serve in soup bowls with an additional grinding of black pepper on top and perhaps with some fresh rosemary leaves as garnish.

Shallots Diced the French Way

Shallots are perhaps underused in American kitchens, but there is no replacement for them once you are familiar with their flavor. They are an absolutely essential ingredient in some vinaigrettes. In South India, they are called "sambar onions" and are equally essential to the flavor of sambars.

Shallots are those little copper-brown, onion-looking things at the market. They sometimes grow in single bulbs, but more often the bulb is divided into two sections, each of which has a papery skin around it.

When dicing shallots for a sauce or vinaigrette, the French use this technique:

1. Peel the shallots and discard the skin.

2. Place the bulb on its end, and using your sharpest small knife, slice the bulb downward toward the base in very thin slices, but do not slice all the way through the bulb. Leave a small bit of the base intact. Turn the bulb 90° and slice it again, at right angles to your first series of slices. Again, do not slice all the way through the bulb. You should be able to pick up the bulb from the base with the tip of your knife without it falling apart.

3. Turn the bulb down lengthwise and, holding the strands together with your free hand, slice downward, making thin slices. The result will be finely diced shallots of uniform size, which will melt evenly into your sauce or float nicely in your vinaigrette.

Bon morale, bon courage, et bonne chance!

Creamy Corn Chowder with Green Chilies

If you can find canned hatch green chilies for this soup, you will be very happy with the result. However, any sort of canned mild green chilies, or freshly roasted ones that you prepare yourself, will work fine. Drain the canned chilies well and chop them into ¼-inch (.5-cm) dice for this recipe.

YIELD: 3 QUARTS (2.85 L)

4 tablespoons (60 mL) canola or olive oil

6 tablespoons (90 mL) white spelt flour or other white flour

1 white onion, peeled and diced

1 teaspoon (5 mL) ground cumin

1 teaspoon (5 mL) paprika

1 teaspoon (5 mL) white pepper

1 teaspoon (5 mL) nutmeg

½ teaspoon (2.5 mL) cayenne pepper

2 quarts (1.9 L) soy or rice beverage, heated

2 large potatoes, peeled and diced into ½-inch (1-cm) cubes

¾ cup (177 mL) diced green chilies or 1 (6-ounce [171-g]) can, drained

4 cups (0.95 L) fresh or frozen sweet corn kernels, fresh (about 3 large ears) or frozen (if using fresh corn, you will want to use a very sharp, broad-bladed knife and, standing the ear on end, trim down the sides of it to remove the kernels)

½ cup (118 mL) fresh cilantro, finely chopped

Salt, to taste

Hot sauce, to taste (optional)

1. In a large, heavy-bottomed soup pot, heat the oil over medium-high heat. Add the flour, whisking together to make a roux. Cook the roux for a few minutes, whisking constantly.

2. Add the onions and the dry spices to the roux and cook for 8 to 10 minutes, or until the onions start to soften.

3. Add the hot soy or rice beverage in 2-cup (473-mL) batches, whisking to combine thoroughly after each addition. If the mixture is too thick, add hot water until you achieve a consistency about the texture of heavy cream.

4. Add the potatoes, chilies, and corn and simmer until the potatoes are tender, about 40 minutes. At the end of the cooking time, add the cilantro.

5. Taste for seasonings and add salt until you achieve the flavor you desire. If you like a spicier soup, add hot sauce or have it available at your table. If the soup has thickened too much during cooking, you may thin it with more soy, rice beverage, or water.

Cooks' Note

Serve in bowls with crackers, warm corn tortillas, or warm bread.

Fourth Avenue Chowder

This soup was always a big hit at the restaurant. We used a vegan tuna substitute cut into 1-inch (2.5-cm) pieces in place of clams, but you may use any good-quality vegan fish substitute. This is a Manhattan-style chowder that should please even the most discriminating palate. I extend gratitude to Chef Jacques Pépin, from whose recipe I have adapted this version. Just writing down the recipe makes me wish I had a bowl of it in front of me.

YIELD: 3 QUARTS (2.85 L)

> 4 tablespoons (60 mL) olive oil
>
> 4 slices tempeh bacon or 4 slices diced vegan Canadian bacon (or use slices from the Vegan "Bacon" Loaf recipe on page 153)
>
> 1 onion, peeled and finely diced
>
> 2 carrots, peeled and finely diced
>
> 1 turnip, peeled and finely diced
>
> 2 stalks celery, finely diced
>
> 1 small eggplant or half a large one, peeled and finely diced
>
> 1 green zucchini, finely diced
>
> 1 green pepper, stemmed, seeded, and finely diced
>
> 1 fennel bulb, stalks, fronds, and coarse outer parts removed and discarded, finely diced
>
> 4 tablespoons (60 mL) tomato paste
>
> 2 large tomatoes, seeded and diced
>
> 2 bay leaves
>
> 1 teaspoon (5 mL) oregano
>
> 1 teaspoon (5 mL) thyme
>
> 1 teaspoon (5 mL) salt
>
> 1 teaspoon (5 mL) black pepper
>
> 1 pound (454 g) vegan tuna or other vegan fish substitute, cut into 1-inch (2.5-cm) pieces
>
> 2 quarts (1.9 L) rich vegetable stock
>
> 2 tablespoons (30 mL) dulse powder*
>
> Salt, to taste
>
> Seasoned rice vinegar, to taste

1. Heat the olive oil in a large, heavy-bottomed soup pot over medium heat. Add the bacon substitute and onions and sauté for 5 minutes.

2. Add the remaining ingredients (up to the dulse powder) and simmer, covered, for 1½ hours. Add water as needed if the soup becomes too thick.

3. Taste for seasonings and add salt and seasoned rice vinegar as needed.

Dulse powder is made of dried, ground, and edible seaweed.

French Seven-Vegetable Soup

I learned to make this soup at the Ritz-Escoffier School of French Gastronomy, and I have since served it hundreds of times. I was delighted while traveling in Morocco to be served precisely the same soup in Africa that I had grown to love in Paris. It is among my favorite soups, simple to prepare and always a crowd pleaser.

YIELD: 4 QUARTS (3.8 L)

2 quarts (1.9 L) good-quality vegetable stock or water

4 tablespoons (60 mL) olive oil

2 large leeks, white and pale green parts only, washed and sliced into rounds

1 tablespoon (15 mL) salt, or to taste

4 large baking potatoes, peeled and sliced into ¼-inch (.5-cm) rounds

4 large carrots, peeled and sliced

2 large turnips, peeled and sliced

4 large tomatoes, peeled, seeded, and diced, or 1 (12-ounce [336-mL]) can diced tomatoes

1 cup (236 mL) fresh or frozen green peas

1 cup (236 mL) fresh or frozen green beans

2 tablespoons (30 mL) ground white pepper

Apple cider vinegar, to taste

Italian parsley, for garnish

1. Heat the water or stock to a boil in a saucepan. Heat the olive oil in a large, heavy-bottomed soup pot over medium heat. Add the leeks and sauté until soft, about 6 to 8 minutes, stirring frequently. Salt the leeks liberally.

2. Add the hot water or stock to the soup pot, followed by the potatoes, carrots, turnips, and tomatoes. Bring to a boil and cook until the potatoes are beginning to break up, about 45 minutes.

3. Add the peas and green beans and cook for an additional 12 minutes.

4. Blend the soup with an immersion blender or in a food processor, and return the soup to serving temperature.

5. Taste the soup for seasonings and add salt and apple cider vinegar as needed.

6. Garnish with a few whole leaves of Italian parsley and serve.

Cooks' Note

A warmed crusty baguette on the side is perfect.

Basque Region Hemingway Potato, Garlic, and Green Bean Soup

According to legend, this was one of Ernest Hemingway's favorite soups. It's a memorable soup that makes an entire meal all by itself. The addition at the very end of the cooking process of thinly sliced garlic sautéed in extra virgin olive oil fills the kitchen with that gorgeous garlic aroma right before serving.

YIELD: 3 QUARTS (2.85 L)

½ cup (118 mL) extra virgin olive oil

2 leeks, washed thoroughly and sliced into ⅛-inch (.25-cm) rounds

½ pound (226 g) seitan, diced in ½-inch (1-cm) cubes

1 teaspoon (5 mL) salt, plus more to taste

8–10 small to medium red potatoes, peeled and diced in ½-inch (1-cm) cubes

2 cups (473 mL) finely shredded white cabbage

2 quarts (1.9 L) water or good-quality vegetable stock

2 cups (473 mL) fresh or frozen green beans, diagonally sliced into 1-inch (2.5-cm) slices

1 bunch Italian parsley, washed, dried, stemmed, and finely chopped

10 cloves garlic, peeled and very finely sliced

Freshly ground black pepper, to taste

1. Heat 4 tablespoons (60 mL) of the olive oil in a large, heavy-bottomed soup pot.

2. Add the leeks, the seitan, and 1 teaspoon (5 mL) of salt, and sauté until the leeks are softened.

3. Add the potatoes, cabbage, and water or stock, and bring to a boil. Reduce to a simmer, and simmer until the potatoes are tender, about 35 minutes.

4. Add the green beans and parsley and cook for 10 more minutes.

5. While the soup is finishing up, heat the remaining olive oil in a sauté pan over low heat. Add the finely sliced garlic and sauté until it is just beginning to turn golden.

6. Add the garlic oil to the soup and stir well.

7. Season the soup to taste with salt and freshly ground black pepper.

Cooks' Note

Serve with crusty bread and sit back to enjoy a soup with literary pretensions.

High Summer Gazpacho

There are just as many recipes for gazpacho as there are devoted creators of this Spanish delight. This version was perfected over a number of years at the restaurant and was always very popular, especially on hot summer days. This raw soup is packed with vitamin C and minerals.

YIELD: 3 QUARTS (2.85 L)

2 (16-ounce [454-g]) cans diced tomatoes or 9 large, ripe tomatoes, blanched, chilled, peeled, and seeded (you'll want about 32 ounces of tomatoes total)

1 (20-ounce [560-mL]) can tomato juice or vegetable juice

1 (32-ounce [1.1-kg]) jar roasted red peppers, diced or 6 red peppers, roasted, peeled, and diced (see page 99 for roasting instructions)

2 cups (473 mL) ice

¼-inch (.5-cm) dice fresh cucumbers, peeled and seeded

1 red onion, peeled and diced finely

2 jalapeño peppers, seeded and diced finely

½ cup (118 mL) fresh cilantro, stemmed and finely chopped

½ cup (118 mL) fresh basil, stemmed and finely chopped

½ cup (118 mL) fresh parsley, stemmed and finely chopped

Juice of 4 limes

Seasoned rice vinegar, to taste

Salt, to taste

Hot pepper sauce, to taste (optional)

2 medium-ripe avocados, peeled, pitted, and cut into ½-inch (1-cm) dice, for garnish

Lime wedges, for garnish (optional)

1. Place the cans of diced tomatoes, roasted red peppers, and tomato or vegetable juice in the freezer, along with the pot in which you intend to make the gazpacho, for 30 to 45 minutes.

2. Remove the cans and pot from the freezer. Place the contents of the cans and the ice into the cold pot, and blend until smooth. After blending, add the cucumbers, onion, jalapeño peppers, and herbs and stir well.

3. Taste for seasonings and add salt, seasoned rice vinegar, and hot pepper sauce as needed (I use green jalapeño hot sauce).

4. Serve in chilled bowls with a few slices of diced avocado floating on top and a lime wedge, if desired.

Cooks' Note

The gazpacho should be thick and chunky, but if it is too thick for your liking, you may add ice-cold water to thin it a bit.

Mexican Potato and Greens Soup with Poblano Chilies

This soup is adapted from a recipe published by Rick Bayless, celebrity chef and owner of Chicago's Frontera Grill. It is dense, very flavorful, and just the thing for a cold winter night. The greens and potatoes are a great combination, and the unique flavor of poblano chilies gives the entire soup a rich underpinning. You may use green kale, collard greens, or mustard greens in this soup.

YIELD: 4 QUARTS (3.8 L)

4 tablespoons (60 mL) olive or canola oil

2 white onions, peeled and finely diced

6 cloves garlic, peeled and crushed

1 tablespoon (15 mL) dried oregano (Mexican oregano is preferred, but Greek will do)

1 tablespoon (15 mL) dried ground cumin

1 tablespoon (15 mL) dark chili powder

4 poblano chilies, roasted, peeled, seeded, and diced (see page 99 for roasting instructions)

1 bunch greens, stemmed and finely sliced

1 quart (.95 L) good-quality vegetable stock, heated

1 quart (.95 L) soy or rice beverage, heated

4 large potatoes, peeled and diced into ½-inch (1-cm) cubes

2 cups (473 mL) fresh (about 2 large or 3 small ears) or frozen corn kernels

Salt, to taste

Fresh cilantro leaves, for garnish

1. Heat the oil in a large, heavy-bottomed soup pot over medium heat. Add the onions, garlic, and dry spices and cook until the onions are softened.

2. Add the roasted, diced poblano chilies and greens. Sauté until the greens are wilted.

3. Add the hot stock, hot soy or rice beverage, and potatoes. Cook, stirring occasionally, until the potatoes are tender, about 30 minutes.

4. Stir in the corn kernels and cook for an additional 10 minutes.

5. Taste for seasonings and add salt as needed. Ladle into individual soup bowls and garnish with cilantro leaves.

Cooks' Note
Warm, fresh corn tortillas or perhaps fresh-baked cornbread would make a nice side.

CHAPTER 2

Salads

Creamy Potato Salad

The trick with potato salad is to cook the potatoes just to the point of tenderness. Over- and undercooking give equally unsatisfactory results. Take a potato chunk out of the water while you are cooking them and pierce it with a fork. The potatoes are done when the fork goes through with just a little pressure. At that point, drain the potatoes immediately and rinse them under cold running water. Or better still, drain them and plunge them into a large quantity of iced, salted water.

YIELD: 3½ POUNDS (1.6 KG)

> 3 pounds (1.4 kg) potatoes, peeled and cut into ½-inch (1-cm) dice
>
> 2 tablespoons salt (30 mL), plus more to taste
>
> 2 teaspoons (10 mL) white pepper
>
> 2 teaspoons (10 mL) dry mustard
>
> 1 cup (236 mL) finely diced celery
>
> ¼ cup (59 mL) finely diced red onion
>
> 4 scallions, thinly sliced
>
> 1 cup (236 mL) Veganopolis Mayo (page 91) or store-bought vegan mayonnaise

1. Place the potatoes in a large pot, and fill it with cold water to cover.

2. Add 2 tablespoons (30 mL) salt to the water, and set the pot over high heat. Bring to a boil, and then reduce the heat to a simmer. Begin checking the potatoes for doneness after about 8 minutes.

3. When the potatoes are fork tender, drain them in a colander and rinse them under cold running water until they are cool. Alternatively, drain them and plunge them into a large quantity of iced water, then drain again once they have cooled.

4. Shake the colander well to remove the excess water.

5. Transfer the potatoes to a large bowl. Season them with the white pepper and dry mustard. Add salt to taste.

6. Add the celery, onions, and scallions and mix gently. Add the Veganopolis Mayo, gently stir everything together, and you are ready to serve!

Old School Veganopolis Ham Salad

While one might think of ham salad as straight from the 1950s, there is a reason it appears in all those old cookbooks. It is really good! Try a Veganopolis ham salad sandwich on rye bread with fresh romaine and mustard.

YIELD: 2 POUNDS (1.1 KG)

> 1 recipe Vegan "Bacon" Loaf (page 153), diced into ½-inch (1-cm) cubes
>
> 3 stalks celery, finely diced
>
> 1 red onion, peeled and finely diced
>
> 1 cup (236 mL) Veganopolis Mayo (page 91) or store-bought vegan mayonnaise
>
> ½ cup (125 mL) finely chopped Italian parsley
>
> 4 tablespoons (60 mL) sweet pickle relish
>
> 1 tablespoon (15 mL) Dijon mustard
>
> 2 teaspoons (10 mL) white pepper

1. Combine all the ingredients and stir well. Taste the mixture, and add pickle relish and mustard as needed until you get the flavor you desire. This salad keeps, if covered and refrigerated, for up to 5 days.

Roasted Potato Salad

This recipe produces a fabulously flavored potato salad. The potatoes are roasted instead of boiled, and a simple vinaigrette replaces the mayonnaise. It is also a little lower in fat than a creamy potato salad.

YIELD: 2 POUNDS (1.1 KG)

For the salad:

> 4 large potatoes (about 2 pounds [1.1 kg] total weight), rinsed and cut into ½-inch (1-cm) pieces
>
> 2 teaspoons (10 mL) salt
>
> 2 teaspoons (10 mL) ground white pepper
>
> ¼ cup (59 mL) olive oil
>
> ⅓ cup (79 mL) apple cider vinegar
>
> ½ cup (118 mL) finely chopped parsley
>
> ½ cup (118 mL) finely diced celery
>
> ¼ cup (59 mL) finely diced shallots

For the vinaigrette:

> 1 tablespoon (15 mL) Dijon mustard
>
> 1 teaspoon (5 mL) agave syrup
>
> ½ cup (118 mL) olive oil
>
> 2 tablespoons (30 mL) apple cider vinegar

1. Preheat the oven to 400°F (200°C). Line a baking sheet with parchment paper.

2. Spread the potato pieces out on the baking sheet and pat dry. Season with the salt and white pepper. Drizzle with olive oil and, using your hands, toss the potato pieces around on the sheet to make sure they are all evenly coated with oil and seasonings.

3. Roast for 35 to 45 minutes, or until the potatoes are lightly browned and fork tender. Remove them from the oven and, while the potatoes are still warm, drizzle them with the apple cider vinegar. Let cool.

4. To make the vinaigrette, combine the Dijon mustard and the agave syrup in a mixing bowl. Whisk in the olive oil, forming an emulsion as you go. Add the apple cider vinegar and whisk again to combine.

5. Combine the roasted potatoes, parsley, celery, shallots, and vinaigrette in a large mixing bowl. Serve and enjoy!

CONTINUED ON PAGE 60

CONTINUED FROM PAGE 59

Cooks' Note

Add chopped fresh rosemary, thyme, and/or basil for different flavors. Add finely sliced scallions and a few tablespoons of grainy mustard for a Bavarian-style potato salad. Try substituting roasted sweet potatoes for the regular potatoes. Or, best of all, use your imagination and invent your own combinations.

Veganopolis Caesar Salad

YIELD: 4 SERVINGS

> 1 head fresh romaine lettuce, thoroughly washed
>
> 1 cup (236 mL) Veganopolis Caesar Dressing (page 79)
>
> ½ cup (118 mL) Pine Nut Parmesan (page 154)
>
> 1 cup (236 mL) Veganopolis Croutons (page 240)
>
> Freshly ground black pepper, to taste
>
> Lemon wedges, for garnish

1. Lay the romaine down lengthwise and slice leaves into 1-inch-wide (2.5-cm-wide) segments. Discard the stem end. Transfer the romaine to a bowl and add the dressing. Toss well.

2. Mound the salad on 4 chilled serving plates, and crumble the Pine Nut Parmesan on top.

3. Sprinkle 5 or 6 fresh crisp Veganopolis Croutons on top of each serving.

4. Add a generous grind of black pepper and serve with lemon wedges on the side.

Cooks' Note

Lay strips of sautéed Cheitan Patties (page 163) across the top for a Cheitan Caesar salad.

Vegan 2na Salad

This salad is perfect scooped on a salad plate, in a cold sandwich, or on our 2na Melt (page 131). Vegan tuna substitutes, generally made from mushroom and soy, are commonly available in Asian markets. The one distributed by All Vegetarian Inc., in El Monte, California, is of superior quality.

YIELD: 1½ POUNDS (681 G)

1 (20-ounce [567-g]) can chickpeas or 1 pound (454 g) vegan tuna substitute (if you use vegan tuna substitute, omit the salt)

2 teaspoons (10 mL) salt

4 stalks celery, finely diced

2 shallots, peeled and finely diced

Juice of 1 lemon

1 cup (236 mL) Veganopolis Mayo (page 91) or store-bought mayonnaise

½ cup (118 mL) finely chopped Italian parsley

2 teaspoons (10 mL) white pepper

½ teaspoon (2.5 mL) dry mustard

1 tablespoon (15 mL) finely chopped fresh dill (optional)

1. If you are using chickpeas, rinse them and place them in a saucepan with enough water to cover them by 1 inch (2.5 cm). Bring to a boil, then lower the heat and simmer for 15 minutes. Drain and rinse in cold water, mash to chunks with a fork, and add the salt. If you are using vegan tuna substitute, remove any seaweed skin, then chop the pieces into roughly ¼-inch (.5-cm) cubes.

2. Add the remaining ingredients and mix well. This salad will keep for 4 days if covered in the refrigerator.

Black-Eyed Betty Salad

This colorful salad features a robust pesto and offers high nutritional value. It may also be heated and served atop a plate of sautéed greens or mashed potatoes. Served cold, this salad is a popular item on our lunch menu.

YIELD: 6 SERVINGS

1 cup (236 mL) Basil Pesto (page 96)

1 (15-ounce [426-g]) can black-eyed peas

½ pound (226 g) dried black-eyed peas, cooked

½ cup (118 mL) finely diced red bell pepper

½ cup (118 mL) finely diced yellow bell pepper

¼ cup (59 mL) finely diced red onion

¼ teaspoon (1.25 mL) nutmeg

1. Rinse and drain the canned black-eyed peas and place them in a saucepan. Add water to cover by 1 inch (2.5 cm) and bring to a simmer.

2. Simmer for 10 minutes, then drain and rinse well under cold running water until the peas are cool.

3. Transfer the peas to a bowl and stir in the pesto.

4. Fold in the remaining ingredients.

5. Taste the salad for seasoning and adjust as necessary.

Cooks' Note

Serve over a bed of fresh spinach. Garnish with Veganopolis Croutons (page 240). This salad also makes a nice wrap filling.

Blue Pear Walnut Salad

This salad depends on a vegan blue cheese substitute for its flavor. The only one currently on the market is offered by a Scottish manufacturer called Isle of Butte and marketed under the name Scheese. Black Duck Imports distributes it in the United States. Ask your grocer if it can be made available in your local store. You may also find Chicago Soydairy's Teese Vegan Mozzarella a wonderful substitute.

YIELD: 2 SERVINGS

> 1 ripe Bartlett, D'Anjou, or red pear
>
> 3 ounces (84 g) fresh leaf spinach or mesclun mix
>
> 2 ounces (57 g) vegan blue cheese substitute, finely diced
>
> ½ cup (118 mL) toasted walnuts, chopped
>
> ½ cup (118 mL) Balsamic Vinaigrette (page 78)
>
> 1 cucumber, stripe peeled and sliced
>
> Freshly ground black pepper, to taste

1. Using a very sharp paring knife, quarter the pear and remove the seeds and the line of fibrous material that runs up to the stem. Turn each pear quarter down on one of its faces and carefully slice it thinly.

2. To assemble the salad, toss a few handfuls of spinach leaves in a bowl with balsamic vinaigrette and transfer it to the center of a chilled plate.

3. Arrange the thinly sliced pear in fans on each side of the plate. (Two sliced pear quarters should be enough for each salad.) Cover the rest of the plate with the sliced cucumbers.

4. Mound the toasted walnuts at the center of the salad, and scatter the vegan blue cheese substitute over all.

5. Finish with a grinding of fresh black pepper and serve.

Taco Salad

This recipe is a bit of a production, but all your work will be rewarded with satisfied smiles from your guests. It's a great choice for brunch buffets. Prepare the Achiote Rice, Pico de Gallo Salsa, and Cilantro Vinaigrette while the beans cook.

YIELD: 8 SERVINGS

1 pound (454 g) dry pinto beans, soaked overnight

4 tablespoons (60 mL) canola oil

1 red onion, peeled and chopped

8 cloves garlic, peeled and minced

1 tablespoon (15 mL) dried oregano

1 tablespoon (15 mL) ground cumin

1 tablespoon (15 mL) dark chili powder

Salt, to taste

3 cups (708 mL) Cheitan Patties (page 163) or vegan chicken substitute, shredded

Freshly ground black pepper, to taste

2 heads romaine lettuce

8 tortilla shell crowns (available in Latin markets)

1 recipe Achiote Rice (page 174)

2 fresh, ripe tomatoes, sliced into 8 wedges each

2 fresh, ripe avocados, peeled, pitted, and sliced into 8 wedges each

4 serrano chilies, stems removed and sliced into thin rounds

2 cups (473 mL) Pico de Gallo Salsa (page 93)

2 cups (473 mL) Cilantro Vinaigrette (page 82)

1. Drain the soaked pinto beans and rinse them well.

2. In a large, heavy-bottomed saucepan, heat 2 tablespoons of the canola oil over medium heat and add the onion, garlic, and dry spices. Sauté until the onion is soft, about 10 minutes. Add the pinto beans and water to cover them by 3 inches (7.5 cm), and stir. Bring to a boil, skim any foam off the surface, and reduce the heat to a simmer.

3. Simmer, adding more water if necessary, until the beans are soft and palatable, about 1 hour. Taste for seasoning and add salt as needed.

4. In a large sauté pan, heat the remaining 2 tablespoons (30 mL) canola oil over medium heat. Add the shredded Cheitan Patties or vegan chicken and sauté until nicely browned. Season with salt and pepper. Keep warm.

5. Chop the romaine lettuce.

6. Place the tortilla shell crowns on a baking sheet and warm in a 350°F (180°C) oven for 3 minutes. These tortillas will burn quite easily, so watch them carefully.

7. To serve, place a handful of chopped romaine at the bottom of each tortilla shell crown. Follow with a few spoonfuls of Achiote Rice, then a few spoonfuls of the pinto beans, and then a scattering of the sautéed vegan chicken. Garnish the salad with the tomato and avocado wedges and the sliced serrano chilies. The chilies are hot, so ask your guests if they want them or offer them on a separate plate. Serve the Pico de Gallo Salsa and the Cilantro Vinaigrette at the table so that your guests can help themselves. You may also offer any hot sauces that you have on hand.

Brunch Tofu Salad

This salad makes a highly nourishing and delicious treat anytime. Use it on sandwiches or wraps, or serve it on toast as a starter.

YIELD: 3 CUPS (708 ML)

 1 pound (454 g) firm tofu, drained, rinsed, and cut into ¼-inch (.5-cm) dice

 1 cup (226 mL) finely diced celery

 ¼ cup (59 mL) finely chopped fresh parsley

 ¼ cup (59 mL) very finely diced shallots

 4 tablespoons (60 mL) finely diced red or orange bell peppers

 2 teaspoons (10 mL) ground turmeric

 1 teaspoon (5 mL) ground white pepper

 2 teaspoons (10 mL) onion powder

 1 clove garlic, minced, or 1 teaspoon (5 mL) garlic powder

 ½ teaspoon (5 mL) salt, to taste

 1 pinch cayenne pepper or a few red pepper flakes

 1 cup (236 mL) Veganopolis Mayo (page 91) or store-bought vegan mayonnaise

1. In a large bowl, combine the tofu, celery, parsley, shallots, and bell peppers.

2. Add the dry spices (and the minced garlic, if using) to the Veganopolis Mayo and stir well until you achieve a pale yellow mixture. Add the seasoned Veganopolis Mayo to the tofu mixture and stir to combine. Check the salad for seasoning and add salt as necessary.

3. Serve as a sandwich or as a salad. This salad also works well in a wrap with romaine or spinach. It will keep, if covered and refrigerated, for 3 days or longer.

Variation

Add rinsed capers, Kalamata olives, or diced pickles for flavor and visual appeal.

Bolshevik Beet Salad with Citrus Vinaigrette and Toasted Hazelnuts

What to do with all those lovely deep-red and golden beets that arrive in the markets during the late summer? Here's one suggestion.

YIELD: ABOUT 6 SERVINGS

> **4 beets, red, golden, or a combination, peeled and cut into 2-inch-long (5-cm-long) and ½-inch-wide (2.5-cm-wide) pieces**
>
> **2 cups (473 mL) orange juice**
>
> **1 cup (236 mL) roasted and chopped hazelnuts**
>
> **10 ounces (280 g) mesclun lettuce mix**
>
> **1 large cucumber, sliced**
>
> **½ cup (118 mL) Veganopolis Cashew Ricotta (page 162), seasoned to taste with dill and black pepper**
>
> **2 cups (473 mL) Citrus Vinaigrette (page 83)**
>
> **Fresh dill sprigs, for garnish (optional)**

1. Preheat the oven to 350°F (180°C). Line a roasting pan with parchment paper.

2. Place the sliced beets in the roasting pan. (Note: If you are using a combination of golden and red beets, roast them in separate pans to prevent the red beets from staining the golden beets.) Pour the orange juice over the beets, and cover the pan tightly with aluminum foil. Place the pan in the oven and roast for at least 45 minutes.

3. Check the beets by taking one piece out and piercing it with a fork. The fork should penetrate the piece with just a little pressure. Remove the pan from the oven, remove the foil, and allow the beets to cool to room temperature. At this point, you may cover and refrigerate the beets for up to four days. The acid in the orange juice helps to preserve their flavor.

4. Toss a handful of the spring mix with the citrus vinaigrette and place it on a chilled plate.

5. Arrange a handful of the beets on top and a few cucumber slices around the edge of the plate.

6. Scoop two tablespoons of the seasoned Veganopolis Cashew Ricotta on each side of the salad plate, making little quenelles of the mixture with two spoons. Garnish each quenelle with a sprig of fresh dill, if desired. Add salt to taste.

7. Scatter some of the toasted chopped hazelnuts over the salad, and serve with a warmed baguette or bread of your choice.

Cabbage, Carrot, and Parsley Slaw

We make this fresh every morning at the restaurant. The raw, organic apple cider vinegar gives the slaw a bright flavor and promotes digestion.

YIELD: 5 CUPS (1.18 L)

2 cups (473 mL) shredded red cabbage

2 cups (473 mL) shredded green cabbage

4 large carrots, peeled and finely julienned or shredded in a food processor

1 cup (236 mL) fresh Italian parsley, washed, dried, and finely chopped

¼ cup (59 mL) raw, organic apple cider vinegar

½ cup (118 mL) seasoned rice vinegar

2 tablespoons (30 mL) liquid amino acids (available from many grocers)

2 tablespoons (30 mL) turbinado sugar

1. Combine all the ingredients in a large bowl and stir well. Serve alongside sandwiches, soups, or entrées.

Cheitan Vegan Waldorf Salad

YIELD: 8 CUPS (1.9 L)

1 cup (236 mL) Veganopolis Mayo (page 91) or store-bought vegan mayonnaise

1 tablespoon (15 mL) lemon juice

2 teaspoons (10 mL) Dijon mustard

2 teaspoons (10 mL) agave or maple syrup

1 cup (236 mL) cooked Cheitan Patties (page 163), diced into ½-inch (1-cm) cubes

1 cup (236 mL) lightly roasted, chopped pecans or walnuts

1 cup (236 mL) peeled, cored, and sliced firm apples

1 cup (236 mL) finely diced celery stalks

1 cup (236 mL) seedless green or black grapes, halved

Salt, to taste

Freshly ground black pepper, to taste

Finely chopped parsley, for garnish

1. In a large bowl, stir together the Veganopolis Mayo, lemon juice, Dijon mustard, and agave syrup.

2. Add the Cheitan Patties, nuts, apples, and celery one by one, blending gently with the dressing.

3. Add the grapes. Taste for seasoning and add salt and pepper as needed.

4. To serve, scoop the salad onto a bed of red leaf or romaine lettuce. Garnish with the finely chopped parsley.

Farmer Cranberry Walnut Salad

This recipe is a delicious variation on cranberry sauce for a holiday meal.

YIELD: 2 CUPS (473 ML)

>   1 (14-ounce [392-g]) can vegan jellied cranberries
>
>   ½ cup (118 mL) chopped toasted walnuts
>
>   ½ cup (118 mL) finely diced celery
>
>   1 tablespoon (15 mL) agave syrup or turbinado sugar
>
>   1 teaspoon (5 mL) salt (optional)
>
>   2 tablespoons (30 mL) orange juice
>
>   1 tablespoon (15 mL) orange zest

1. Combine all the ingredients in a bowl. Taste for seasoning and adjust as needed.

2. Serve chilled.

To create a holiday mold:

1. Soak 2 tablespoons (30 mL) agar powder or flakes in a blend of ¼ cup (59 mL) orange juice and 2 tablespoons (30 mL) water. Heat the mixture to a boil.

2. Reduce the heat and simmer for 5 minutes. Add to the salad. Stir well, pour into the mold, and chill for a few hours before serving. At serving time, invert the mold on a chilled plate and garnish with whole cranberries and orange peel.

Variation

Add chopped apples, blueberries, or firm pears.

Old-Fashioned French Lentil Salad

This most likely goes back centuries. It's typically French and absolutely delicious. Use only French green lentils in preparing this, because the common brown lentils will turn to mush after cooking, while the green ones will hold their shape.

YIELD: 6 CUPS (1.4 L)

For the lentils:

> 2 cups (473 mL) French green lentils
>
> 1 carrot
>
> 1 stalk of celery
>
> ½ onion
>
> 4 cloves garlic, peeled
>
> 1 shallot, peeled
>
> 4 sprigs fresh parsley

For the vinaigrette:

> 4 tablespoons (60 mL) red wine vinegar
>
> 2 shallots, peeled and finely minced
>
> 2 tablespoons (30 mL) Dijon mustard
>
> 1 tablespoon (15 mL) freshly ground black pepper
>
> ¾ cup (177 mL) extra virgin olive oil
>
> Salt, to taste

To finish:

> 3 tablespoons (45 mL) canola oil
>
> 1 cup (236 mL) Fly Façon (page 118), vegan bacon, or tempeh bacon, cut into ¼-inch (.5-cm) pieces
>
> 1 head fresh green leaf lettuce, washed and separated into leaves
>
> 3 large, ripe tomatoes, quartered and lightly salted
>
> 2 shallots, peeled and finely minced
>
> ¼ cup (59 mL) finely chopped fresh parsley
>
> 1 cup (236 mL) baby croutons

1. In a pot, combine the lentils with 2 quarts (1.9 L) water and bring to a boil.

2. Lower the heat, add the vegetables, and cook until the lentils are tender, about 35 to 40 minutes. Drain and remove the vegetables.

CONTINUED ON PAGE 72

CONTINUED FROM PAGE 71

3. To make the vinaigrette, place the minced shallots in a small bowl and add the red wine vinegar. In a separate bowl, combine the Dijon mustard and black pepper. Whisk in the olive oil, a little at a time, until you have a smooth emulsion. Add the shallots and red wine vinegar, whisk everything together, and season with salt to taste.

4. Heat the canola oil in a sauté pan over medium heat. Add the bacon substitute and cook until the pieces are well browned and crisp. Drain and reserve.

5. Pour the oil from the sauté pan into the reserved lentils and stir. Stir the vinaigrette into the lentils. Add the browned bacon substitute to the lentils and stir.

6. To serve, place a mound of the lentil salad on a bed of lettuce and surround it with fresh quartered tomatoes. Garnish the salad with the minced shallots, chopped parsley, and baby croutons and serve warm or at room temperature.

Cooks' Note

You can quickly prepare baby croutons by sautéing finely diced day-old baguette in a large sauté pan with olive oil, salt, and pepper.

Grilled Tofu Salad with Avocado

This salad recipe produces a nice combination of temperature, texture, and color for your family or your guests.

YIELD: 1 SERVING

⅓ **pound (152 g) extra-firm tofu, marinated (page 141)**

Generous handful mesclun lettuce mix

2 tablespoons (30 mL) seasoned rice vinegar

1 fresh avocado, peeled, pitted, quartered, and sliced lengthwise

1 fresh tomato, sliced

1 cucumber, stripe peeled and sliced

Finely chopped parsley, for garnish

1. Preheat the grill or broiler.

2. Grill the tofu on each side until it is fully cooked and firm. Slice it lengthwise in half and grill the newly cut sides. Remove it from the grill and slice it into triangles.

3. Dress a handful of mesclun with the seasoned rice vinegar or dressing of your choice, and mound it in the center of a chilled plate.

4. Arrange one quarter of a sliced avocado and a few slices of tomato and cucumber on one side of the plate.

5. Top the salad with the grilled tofu triangles.

6. Garnish with finely diced parsley and serve.

Groovy Asian Slaw

YIELD: ABOUT 2 POUNDS (1.1 KG)

2 cups (473 mL) shredded green cabbage

1 cup (236 mL) thinly sliced or shredded red cabbage

2 carrots, peeled and grated

½ cup (118 mL) finely chopped cilantro

⅓ cup (79 mL) thinly sliced red onion

½ cup (118 mL) medium-sized fresh or canned pineapple chunks

1 cup (236 mL) roasted, chopped peanuts or almonds

½ cup (118 mL) seasoned rice vinegar

1 tablespoon (15 mL) apple cider vinegar

1 tablespoon (15 mL) liquid amino acids or tamari

2 teaspoons (10 mL) fresh ginger, peeled and finely chopped (optional)

1 tablespoon (15 mL) agave syrup or turbinado sugar

2 teaspoons (10 mL) salt

1 teaspoon (5 mL) curry powder

1 pinch cayenne pepper

1. Place all the ingredients in a large bowl and stir to combine.

2. Chill the mixture for 30 minutes and serve.

Variation

This salad makes a nice wrap filling with a leaf of romaine lettuce.

CHAPTER 3

Dressings, Sauces, and Gravy

Veganopolis Sauces and Dressings

These are some of the sauces and dressings we make fresh three times per week in the restaurant kitchen. Of course, we make many variations and hundreds of other sauces, but these are the basics you can add to, subtract from, or otherwise alter. We encourage you to experiment once you have a basic recipe down.

At Veganopolis, it is interesting to taste test the results among the various palates on staff. Any restaurant with well-balanced and consistent dressings and sauces, be they simple or complicated, has a dedicated chef and staff.

Our kitchen chef, Santos, owns hands-down the most articulated palate for the delicate balance of a vinaigrette. Isabel was our pesto specialist and top raw-slaw and dressing chef. Santos and Isabel followed this important procedure every single time they produced a recipe:

Test, wait, test, adjust, and test again.

Our recipes, never written down before this time, were tested daily and improved over time as we streamlined the production in the restaurant kitchen. Though most of the recipes in this chapter are simple classics, your own attention to tasting them will bring that special zing to the end result.

Different vinegars by different manufacturers—and even the same vinegars—can vary to your taste, bottle by bottle and year by year. The type, brand, and age of vinegars, oils, and tahinis will often call for slight adjustments in the ratios listed in the recipes.

Taste the sauce on a spoon. Wait a few minutes, then taste again on a slice of baguette or on some greens. Adjust if needed, wait for a moment, and taste again. Our motto is, "Never send it to 'the line' until it is perfect." Let 'em wait!

Concentrate on the dimensional quality and balance. It is also best to allow a vinaigrette to stand for 30 minutes to meld flavors. For marinara, béchamel, and enchilada sauces, cooking time is a factor. Some sauces are ready to use as soon as the texture and flavor are right. Some benefit from longer cooking times, which allow the flavors to meld and present themselves to the palate. As you cook, you will discover what works best for you in your kitchen.

Balsamic Vinaigrette

This vinaigrette is fantastic with many salads. It goes particularly well with spinach. Use it warmed for a German-style spinach salad. To make this dressing, you will need a whisk; two stainless steel bowls (one small and one medium); a heavy pot into which the larger bowl will almost fit; and a clean, dry kitchen towel.

YIELD: 1½ CUPS (354 ML)

> **2 shallots, peeled and very finely diced**
>
> **⅓ cup (79 mL) balsamic vinegar**
>
> **2 teaspoons (10 mL) Dijon mustard**
>
> **Freshly ground black pepper, to taste**
>
> **1 teaspoon (5 mL) agave syrup**
>
> **1 cup (236 mL) extra virgin olive oil**
>
> **Salt, to taste**

1. In a small stainless steel bowl, combine the diced shallots and balsamic vinegar. Let them rest for a few minutes while the aromatics of the shallot penetrate the vinegar.

2. Place a clean, dry kitchen towel across the opening of a heavy pot and sink a medium stainless steel bowl into it so that the towel holds the bowl in place.

3. In the larger bowl, whisk together the Dijon mustard, black pepper, and agave syrup to form a smooth mixture.

4. While whisking the mustard mixture constantly, add the olive oil in a thin stream. If the mixture starts to break, stop adding the oil and whisk furiously until every bit of it is incorporated into the emulsion. Then begin adding oil again in small batches, whisking between each addition.

5. Whisk in the vinegar/shallot mixture and combine thoroughly.

6. Taste for seasoning and add salt if necessary. This vinaigrette will keep for weeks if sealed, stored, and refrigerated.

Veganopolis Caesar Dressing

This recipe produces a classic, creamy Caesar dressing. Olive oil, garlic, lemon juice, and red wine vinegar are essential. Use this dressing for Veganopolis Caesar Salad (page 60) and the Veganopolis Chicken Caesar Sandwich (page 132).

YIELD: 4 CUPS (.95 L)

8 ounces (224 g) firm tofu, drained and rinsed

8 ounces (224 g) soft tofu, drained and rinsed

⅓ cup (79 mL) freshly squeezed lemon juice

⅓ cup (79 mL) red wine vinegar

1 tablespoon (15 mL) vegan Worcestershire sauce*

1 tablespoon (15 mL) freshly ground black pepper

4 cloves garlic, peeled and crushed

1 cup (236 mL) extra virgin olive oil or more as needed

Salt, to taste

1. In a food processor or a large blender, thoroughly blend the tofu until no particles are left in the mixture. With the machine running, add the remaining ingredients, adding enough olive oil at the very end of the process that you can taste it. Your finished Caesar dressing should be creamy but not overly thick, so it will nicely coat your lettuce.

2. Taste the dressing for seasoning and add salt as necessary. This recipe usually requires a good amount of salt to achieve the right flavor.

*Available in many areas. In a pinch, use 1 tablespoon (15 mL) tamari and 1 tablespoon (15 mL) balsamic vinegar.

Cilantro Cashew Pesto Spread

This bright-green spread can be used to top English muffins or Sunshine Crackers, as a sandwich spread or taco topping, or as a garnish for soup or stew.

YIELD: 1 CUP (236 ML)

1 cup (236 mL) raw cashews, soaked in cold water for 1 hour or longer

1 cup (236 mL) fresh cilantro leaves (some stems may be included)

1 clove garlic, peeled and sliced

2 teaspoons (10 mL) onion powder

1½ teaspoons (7.5 mL) cumin

1 teaspoon (5 mL) salt

¼ teaspoon (1.25 mL) cayenne pepper

1 tablespoon (15 mL) lime juice

1 tablespoon (15 mL) seasoned rice vinegar

1 tablespoon (15 mL) grapeseed oil

1 tablespoon (15 mL) seeded and chopped jalapeño pepper or 1 serrano chile, seeded and chopped (optional)

1. Drain the soaked cashews and rinse them well under cold running water.

2. Place all ingredients in a food processor and blend for 2 minutes.

3. Taste for seasoning and adjust salt and acid as necessary.

Cilantro Cream Vinaigrette

YIELD: 1½ CUPS (354 ML)

½ cup (118 mL) raw cashews, soaked in cold water for 1 hour or more

⅓ cup (79 mL) fresh cilantro leaves

1 teaspoon (5 mL) ground cumin

1 teaspoon (5 mL) onion powder

1 clove garlic, peeled and crushed, or 1 teaspoon (5 mL) garlic powder

¼ teaspoon (1.25 mL) ground white pepper

½ teaspoon (2.5 mL) salt

¼ teaspoon (1.25 mL) cayenne pepper

3 tablespoons (45 mL) seasoned rice vinegar

1 tablespoon (15 mL) grapeseed oil

2 teaspoons (10 mL) agave or maple syrup

2 tablespoons (30 mL) lime juice

1. Drain the soaked cashews and rinse them well under cold running water.

2. Place all the ingredients into a food processor and blend for 2 minutes.

3. Taste for seasoning and adjust salt and acid as necessary.

Cilantro Vinaigrette

This gorgeously flavored dressing works well on many salads, but particularly the Taco Salad (page 64). A food processor or blender is essential for this recipe.

YIELD: 2 CUPS (473 ML)

   1 bunch fresh cilantro, stemmed and roughly chopped

   1 jalapeño pepper, seeded and roughly chopped

   10 ounces (226 g) soft tofu, drained

   3 tablespoons (45 mL) seasoned rice vinegar

   1 cup (236 mL) canola or grapeseed oil

   Juice of 1 lime

   Red pepper flakes, to taste

   Salt, to taste

1. In a blender or food processor, blend the cilantro, jalapeño, tofu, and rice vinegar until smooth. With the machine running, add the oil in a thin stream to form an emulsion.

2. Add the lime juice and blend again. Add red pepper flakes to taste and pulse twice.

3. Taste for seasoning and add salt as necessary.

Citrus Vinaigrette

This great summertime vinaigrette is perfect on the Bolshevik Beet Salad (page 67) or any salad that features citrus fruit, such as grapefruit or blood-orange sections.

YIELD: 1½ CUPS (354 ML)

½ cup (118 mL) freshly squeezed orange juice

2 tablespoons (30 mL) fresh lemon juice

1 shallot, peeled and very finely diced

1 teaspoon (5 mL) fine Dijon mustard

2 teaspoons (10 mL) agave syrup

1 cup (236 mL) extra virgin olive oil

Salt, to taste

1. In a small bowl, combine the orange and lemon juices and the shallots. Set aside.

2. In a medium bowl, stir together the mustard and agave syrup.

3. Add the olive oil in a thin stream to the mustard mixture, whisking constantly to create an emulsion.

4. Slowly add the juice and shallots to this mixture and whisk together.

5. Taste for seasoning and add salt as necessary. Covered and refrigerated, this vinaigrette will last for 2 weeks.

Veganopolis Ranch Dressing

Scallions and chopped parsley enhance this vegan version of the American standard.

YIELD: 2 CUPS (473 ML)

8 ounces (224 g) soft tofu

8 ounces (224 g) firm tofu

Juice of 1 lemon

2 teaspoons (10 mL) agave syrup

1 cup (226 mL) sliced scallions

½ cup (118 mL) finely chopped parsley

2 tablespoons (30 mL) seasoned rice vinegar

2 teaspoons (10 mL) ground white pepper

1½ cups (354 mL) grapeseed or canola oil

¼ cup (59 mL) water

Salt, to taste

1. Combine the soft and firm tofu in a food processor and blend until very smooth.

2. Add the lemon juice, agave syrup, scallions, parsley, vinegar, and white pepper, and blend again until well mixed.

3. With the machine running, add the grapeseed or canola oil in a thin stream until it is completely incorporated. The dressing should be shiny and smooth.

4. Taste for seasoning and add salt in small amounts, blending after each addition, until you get the result that pleases you. Your finished dressing should be thick enough to nicely coat the lettuce—thinner than a mayonnaise, but thicker than a vinaigrette. You may add water to adjust the density.

Veganopolis Thousand Island Dressing

I have often mused about the origin of Thousand Island dressing. It is, after all, comparatively vulgar in relation to rémoulades, aiolis, and other elegant dressings; but there is really something appealing about it. It is as essential as sauerkraut on the Vegan New York Reuben Sandwich (page 134).

YIELD: 3⅓ CUPS (787 ML)

> **2 cups (473 mL) Veganopolis Mayo (page 91)**
>
> **1 cup (236 mL) ketchup**
>
> **⅓ cup (79 mL) dill pickle relish**

1. Combine the three ingredients and blend well.

Dijon Vinaigrette

Classic vinaigrette is always made with 1 part vinegar to 3 parts oil. You can scale this one up by using champagne vinegar, but white wine vinegar works fine. Dijon has been making mustard for at least two centuries and most likely much longer than that. It is the favorite condiment at the table in France.

YIELD: 1½ CUPS (354 ML)

3 shallots, peeled and finely diced

⅓ cup (79 mL) champagne or white wine vinegar

¼ cup (59 mL) Dijon mustard

1 teaspoon (5 mL) ground white pepper

1 teaspoon (5 mL) agave syrup

1 cup (236 mL) extra virgin olive oil

Salt, to taste

1. In a small stainless steel bowl, combine the diced shallots and balsamic vinegar. Let the mixture rest for a few minutes while the aromatics of the shallot penetrate the vinegar.

2. Place a clean, dry kitchen towel across the opening of a heavy pot and sink a medium stainless steel bowl into it so that the towel holds the bowl in place.

3. In the larger bowl, whisk together the Dijon mustard, white pepper, and agave syrup to form a smooth mixture.

4. While whisking the mustard mixture constantly, add the olive oil in a thin stream. If the mixture starts to break, stop adding the oil and whisk furiously until every bit of it is incorporated into the emulsion. Then begin adding oil again in small batches, whisking between each addition.

5. Whisk in the vinegar/shallot mixture and combine thoroughly. Taste for seasoning and add salt as needed.

Cooks' Note

This vinaigrette works well on any green salad and is wonderful on avocados. For a summer treat, slice a medium-ripe avocado in half and remove the pit and skin carefully. Place the halves face up on a bed of mixed lettuces, which have been lightly tossed in Dijon vinaigrette. Fill the half sphere in the center of each avocado half with Dijon vinaigrette and sprinkle the whole plate with finely diced parsley. Garnish with ripe cherry or grape tomatoes. As a child, I was served a dish like this at a restaurant in Canada, and I have never forgotten how simple, elegant, and delicious it was.

Simple Herb Vinaigrette

This dressing is great on sandwiches or salads and super simple to make.

YIELD: 1⅓ CUPS (317 ML)

> 1 cup (236 mL) olive oil
>
> ⅓ cup (79 mL) red wine vinegar
>
> 2 teaspoons (10 mL) dry Italian seasoning
>
> 1 teaspoon (5 mL) salt

1. Combine all the ingredients in a bottle. (A plastic squeeze bottle is perfect for this.) Whisk or shake vigorously directly before using.

Tahini Dressing

YIELD: 1½ CUPS (354 ML)

½ shallot, finely diced

1 cup (226 mL) raw tahini

3 tablespoons (45 mL) seasoned rice vinegar or red wine vinegar

1 tablespoon (15 mL) parsley or cilantro, chopped, or 2 teaspoons (10 mL) dried oregano

1 tablespoon (15 mL) liquid amino acids or soy sauce

2 teaspoons (10 mL) agave syrup, maple syrup, turbinado sugar, or pineapple juice

1 teaspoon (5 mL) turmeric (optional)

1 teaspoon (5 mL) salt

1 teaspoon (5 mL) ground white pepper

1 teaspoon (5 mL) ground cumin

⅓ cup (79 mL) water

1 tablespoon (15 mL) olive oil

1. In a mixing bowl, combine all the ingredients except the water and olive oil.

2. Slowly whisk in the water until well combined.

3. Slowly whisk in the olive oil.

4. Taste for seasoning and adjust as needed.

Cooks' Note

Add more water or lemon juice, if necessary, to achieve a smoother result.

Veganopolis Béchamel Sauce

This sauce can be substituted for any savory white sauce. I use it as the base for many dishes, including the Veganopolis Mac and Cheese with Green Peas (page 196). You can add crushed garlic for a delicious creamy garlic sauce or melt shredded vegan cheese into it and use it as a vegan Mornay sauce.

YIELD: 2 QUARTS (1.9 L)

> 2 quarts (1.9 L) soy or rice beverage
>
> ⅓ cup (79 mL) olive oil
>
> ⅔ cup (158 mL) white spelt flour or other white flour
>
> 4 shallots, peeled and very finely diced
>
> 2 teaspoons (10 mL) ground white pepper
>
> 2 teaspoons (10 mL) ground nutmeg
>
> Salt, to taste

1. In a saucepan over medium-high heat, heat the soy or rice beverage to a boil, then reduce the heat to a simmer.

2. In a large, heavy-bottomed saucepan, heat the olive oil over medium-high heat. Whisk in the flour to form a roux.

3. Add the shallots and dry spices and cook everything together, whisking constantly, for about 5 minutes or until the roux is fragrant and just beginning to darken.

4. Add the hot soy or rice beverage in 1-cup (236-mL) batches, whisking to incorporate after each addition. Continue adding and whisking until all the liquid is incorporated. Add salt until you achieve the flavor you desire.

Cooks' Note

To augment the flavor of the béchamel, try studding a small, whole, peeled onion with whole cloves and placing it in the finished sauce. Cook the sauce over very low heat for an additional 30 minutes, stirring occasionally. Remove and discard the onion. You may also try adding a few bay leaves when you add the onion, removing them before using the sauce.

This recipe makes a large quantity for a full pan casserole. We suggest making this large batch and freezing the unused portion.

New Orleans–Style Vegan Barbecue Sauce

This sauce is great for barbecued anything. My favorite use for it is on sliced seitan, which makes a remarkably good sandwich. Barbecued tofu is also really good as a sandwich or cubed and served over rice.

YIELD: 3 CUPS (708 ML)

> 2 tablespoons (30 mL) canola oil
>
> 1 large onion, peeled and finely diced
>
> 2 teaspoons (10 mL) garlic powder
>
> 2 teaspoons (10 mL) onion powder
>
> 2 teaspoons (10 mL) freshly ground black pepper
>
> 1 teaspoon (5 mL) ground white pepper
>
> ½ teaspoon (2.5 mL) cayenne pepper
>
> 2 cups (473 mL) vegetable stock
>
> 1½ cups (354 mL) bottled mild chili sauce (in a pinch, use 1 [6-ounce (168-g)] can tomato paste)
>
> ¼ cup (59 mL) agave syrup or maple syrup
>
> Juice of 1 orange
>
> Juice of 1 lemon
>
> 4 tablespoons (60 mL) apple cider vinegar
>
> ¾ cup (177 mL) chopped roasted almonds
>
> 1 tablespoon (15 mL) crushed fresh garlic
>
> 1 tablespoon (15 mL) liquid smoke flavoring
>
> 2 teaspoons (10 mL) hot sauce
>
> Salt, to taste

1. In a large, heavy-bottomed saucepan, heat the canola oil over low heat. Add the onions and sauté until they begin to caramelize, about 15 minutes, stirring frequently.

2. Stir in the dry spices.

3. Stir in the stock, agave or maple syrup, chili sauce, orange juice, lemon juice, vinegar, almonds, and garlic.

4. Cook everything together until you achieve the texture you want for your barbecue sauce.

5. Using an immersion blender or a food processor, blend the sauce.

6. Taste for seasoning and add salt, liquid smoke flavoring, and hot sauce as needed.

Veganopolis Mayo

One nice thing about making your own mayonnaise is that you can season it just to your taste. It's also very economical.

YIELD: 3 CUPS (708 ML)

> **8 ounces (224 g) firm tofu, drained and rinsed**
>
> **8 ounces (224 g) soft tofu, drained and rinsed**
>
> **4 tablespoons (60 mL) apple cider vinegar**
>
> **2 teaspoons (10 mL) agave syrup**
>
> **1 tablespoon (15 mL) fresh lemon juice**
>
> **½ teaspoon (2.5 mL) dry mustard**
>
> **2 teaspoons (10 mL) ground white pepper**
>
> **1 cup (226 mL) grapeseed or canola oil**
>
> **Salt, to taste**

1. In a blender or food processor, blend the firm and soft tofu together until smooth.

2. Add the vinegar, agave syrup, lemon juice, and dry spices and blend again.

3. While the machine is running, add the grapeseed or canola oil in a thin stream until it is incorporated. If the mayonnaise is too thick at this point, you may add a little water.

4. Season to taste with salt and perhaps a little more fresh lemon juice.

Veganopolis Dijonnaise

This is great on many sandwiches and burgers. It will keep nicely for weeks.

YIELD: 2 CUPS (473 ML)

  1 cup (236 mL) Veganopolis Mayo (page 91)

  1 cup (236 mL) Dijon mustard

1. Blend the two ingredients. Store sealed and refrigerated.

Pico de Gallo Salsa

Pico de gallo *means "rooster's beak" in Spanish, and this does not refer to any ingredient in the salsa—especially in a vegan cookbook. Rather, it refers to the sound of your knife tapping the cutting board rapidly as you dice the tomatoes, chilies, and onions. Imagine hens and cocks in the yard tapping away at their corn, and you get the idea. Hats off to Isabel Trujillo Chaves, who made the very best pico de gallo in our kitchen several times a week.*

YIELD: 2 CUPS (473 ML)

4 ripe tomatoes, finely diced

2 jalapeño peppers, stems removed, seeded, and finely diced

1 large white onion, peeled and finely diced

1 bunch fresh cilantro, rinsed, shaken dry, stemmed, and finely diced

2 tablespoons (30 mL) fresh lime juice or seasoned rice vinegar

1 tablespoon (15 mL) ground cumin, toasted (toasting instructions follow)

Salt, to taste

1. In a large bowl, stir together the tomatoes, peppers, onion, and cilantro.

2. Stir in the lime juice or vinegar and then the toasted cumin. Taste for seasoning and add salt as desired.

Cooks' Note

To toast cumin, heat a small, dry sauté pan (a cast-iron skillet is ideal) over medium heat and add the ground cumin. Stir the cumin around in the hot pan until it darkens a little, then remove the pan from the heat and scrape the cumin into a clean container.

Roasted Garlic Ketchup

This is just grand on potatoes and burgers.

YIELD: 24 OUNCES (672 G)

> 1 (24-ounce [672-g]) bottle ketchup
>
> 2 tablespoons (30 mL) crushed garlic
>
> 2 tablespoons (30 mL) balsamic vinegar
>
> 1 tablespoon (15 mL) Roasted Garlic Paste (page 95)

1. Combine all the ingredients and stir well. Refrigerate until ready to use.

Roasted Garlic Paste

YIELD: 6 OUNCES (168 G)

> **4 heads fresh garlic**
>
> **½ cup (118 mL) water**
>
> **¼ cup (59 mL) olive oil**

1. Preheat oven to 350°F (180°C).

2. Slice off the top ¼ of the heads of garlic, exposing the cloves. Discard the tops.

3. Place the prepared heads of garlic in an oven-safe pan, such as a small loaf pan. Add the water and olive oil. Tightly seal the pan with aluminum foil, and cook the heads for approximately 45 minutes. (When they're ready, the garlic heads should be soft and beginning to brown a little. If the heads are still firm and the cloves are still bright white, return the pan to the oven for an additional 15 minutes.) Remove the pan from the oven, remove the foil, and transfer the roasted garlic heads to a surface where they can cool to room temperature.

4. Once they are cool enough to handle, squeeze the softened garlic cloves out of their papery skin into a bowl. Crush the softened garlic cloves with a fork, or place the entire contents of the bowl into a food processor and process until blended smooth. Transfer the garlic paste to a clean container and store, covered, in the refrigerator.

Basil Pesto

A chef friend of mine used to come to the restaurant a few times a month to buy a half-pound of this pesto because he liked it so much. I would always joke with him about the recipe, detailing all the ingredients until I got to the end of the list at which point I would say, "and then of course the secret ingredient. . . ." Well, here's the entire recipe, including the secret ingredient, which is seasoned rice vinegar.

Rice vinegar is primarily used in Japanese kitchens. It is sold in 2 varieties: plain and seasoned. The seasoned variety is what makes sushi rice taste the way it does. Its sweet/salty/acid flavor is unique among vinegars and adds just the right touch to this pesto. Of the two most common brands of rice vinegar in the United States, I prefer Marukan for its consistent quality and flavor.

This pesto is great for pastas, pizzas, and sandwiches. It's also an essential ingredient in the Mediterranean Sandwich (page 125) and the Vegan Chicken Pesto Sandwich (page 133).

YIELD: 2 CUPS (473 ML)

> **8 cloves garlic, peeled and minced**
>
> **2 bunches fresh basil, stemmed (about 3 cups [750 g])**
>
> **2 ounces (57 g) pine nuts**
>
> **¼ cup (59 mL) seasoned rice vinegar**
>
> **3 tablespoons (45 mL) red wine vinegar**
>
> **1½ cups (375 mL) extra virgin olive oil, or more as needed**
>
> **Salt, to taste**

1. In a food processor, blend the garlic, basil leaves, pine nuts, and vinegars until smooth.

2. With the machine still running, add the olive oil in a thin stream until you achieve the texture you want. What you are looking for is a fairly dense mixture that coats a spoon thickly.

3. Add salt as needed to bring out the flavors.

Cooks' Note

This pesto will keep, if covered and refrigerated, for at least a week. If you place it in sterile, sealed jars, it will keep even longer. If the top of the pesto oxidizes over time, simply spoon the very top layer off and discard. The remainder should be fine.

Variation

Add ½ cup (118 mL) soaked and drained sun-dried tomatoes.

Mushroom Gravy

This is easy to make, and your friends and family will love you for it. It goes great with Veganopolis Spelt and Scallion Biscuits (page 107) or Savory Bread Pudding (page 103).

YIELD: 8 CUPS (1.9 L)

6 cups (1500 mL) best-quality vegetable stock

¼ cup (59 mL) olive or canola oil

½ cup (118 mL) spelt flour or other flour

½ cup (118 mL) finely diced shallots

1 tablespoon (15 mL) garlic powder

1 tablespoon (15 mL) onion powder

2 teaspoons (10 mL) ground white pepper

1 teaspoon (5 mL) freshly ground black pepper

½ teaspoon (2.5 mL) cayenne pepper

1 cup (226 mL) fresh button or crimini mushrooms, stemmed and quartered

2 tablespoons (30 mL) tamari

1. In a saucepan, bring the stock to a boil.

2. In a second saucepan, heat the oil over high heat. Add the flour and whisk to form a roux.

3. Cook the roux for about 3 minutes to eliminate any raw flour taste in the finished gravy.

4. Add the shallots and the dry spices, and cook for another 2 to 3 minutes. Add the mushrooms and cook for another 5 minutes, stirring constantly with a steel or wooden spoon.

5. Ladle about ¼ of the boiling stock into the mushrooms, and stir until it's completely blended. Blend in another ⅓. Little by little, add the rest of the stock until you reach a consistency you like.

6. Stir in the tamari.

Roasted Red Pepper Sauce

This tangy, rich sauce is great on the Roasted Eggplant Sandwich (page 126).

YIELD: 3 CUPS (708 ML)

> 2 cups (473 mL) roasted red peppers, stemmed, peeled, and seeded (or use the bottled equivalent)
>
> 4 tablespoons (60 mL) balsamic vinegar
>
> 3 cloves garlic, peeled and crushed
>
> 2 tablespoons (30 mL) Roasted Garlic Paste (page 95)
>
> ½ cup (118 mL) olive oil
>
> Salt, to taste

1. In a blender or food processor, blend the peppers until smooth.

2. Add the vinegar, garlic, and garlic paste and blend again. With the machine running, add the olive oil in a thin stream until it is all incorporated into the mixture.

3. Taste for seasoning and add salt as necessary.

Veganopolis Recipe Enchilada Sauce

This sauce is made using all fresh vegetables and chilies and will fill your kitchen with the most delightful aromas. (Canned enchilada sauces seem like tomato juice by comparison.) Use this sauce on Enchilada Lasagna (page 207) or on your own creations. This sauce freezes nicely.

YIELD: 8 CUPS (1.9 L)

¼ cup (59 mL) olive oil

6 large, ripe tomatoes or 8 Roma tomatoes

4 poblano peppers (also called pasilla chilies)

4 jalapeño peppers

2 white onions, peeled and quartered

12 cloves garlic, peeled

1 tablespoon (15 mL) ground cumin

1 tablespoon (15 mL) oregano

1 tablespoon (15 mL) dark chili powder

1 (32-ounce [.1-kg]) can tomato juice

Salt, to taste

1. Preheat the oven to 450°F (240°C). Line a large roasting pan with parchment paper and coat with olive oil.

2. Arrange the tomatoes, peppers, onions, and garlic in the pan and coat them lightly with olive oil.

3. Roast the vegetables for about 35 minutes, or until the skins of the peppers are about 75 percent blackened, turning once. Remove the pan from the oven and transfer the peppers to a bowl. Cover it with plastic wrap or an inverted plate and set aside.

4. When the peppers are cool enough to handle, strip the skins and remove the seeds. Remove the skins and seeds from the tomatoes. Chop all of the vegetables roughly. Try to retain as much of the liquid from the roasting pan and your cutting board as possible, and use all the juices in the sauce.

5. In a large saucepan, heat 2 tablespoons (30 mL) olive oil over medium heat and add the dry spices. Cook until fragrant. Add the chopped vegetables and the tomato juice and bring to a boil.

6. Blend the sauce thoroughly with an immersion blender or in a food processor, thinning it with water if necessary.

7. Taste for seasoning and add salt as needed.

Marinara Sauce

This all-purpose Italian red sauce may be varied in countless ways. Of course, using fresh, blanched, peeled, seeded, and diced tomatoes will always result in a better tasting sauce, but best-quality canned diced tomatoes are acceptable and even preferable in the winter months when tomatoes are unavailable or absurdly expensive. I always use diced tomatoes rather than crushed tomatoes, whole tomatoes, or tomato sauce because they cook down into an appealing, chunky sauce you can serve as is or blend smooth.

YIELD: 6 CUPS (816 ML)

½ cup (118 mL) extra virgin olive oil

1 large red onion, peeled and finely diced

4 cloves garlic, peeled and crushed

1 tablespoon (15 mL) Italian seasoning blend

1 teaspoon (5 mL) freshly ground black pepper

1 small pinch red pepper flakes

1 (32-ounce [1.1-kg]) can diced tomatoes or an equivalent amount diced, fresh tomatoes

Salt, to taste

1. In a large saucepan, heat the oil over medium heat.

2. Add the onions, garlic, and dry spices. Cook until the onions are softened. Add the diced tomatoes and stir well.

3. Simmer for at least 40 minutes, and add salt as needed before serving.

Cooks' Note
You can spike the sauce at the end with a splash of balsamic vinegar or fresh chopped basil, if desired.

CHAPTER 4

Breakfast Sensations

Savory Bread Pudding

Always one of the most popular dishes on our Saturday brunch menu, this recipe is an attempt at a soufflé without eggs. Upon first tasting this, sensitive persons may get a little teary eyed. It is just that good! It's another grand way to use up stale baguette or other good breads. Fresh herbs and cracked black pepper add a nice sharpness to the overall dish. This recipe uses sautéed leeks, but you may substitute blanched asparagus stalks that have been halved lengthwise to make a more elegant offering. One of my chefs always called leeks "the poor man's asparagus."

YIELD: 6–8 SERVINGS

2 or more baguette, focaccia, or ciabatta loaves or a combination, sliced 1 inch (2.5 cm) thick (if using a baguette, slice on a diagonal to make longer pieces)

1 quart (.95 L) rice or soy beverage

½ cup (118 mL) olive or canola oil, divided, plus more to oil the pan

2 large leeks, well washed, drained, and thinly sliced, or ¾ pound (339 g) asparagus

1 pound (454 g) mushrooms, stemmed and quartered

Salt, to taste

Freshly ground black pepper, to taste

8 ounces (224 g) soft tofu

8 ounces (224 g) firm tofu

6 cloves garlic, crushed

2 tablespoons (30 mL) vegan Worcestershire sauce

2 tablespoons (30 mL) fresh lemon juice

1 tablespoon (15 mL) ground turmeric

½ teaspoon (2.5 mL) cayenne pepper

2 teaspoons (10 mL) white pepper

2 teaspoons (10 mL) paprika

6 ounces (168 g) each vegan mozzarella and vegan cheddar, sliced or grated, or 12 ounces (336 g) total other vegan cheese substitute

¼ cup (59 mL) stemmed and chopped fresh rosemary

¼ cup (59 mL) stemmed and chopped fresh parsley

CONTINUED ON PAGE 104

CONTINUED FROM PAGE 103

1. Preheat the oven to 400°F (200°C). Lightly coat a shallow baking pan with olive or canola oil.

2. Soak the sliced bread pieces in the rice or soy beverage while you prepare the other ingredients.

3. Heat the oil over medium heat in a sauté pan. Sauté the leeks and the mushrooms until the leeks are softened and the mushrooms are cooked through. Season liberally with salt and pepper.

4. In a food processor, blend thoroughly the soft and firm tofu, garlic, remaining ¼ cup (59 mL) oil, Worcestershire sauce, lemon juice, turmeric, cayenne pepper, white pepper, and paprika. You may add soy or rice beverage to thin the mixture if necessary. The result you are looking for is a beaten-egg texture. Taste the mixture for seasoning and add salt as necessary.

5. Layer the soaked bread slices in the bottom of the prepared baking pan, followed by half the tofu mixture, half the vegetables, and half the vegan cheese. Sprinkle with half the chopped rosemary and parsley, and give the layer a good grinding of black pepper.

6. Repeat the layering with the remaining ingredients.

7. Bake, uncovered, until the bread pudding is heated through and the top is nicely golden brown, about 45 minutes. Cut into square serving pieces, and serve as is or with a large spoonful of Mushroom Gravy (page 97) ladled on top.

Variation

For a soy-free version, replace the tofu with 2 cups (473 mL) rice beverage. Heat the rice beverage in a saucepan, stirring in 2 tablespoons (30 mL) flax meal or quinoa flour and 2 teaspoons (10 mL) ground turmeric. Simmer for 2 minutes, or until well blended. Replace the vegan soy cheese with vegan rice, hemp, or almond cheese.

Vegan Benedict

Benedict is perfect for Sunday brunch. Pass the champagne cocktail, dear, the sun is coming out.

YIELD: 6 SERVINGS

     Vegan Hollandaise Sauce (page 106)

     1 recipe Vegan "Bacon" Loaf (page 153)

     6 English muffins

     1 recipe Golden Tofu Patties (page 166)

     ½ cup (118 mL) chopped Italian parsley, for garnish

     12 cherry tomatoes, sliced in half and lightly salted, for garnish

1. Make the Vegan Hollandaise Sauce and keep it warm.

2. Slice the Vegan Bacon Loaf into ¼-inch-thick (.5-cm-thick) slices and grill or sauté them until browned on a lightly oiled hot grill or in a lightly oiled sauté pan set over medium heat.

3. Slice the English muffins and toast or grill them. Set the 2 muffin halves down on a warmed plate and lay a slice of Vegan Bacon on each one, followed by a warm Golden Tofu Patty.

4. Ladle dollops of Vegan Hollandaise Sauce on each muffin half. Garnish with fresh chopped parsley and cherry tomatoes, and serve.

Vegan Hollandaise Sauce

YIELD: 12 OUNCES (336 G)

> 10 ounces (280 g) soft tofu
>
> 4 tablespoons (60 mL) vegan margarine, melted
>
> Juice of 1 lemon
>
> 1 tablespoon (15 mL) ground turmeric
>
> 1 pinch cayenne pepper
>
> Salt, to taste

1. In a food processor, combine all the ingredients and blend until you achieve a thick sauce that will coat a spoon.

2. Transfer to a saucepan and heat very gently over low heat, whisking constantly. If the mixture becomes too grainy, add a bit of hot water and continue to stir. Before serving, taste for seasoning and add salt and lemon as necessary.

Variation

Vegan Florentine Version: Proceed as above, but add to the finished hollandaise 8 ounces (224 g) stemmed, finely sliced, sautéed spinach that has been seasoned with 1 teaspoon (5 mL) grated nutmeg and 1 teaspoon (5 mL) white pepper and drained well. Keep the sauce warm while you prepare the finished plates.

Veganopolis Spelt and Scallion Biscuits

This standard offering at the restaurant is adored by the customers. They are spectacular with Mushroom Gravy (page 97).

YIELD: 10–12 BISCUITS

¼ cup (59 mL) fresh scallions, sliced

1 tablespoon (15 mL) turbinado sugar

1 tablespoon (15 mL) onion powder

3 cups (708 mL) unbleached white spelt flour or other flour

1 tablespoon (15 mL) brewer's yeast flakes

2 teaspoons (10 mL) salt

2 teaspoons (10 mL) baking soda

1½ teaspoons (7.5 mL) baking powder

1¼ cups (295 mL) rice or soy beverage

3 tablespoons (45 mL) lemon juice

1. Preheat the oven to 350°F (180°C). Line a baking sheet with parchment paper.

2. In a large bowl, combine the scallions, turbinado sugar, onion powder, flour, brewer's yeast, salt, baking soda, and baking powder.

3. In a separate small bowl, combine the rice or soy beverage with the lemon juice and stir them together.

4. Make a well in the center of the dry ingredients and quickly fold in the liquid ingredients until just combined.

5. With a spoon or an ice cream scooper, scoop the batter onto the prepared baking sheet, placing them 1 to 2 inches (3 to 5 cm) apart. Bake for 9 to 12 minutes, or until the biscuits are just lightly browned and still soft (but not wet) inside.

Veganopolis Tofu Scramble

This is our recipe for tofu scramble. Of course, there are as many variations for a standard like this as there are ideas in your head. Try adding spinach, mushrooms, tomatoes, fresh herbs, cubed zucchini, or whatever else you think will go well.

YIELD: 2½ POUNDS (2.3 L) OR 8 SERVINGS

¼ cup (59 mL) canola or olive oil

4 shallots, peeled and finely diced

1 yellow pepper, finely diced

1 red pepper, finely diced

2 teaspoons (10 mL) ground turmeric

2 teaspoons (10 mL) paprika

2 teaspoons (10 mL) white pepper

2 teaspoons (10 mL) garlic powder

¼ teaspoon (1.25 mL) cayenne pepper

2 pounds (1.1 kg) firm tofu, crumbled into approximately ¼-inch (.5-cm) pieces

Juice of 1 lemon

2 teaspoons (10 mL) vegan Worcestershire sauce

⅓ cup (79 mL) finely chopped parsley

Salt, to taste

1. In a large sauté pan, heat the oil over medium heat and sauté the shallots and peppers until they are soft.

2. Add the dry spices. Cook, stirring constantly, for 1 to 2 minutes.

3. Add the tofu and stir well, evenly distributing the dry spices through the dish.

4. Stir in the lemon juice, Worcestershire sauce, and parsley.

5. Taste for seasoning and add enough salt to bring out the flavors. Serve immediately with toasted bread, potatoes, and perhaps your favorite hot sauce.

Rosti Hash

This is a very tasty brunch dish or dinner side dish that features those delectable root vegetables that are so prevalent in the fall. It is loosely derived from the Swedish dish rosti, *which is similar to hash browns, but with the kick of all those colors and flavors. For best results, after shredding the vegetables, press them between two large, clean kitchen towels to extract some of the moisture. This step will result in a crisper finished hash.*

YIELD: ABOUT 12 SERVINGS

1 cup (236 mL) canola oil, divided, plus more to oil pan

1 large red onion, peeled and finely diced

1 tablespoon (15 mL) salt

1 tablespoon (15 mL) dill weed

2 teaspoons (10 mL) garlic powder

2 teaspoons (10 mL) ground white pepper

1 teaspoon (5 mL) grated nutmeg

4 parsnips, peeled and shredded

4 carrots, peeled and shredded

2 turnips, peeled and shredded

1 rutabaga, peeled and shredded

4 potatoes, peeled and shredded

1. Preheat the oven to 400°F (200°C). Line a flat baking pan with parchment paper and lightly coat it with canola oil.

2. Heat ½ cup (118 mL) of the canola oil in a sauté pan over medium heat. Add the diced onion and sauté until soft. Stir in the salt and dry spices.

3. In a large bowl, toss the shredded vegetables with the sautéed onions until evenly mixed. Add the remaining ½ cup (118 mL) canola oil and toss again. Spread the mixture evenly over the baking sheet and roast until the vegetables are tender and beginning to brown, about 45 minutes.

4. Taste for seasoning and add salt as necessary. Alternatively, you may form the mixture into thin patties and fry them in a large sauté pan, about 10 minutes on each side.

City Cinnamon Pecan Rolls

This recipe produces cinnamon rolls that are not overly sweet and that highlight the flavor of the cinnamon and pecans.

YIELD: 6–7 LARGE ROLLS OR 14 MINIATURE ROLLS

1 cup (236 mL) rice, soy, or almond beverage, divided

⅓ cup (79 mL) plus 1 teaspoon (5 mL) turbinado sugar, divided

1 (¼-ounce [7-g]) packet active dry yeast

3 cups (750 mL) all-purpose flour

1 teaspoon (5 mL) salt

1 tablespoon (15 mL) ground cinnamon, divided

10 tablespoons vegan margarine, divided

2 teaspoons (10 mL) pure vanilla extract, divided

3 cups (708 mL) white spelt flour or other white flour

2 tablespoons (30 mL) quinoa flour (optional)

1 teaspoon (5 mL) salt

2 teaspoons (10 mL) ground cinnamon

2 tablespoons (30 mL) agave or maple syrup

1½ cups (354 mL) chopped pecans

1½ cups (354 mL) raisins (optional)

1. In a small saucepan over low heat, warm ½ cup (118 mL) of the rice, soy, or almond beverage to 105°F (40°C).

2. Stir in 1 teaspoon (5 mL) of the turbinado sugar and the yeast. Set aside for 10 minutes until bubbles form.

3. In a bowl, stir together the all-purpose flour, salt, and 1 teaspoon of the cinnamon. Set aside.

4. In a saucepan over low heat or in the microwave, gently warm the remaining ½ cup (118 mL) soy, rice, or almond beverage; 6 tablespoons (60 mL) of the vegan margarine; and 1 teaspoon (5 mL) of the pure vanilla extract. Heat just enough to melt the margarine. Do not simmer.

5. Add the liquid ingredients to the dry ingredients. Slowly work the two together to form a dough. Sprinkle with flour as necessary to keep the dough from sticking. Add a very small amount of water if the flour is not fully incorporated.

6. Knead for 2 minutes on a clean, lightly floured surface, and then form the dough into a ball. Lightly oil the sides of a large bowl. Transfer the dough to the bowl, cover with plastic wrap or a clean towel, and place in a warm area until the dough doubles in size. This will take 30 minutes to 1 hour.

7. Punch the dough down and let rise another 25 minutes in the refrigerator. Alternatively, at this point the dough can be covered and left in the refrigerator overnight, if desired.

8. Place the dough on a clean, floured surface or on a sheet of lightly oiled parchment paper. Roll out the dough into a ½-inch-thick (1-cm-thick) rectangle. Let rest.

9. In a microwaveable bowl, melt the remaining 4 tablespoons vegan margarine, the agave or maple syrup, the remaining ⅓ cup (79 mL) turbinado sugar, the remaining 2 teaspoons (10 mL) cinnamon, and the remaining 1 teaspoon (5 mL) vanilla extract. Stir together.

10. Preheat the oven to 350°F (180°C). Line a baking sheet with parchment paper and lightly oil the paper.

11. Brush or spoon half of the margarine and syrup mixture to coat the dough rectangle. Sprinkle half the pecans and half the raisins, if using, over the surface. Cut the rectangle vertically into 1½-inch (3.5-cm) strips for large rolls or ¾-inch (1.75-cm) strips for small rolls. Carefully roll each strip tightly and place on the prepared sheet.

12. Sprinkle the remaining chopped pecans and raisins, if using, over the tops of the rolls. Spoon the remaining margarine and syrup mixture over the tops and let drizzle down the sides.

13. Bake for 18 to 20 minutes.

14. Serve fresh from the oven. These rolls can be stored, if cooled and covered, for a day or two. Warm before serving.

Variation

Leave out the pecans and use golden raisins, dried currants, dried cranberries, or dried cherries in their place.

Vegan French Toast

This quick and delicious French toast recipe makes a great breakfast item.

YIELD: 8 SERVINGS

> 2 cups (473 mL) rice beverage
>
> 2 tablespoons (30 mL) vegan margarine
>
> 1 tablespoon (15 mL) flax meal
>
> 2 teaspoons (10 mL) pure vanilla extract
>
> 1 teaspoon (5 mL) ground cinnamon
>
> ¼ teaspoon (1.25 mL) ground nutmeg
>
> ½ teaspoon (2.5 mL) salt
>
> 2 teaspoons (10 mL) agave syrup or 1 tablespoon (15 mL) turbinado sugar
>
> ½ ripe banana
>
> Sliced bread of your choice (whole wheat or other whole-grain bread preferred)
>
> Confectioners' sugar, for dusting (optional)

1. In a saucepan over medium-low heat, warm the rice beverage for 1 minute.

2. Stir in the margarine, flax meal, vanilla extract, cinnamon, nutmeg, salt, and agave syrup or turbinado sugar. Cook, stirring, for 2 minutes.

3. Add the banana and mash it against the sides of the saucepan. Some lumps may remain. Cook, stirring, for 1 minute.

4. Remove the pan from the heat and transfer to a wide, shallow container. Allow to cool for 2 minutes.

5. Warm a lightly oiled skillet over a medium-high flame.

6. Dredge each side of each bread slice slowly through the rice beverage mixture.

7. Brown for a few minutes on each side in the hot skillet.

8. Serve with powdered sugar shaken though a small mesh strainer, if desired.

Variation

Add 1 tablespoon (15 mL) orange juice to the rice beverage in Step 2 for a different flavor.

For added color, flavor, and protein, whisk 2 tablespoons (30 mL) quinoa flour into the rice beverage mixture before adding the banana.

Serve with maple syrup or berry compote.

Good-Day Hash Browns

A plate of fresh hash browns certainly gets the day off to a good start. Quick and easy, these hash browns are ready to come out of the pan before you are fully awake. We've presented our basic recipe, followed by variations we have enjoyed over the years. Keep your favored hash brown spice blend ready to use in a marked shaker.

YIELD: 6 SERVINGS

6 or 7 medium red potatoes or 3 baking potatoes, peeled and halved

⅓ cup (79 mL) diced onion

2 teaspoons (10 mL) salt

1½ teaspoons (7.5 mL) ground white pepper

1½ teaspoons (7.5 mL) garlic powder

1 pinch cayenne pepper

1 pinch ground nutmeg

2 tablespoons (30 mL) chopped fresh parsley

2 tablespoons (30 mL) vegan margarine or canola oil

1. Line a baking dish with two layers of paper towels or a clean towel.

2. Soak the peeled, halved potatoes in cold water for 5 minutes. Rinse well and cover with water until ready to use.

3. In a medium bowl, combine the onion, salt, and dry spices.

4. Drain and pat dry the potato pieces.

5. Grate the potatoes over the prepared baking dish with a hand or box grater. Use your hands to squeeze out any excess moisture.

6. Add the grated potatoes to the spices, chopped parsley, and onion. Stir together or blend with your hands.

7. Heat a heavy skillet over medium heat and melt the margarine or canola oil.

8. Add half the grated potato mixture to the hot skillet and use a spatula to press it flat. The trick is to maintain a thin layer.

9. Cook until browned on one side. Flip and brown the opposite side until crispy.

Cooks' Note

If you are not cooking the potatoes at once, add 2 teaspoons (10 mL) lemon juice to the water to prevent them from discoloring.

Variations

Oven cooking the potatoes is another alternative.

1. Preheat the oven to 400°F (200°C). Line a baking sheet with parchment paper and oil generously.

CONTINUED ON PAGE 114

CONTINUED FROM PAGE 113

2. Spread the grated potatoes in a thin layer on the prepared baking sheet.

3. Bake for 15 minutes. Divide the mixture into manageable pieces and flip them. Return the pan to the oven and bake for an additional 10 minutes until both sides are well browned.

Rosemary-Leek Hash Browns

Add to the basic recipe:

2 tablespoons (30 mL) finely chopped fresh rosemary

1 leek, white and light green parts only

1. Chop the rosemary. Remove outer leaf from leek and slice in ¼-inch-thick (.25-cm-thick) rounds. Rinse the leek rounds well to remove sand.

2. In a lightly oiled skillet set over medium heat, sauté the leeks and rosemary until soft.

3. Add the leeks and rosemary to the grated, uncooked potatoes. Proceed with the basic recipe.

South Indian–Style Hash Browns

2–3 teaspoons (10–15 mL) vegetable oil

1 tablespoon (15 mL) mustard seed

½ cup (118 mL) frozen peas

2 teaspoons (10 mL) ground turmeric

2 teaspoons (10 mL) ground cumin

1 teaspoon (5 mL) cayenne pepper

2 teaspoons (10 mL) salt

1. Heat the oil in a skillet over medium heat. Add 1 tablespoon (15 mL) mustard seeds and cook until they start to pop.

2. Add the peas. Sauté for 1 minute.

3. Add the mustard seeds and peas to the grated, uncooked potatoes.

4. Season with the dry spices, and proceed with the basic recipe.

Cilantro–Carrot–Peanut Hash Browns

2 tablespoons (30 mL) chopped cilantro

⅔ cup (158 mL) grated carrot

¼ cup (59 mL) chopped unsalted, roasted peanuts

1. Add the cilantro, carrot, and peanuts to the grated, uncooked potatoes. Proceed with the basic recipe. A squeeze of fresh lime juice right at the end of cooking would be stellar here.

Quiche

The variations on this fantastic breakfast or lunch dish are limited only by your imagination. Vegan cheese works great in quiches. Lightly sautéed spinach, leeks, mushrooms, onions, peppers, and minced fresh herbs such as parsley, rosemary, and basil are all good candidates for your finished quiche.

YIELD: 6 SERVINGS

> 1 Vegan Pie Crust (page 241)
>
> 1½ pounds (681 g) extra-firm tofu, drained and pressed
>
> 2 teaspoons (10 mL) garlic powder
>
> 1 teaspoon (5 mL) onion powder
>
> ½ teaspoon (2.5 mL) freshly ground black pepper
>
> 1½ teaspoons (7.5 mL) ground turmeric
>
> ¼ teaspoon (1.25 mL) dry mustard
>
> 2 teaspoons (10 mL) lemon juice
>
> 2 teaspoons (10 mL) minced fresh garlic
>
> 1 teaspoon (5 mL) ground smoked or sweet paprika
>
> 1 teaspoon (5 mL) salt, or to taste
>
> 1 tablespoon (15 mL) olive oil
>
> 1 tablespoon (15 mL) warm water
>
> 1 cup (226 mL) vegetables of your choice, chopped
>
> 1 cup (226 mL) vegan protein of your choice (e.g., shredded vegan cheddar-style cheese)

1. Preheat the oven to 350°F (180°C).

2. Press the unbaked Vegan Pie Crust into a pie pan, trim the edges, and finish the edge by pressing it down with the tines of a fork around the top rim. Bake the crust until firm but not browned, about 15 minutes. Remove from the oven and let cool.

3. Over a strainer, squeeze as much moisture as you can from the tofu and break it up into large chunks. Place the tofu, garlic, garlic powder, onion powder, black pepper, turmeric, lemon juice, paprika, and salt in a food processor fitted with the S blade.

4. Pulse 6 times, adding the olive oil a little at a time as you go. Do not overpulse, as the quiche will lose its firmness. Leave the finished mixture a little chunky.

5. Lightly sauté your chosen vegetables and vegan protein (if using a protein other than vegan cheese).

6. Fill the partially baked, cooled crust with half the tofu mixture, then half the vegetables and protein, vegan cheese (if using), and then the remaining tofu mixture. Top with the remaining vegetables and protein.

7. Bake on the top shelf of your oven for approximately 25 minutes or until the mixture is cooked through and firm.

Pancakes

Light, delicious, egg- and dairy-free pancake batter is easy to make and will be popular with the pancake lovers in your home. Add blueberries, sliced bananas, sliced almonds, toasted chopped hazelnuts, lingonberries, or whatever you like to the pancakes for a special treat.

YIELD: 18 PANCAKES

2 cups (473 mL) rice or soy beverage

2 teaspoons (10 mL) apple cider vinegar

3 tablespoons (45 mL) vegan shortening

1 tablespoon (15 mL) vanilla

3 cups (708 mL) white spelt flour or other white flour

1 tablespoon (15 mL) turbinado sugar

2 teaspoons (10 mL) baking powder

1 teaspoon (5 mL) baking soda

1 teaspoon (5 mL) salt

1. Stir the vinegar into the rice or soy beverage and let stand for 5 minutes.

2. Melt the vegan shortening and add the vanilla to it.

3. Mix the flour, sugar, baking powder, baking soda, and salt together.

4. Combine the liquid ingredients. Blend them into the dry ingredients and stir well.

5. Heat a griddle or a very large sauté pan over medium heat. Oil it lightly or coat with canola oil spray.

6. Ladle approximately ¼ cup (59 mL) of the batter into the hot pan and cook the pancake on one side for about 3 minutes, or until there are bubbles across the top and the bottom is golden brown. Flip the pancake with a spatula and cook on the other side for another 2 minutes or so. Repeat with the remaining batter.

Cooks' Note

Serve with maple syrup, vegan margarine, fruit compote, or whatever topping you like.

Corned Hash

Serve this hash for breakfast or brunch. It's great alongside the Veganopolis Tofu Scramble (page 108).

YIELD: 12 SERVINGS

½ recipe Corned Beef Substitute (page 152)

3 pounds (1.36 kg) Oven-Roasted Potatoes (page 171)

Salt, to taste

Freshly ground black pepper, to taste

¼ cup (59 mL) olive or canola oil

1 cup (226 mL) diced red onion

1 cup (226 mL) diced green peppers

½ cup (118 mL) finely chopped Italian parsley

1. Preheat the oven to 350°F (175°C).

2. In a roasting pan, combine the Corned Beef Substitute with the roasted potatoes. Season with salt and black pepper. Cover and bake for about 25 minutes.

3. Heat the canola oil in a sauté pan over medium-high heat. Sauté the onions and green peppers until the onions are softened and transparent.

4. Add the sautéed onions, peppers, and parsley to the roasting pan.

Fly Façon

This easy dish makes a great addition to a breakfast plate.

YIELD: 1 POUND (454 G) OR ABOUT 4 SERVINGS

> 1 pound (454 g) extra-firm tofu
>
> ½ cup (118 mL) seasoned rice vinegar
>
> ¼ cup (59 mL) liquid smoke or liquid hickory seasoning
>
> 2 tablespoons (30 mL) vegetable oil
>
> 2 tablespoons (30 mL) maple syrup
>
> 3 teaspoons (15 mL) salt
>
> 1 teaspoon (5 mL) paprika
>
> 1 teaspoon (5 mL) ground cumin
>
> 1 teaspoon (5 mL) ground black pepper
>
> 4 tablespoons (60 mL) beet juice (optional, for color)
>
> 2 tablespoons (30 mL) canola oil

1. Cover a cutting board or tray with a clean kitchen towel and place the tofu block on it. Cover with another clean kitchen towel and place a heavy object on top. (A cast-iron skillet works well here.) Let sit for about 30 minutes. The idea is to press as much moisture from the tofu as possible.

2. Meanwhile, whisk together the remaining ingredients in a shallow container.

3. Cut the tofu into ½-inch-thick (1-cm-thick) slices along the shorter side and then carefully cut the slices into 3 × 1–inch (7.5 × 2.5–cm) pieces.

4. Place tofu in the shallow container with the marinade for at least one hour at room temperature or up to 4 days in the refrigerator.

5. Heat a skillet with the canola oil over medium-high heat. Gently brown until slightly crisp.

CHAPTER 5

Sandwiches

Vegan BLT

Who doesn't like the classic bacon, lettuce, and tomato sandwich? This one is especially good with the addition of fresh sliced avocado, but it stands on its own as is.

YIELD: 1 SANDWICH

> 2 slices whole wheat, white, or rye bread
>
> 3 slices Fly Façon (page 118), or Vegan "Bacon" Loaf (page 153) or store-bought vegan bacon
>
> Veganopolis Mayo (page 91) or store-bought vegan mayonnaise, for spreading
>
> 2 fresh romaine lettuce leaves
>
> 1 large ripe tomato, sliced

1. Toast or grill the bread slices.

2. Sauté or grill the protein according to the recipe or package instructions.

3. Spread a generous layer of Veganopolis Mayo on one slice of the toasted bread. Layer the romaine leaves, protein, and tomato and top with the remaining slice of toasted bread. Cut diagonally and serve.

Gyros Sandwich

This gyros spice combination will amaze you! We taste-tested this sandwich on our friend and bread deliveryman Stephen, and the next day he asked if we had another one for him. As fortune would have it, we did, and Stephen was happy. For the best results, begin preparation the day before. This sandwich goes great with Oven-Roasted Potatoes (page 171) or Oven-Roasted French Fries (page 219).

YIELD: 6–8 SERVINGS

For the gyros:

> 2 tablespoons (30 mL) dried oregano
>
> 2 tablespoons (30 mL) coarsely ground black pepper
>
> 1 tablespoon (15 mL) ground cumin
>
> 1 tablespoon (15 mL) paprika
>
> 1 teaspoon (5 mL) cinnamon
>
> 1 teaspoon (5 mL) garlic powder
>
> ½ teaspoon (2.5 mL) cayenne pepper
>
> 2 pounds (1 kg) Cheitan Patties (page 163) or seitan, cut into 1-inch (2.5-cm) strips
>
> 1 red onion, peeled and cut into six wedges
>
> 8 cloves garlic, peeled
>
> 1 cup (236 mL) red wine vinegar
>
> Juice of 1 lemon

1. Combine the dry spices and mix well.

2. Rub the strips of Cheitan or seitan well with the dry spices and place them, with the onions and garlic, in a medium-sized roasting pan or loaf pan.

3. Pour the red wine vinegar and lemon juice over all and mix well. Cover and refrigerate overnight. If you are in a hurry to make this, let the pan stand at room temperature for at least 2 hours before cooking.

4. Preheat your oven to 400°F (200°C).

5. Cover the pan tightly with foil and roast for about 1 hour. Remove the pan from the oven and remove the foil. Set aside.

For the sauce:

> 1 cup (236 mL) plain soy yogurt
>
> ¼ cup (50 mL) peeled, seeded, and diced cucumber
>
> 1 teaspoon (5 mL) dill weed
>
> 2 tablespoons (30 mL) fresh lime or lemon juice
>
> ½ teaspoon (2.5 mL) salt
>
> ½ teaspoon (2.5 mL) paprika

1. Combine all ingredients and chill.

For the sandwiches:

> 6–8 sandwich-sized pita pockets
>
> 4 cups (.95 L) chopped romaine lettuce
>
> 2 cucumbers, sliced
>
> 2 large tomatoes, sliced

1. Grill the seitan strips on a well-oiled hot grill or griddle, or sauté over medium-high heat in a large, heavy sauté pan. Grill or sauté some of the onions, too, if you like.

2. Warm the pita bread. Open the pita and spread a bit of the soy yogurt sauce inside.

3. Arrange the chopped romaine, grilled vegan gyros, sliced cucumber, and sliced tomato inside. Serve hot, with a little ramekin of extra sauce on the side.

Walnut Tofu Ball Sandwich

This recipe produces a lunch or dinner sandwich children will love.

YIELD: 3 SANDWICHES

> 1 crusty baguette
>
> ⅓ cup (79 mL) olive oil
>
> 2 cups (473 mL) fresh spinach leaves
>
> 1 recipe Walnut Tofu Balls (page 159)
>
> 1 recipe Marinara Sauce (page 100)
>
> 3 slices vegan mozzarella (optional)

1. Cut off the ends of the baguette and slice the loaf into 6-inch-long (15-cm-long) sections.

2. Slice each section lengthwise, leaving one edge intact, and unfold all.

3. Brush a little olive oil on the exposed surfaces, and grill the baguettes lightly on a medium-hot grill or place them under the broiler for 2 minutes. Layer each with a third of the fresh spinach.

4. Place 3 or 4 Walnut Tofu Balls inside each grilled baguette and cover generously with hot Marinara Sauce. (At this point you may add a slice or two of vegan mozzarella and place the whole sandwich under a broiler until the mozzarella is melted). Serve immediately.

Mediterranean Sandwich

This is a light and delicious summertime sandwich. It is loosely based on the popular sandwich known in Nice as pan bagnat. *The essential ingredient is a large crusty roll, which is stuffed with fresh spinach and the Mediterranean mixture. At the restaurant we use ciabatta rolls.*

YIELD: 12 SANDWICHES

2 cups (473 mL) Veganopolis Cashew Ricotta (page 162)

1 cup (236 mL) Basil Pesto (page 96)

1 cup (236 mL) Roasted Artichoke Hearts (recipe follows)

½ cup (118 mL) julienned sun-dried tomatoes

½ cup (118 mL) pitted Kalamata olives, halved

12 ciabatta rolls, approximately 8 inches (20 cm) in diameter and 3 inches (7.5 cm) tall, or similar large, crusty rolls

3 cups (708 mL) fresh spinach leaves

1. To make the Mediterranean mixture, combine the ricotta, pesto, roasted artichoke hearts, sun-dried tomatoes, and olive halves in a large bowl and stir everything together. The result should be a pale green, spreadable mixture, about the consistency of cream cheese.

2. Cut a ½-inch-thick (1-cm-thick) slice off the top of each roll. Dig out the inside of each roll, leaving a shell about 1 inch thick (2.5 cm) and warm the hollowed-out rolls on a grill. Stuff each roll with a layer of fresh spinach and then the Mediterranean mixture.

3. Replace the tops of the stuffed rolls and diagonally slice each sandwich in half. Serve alone or with a side of roasted potatoes and/or sliced tomatoes or fruit.

Roasted Artichoke Hearts

1 (14-ounce [397-g]) can artichoke hearts, drained

¼ cup (59 mL) olive oil

1 teaspoon (5 mL) salt

1 teaspoon (5 mL) freshly ground black pepper

1. Preheat the oven to 400°F (200°C). Line a baking sheet with parchment paper.

2. In a bowl, toss the artichoke hearts with the olive oil, salt, and pepper. Arrange them on the prepared baking sheet and roast for 15 minutes, or until the edges just begin to brown.

Roasted Eggplant Sandwich

This sandwich is always popular. The combination of flavors and textures makes it unique and memorable.

YIELD: 4 SANDWICHES

> 1 large eggplant, peeled and sliced lengthwise into ⅛-inch-thick (.25-cm-thick) strips
>
> 1 tablespoon (15 mL) Italian seasoning
>
> 1 teaspoon (5 mL) freshly ground black pepper
>
> 2 teaspoons (10 mL) garlic powder or roasted garlic pepper spice mixture (preferred)
>
> 12 thin slices from 1 red onion
>
> 1 large ciabatta roll, sliced lengthwise in half, or fresh baguette sliced lengthwise in half and cut into 6-inch-long (15-cm-long) sections
>
> 1 cup (236 mL) Almond Feta (page 146)
>
> 1 cup (236 mL) Roasted Red Pepper Sauce (page 98)
>
> 1 cup (236 mL) fresh spinach leaves
>
> 1 large, fresh tomato, sliced

1. Preheat the oven to 400°F (200°C). Line a baking sheet with parchment paper.

2. Place the eggplant slices in a single layer on the prepared baking sheet.

3. Combine the Italian seasoning, black pepper, and garlic powder or roasted garlic pepper mixture. Sprinkle both sides of the eggplant slices with the spice mixture. Roast the eggplant slices until the edges begin to brown, about 12 to 15 minutes. Remove from the oven and set aside.

4. Grill or sauté the sliced onion over medium-high heat until soft and lightly browned. Grill the ciabatta roll or baguettes until grill marks appear. Grill the eggplant slices until grill marked.

5. To assemble the sandwich, spread ¼ cup (59 mL) Almond Feta inside the top slice of each roll and Roasted Red Pepper Sauce inside each bottom slice. Over the sauce, layer the fresh spinach, eggplant slices, fresh sliced tomatoes, and grilled onions. Replace the top slice on each sandwich and slice diagonally. Serve alone or with potatoes or slaw.

Sloppy Joe

This delicious sandwich is based on the scores of recipes for this American classic. It's great for a casual lunch or for feeding a group of hungry children.

YIELD: 8–10 SERVINGS

4 tablespoons (60 mL) canola oil

1 red onion, diced

1 red pepper, diced

1 green pepper, diced

2 teaspoons (10 mL) black pepper

1 tablespoon (15 mL) paprika

1 tablespoon (15 mL) dark chili powder

2 teaspoons (10 mL) garlic powder

1 (6-ounce [168-g]) can tomato paste

1 recipe Roadhouse Vegan Burgers (page 155), crumbled

1 cup (236 mL) root beer or cola

Salt, to taste

8–10 crusty rolls or burger buns

Fresh spinach leaves (optional)

Thinly sliced red onion (optional)

1. Heat the canola oil in a large sauté pan over medium-high heat.

2. Add the onions, peppers, and dry spices. Sauté until the onions and peppers are soft and the mixture is fragrant.

3. Stir in the tomato paste.

4. Add the crumbled burger in small handfuls, and cook until the burger is nicely browned and the seasonings are distributed throughout.

5. Add the root beer or cola and mix well. Heat the mixture to serving temperature and taste for seasoning, adding salt as necessary.

6. Serve on your favorite crusty rolls or burger buns. You can dress up each sandwich with some fresh spinach leaves underneath and thinly sliced red onions on top, if you wish.

Spanish Sandwich with Saffron Garlic Aioli

After George and I created this sandwich one morning at our food cart, we decided to offer it as the special sandwich that day. By chance, a food critic from the local paper came by and ordered one. The next week, he wrote up the food cart in his column, describing our creations as "gastroporn." So here's to the creation of a new word for the English vocabulary. This sandwich is fancy enough to serve at a brunch or dinner party and would pair well with a nice Spanish white wine. My favorite Spanish white is made from the Alella grape and produced under the label Marques de Alella. It's so good it makes me want to cry.

YIELD: 4 SANDWICHES

> 6 tablespoons (90 mL) extra virgin olive oil
>
> 10 cloves garlic, peeled and finely minced
>
> 2 large tomatoes, diced
>
> 4 tablespoons (60 mL) Italian parsley, finely chopped
>
> 2 tablespoons (30 mL) seasoned rice vinegar
>
> Freshly ground black pepper, to taste
>
> 1 cup (236 mL) vegetable stock
>
> 1 pound (454 g) Cheitan Patties (page 163), cut into bite-sized pieces
>
> ½ cup (118 mL) dry white wine
>
> Generous pinch saffron
>
> 1 cup (236 mL) Veganopolis Mayo (page 91) or store-bought vegan mayonnaise
>
> 4 ciabatta rolls or similar large, crusty rolls
>
> Fresh leaf spinach, to top
>
> 1 cup (226 mL) roasted red peppers, sliced lengthwise into strips
>
> 1 cup (226 mL) pitted Kalamata olives, halved

1. Preheat the oven to 350°F (180°C). Line a roasting pan with parchment paper.

2. In a sauté pan, heat the olive oil over medium-low heat. Add 2 tablespoons (30 mL) of the garlic. Sauté for a few seconds, then add the diced tomatoes and parsley and cook until the tomatoes start to break up.

3. Add the seasoned rice vinegar and a generous grinding of black pepper. Allow the mixture to cook down for a few minutes, and then add the stock.

4. Bring the mixture to a boil and cook until it is reduced by half. Reserve 3 tablespoons (45 mL) of the mixture in a separate cup or small bowl and cool it down in the refrigerator or freezer.

5. Place the Cheitan Patty pieces in the prepared roasting pan and pour the contents of the sauté pan over it. Mix well with your hands. Cover the pan tightly with aluminum foil and bake for about 30 minutes.

6. While the Cheitan is roasting, prepare the saffron aioli. Heat the white wine in a small saucepan over high heat. Add the saffron and allow it to cook down to just a few tablespoons (15 to 30 mL) of bright orange-colored liquid. Add 1 tablespoon (15 mL) of the minced garlic and the cooled reserved tomato-parsley mixture. Stir well and set aside to cool again.

7. Stir in the mayonnaise. Store the aioli in the refrigerator and stir it well again before using it.

8. To assemble the sandwiches, cut each roll in half and lightly grill them. Cover each bottom half with spinach leaves and place about ¼ pound (112 g) of the Cheitan mixture on top of that. Garnish with a few strips of the roasted red pepper and halved Kalamata olives. Spread a generous amount of the saffron aioli on the inside of the top half of each roll and replace the top on each sandwich. Diagonally slice each sandwich in half and serve.

Saturday Brunch Tofu Salad Sandwich

This sandwich makes an easy and delicious meal for warm weather or anytime you have a taste for it.

YIELD: 3 SANDWICHES

> 6 slices of a good, crusty bread
>
> 3 romaine lettuce leaves
>
> 1 recipe Brunch Tofu Salad (page 66)
>
> Fresh, ripe tomato slices

1. Layer the romaine leaves, tofu salad, and sliced tomatoes on each bottom slice. Cover with the top slice, cut in half, and serve!

2na Melt Sandwich

This sandwich is always popular. For the best result, make sure the vegan cheese is fully melted.

YIELD: 1 SANDWICH

> 2 pieces sliced white, whole wheat, or rye bread
>
> 4 ounces (112 g) Vegan 2na Salad (page 61)
>
> 2 vegan cheese slices (American or cheddar style preferred)
>
> 2 slices ripe tomato
>
> 1 tablespoon (15 mL) canola oil

1. Spoon the Vegan 2na Salad on one slice of the bread. Layer on the tomato slices and the vegan cheese.

2. Heat the canola oil in a sauté pan over medium-low heat. Grill the sandwich on both sides. Slice diagonally and serve with potatoes, chips, slaw, or a cup of soup for a lovely, quick lunch.

Veganopolis Chicken Caesar Sandwich

This recipe uses Cheitan Patties (page 163). You may use a commercially available chicken-style seitan or patty instead, but check the label because these products sometimes contain whey, egg white, casein, or another animal ingredient as a binder. If you make it yourself, you will always know the ingredients.

YIELD: 4 SANDWICHES

>   2 pounds (1.1 kg) Cheitan Patties (page 163), cut into bite-sized chunks
>
>   1 tablespoon (15 mL) turmeric powder
>
>   1 tablespoon (15 mL) garlic powder
>
>   1 tablespoon (15 mL) paprika
>
>   2 teaspoons (10 mL) white pepper
>
>   ½ teaspoon (2.5 mL) cayenne pepper
>
>   2 cups (473 mL) good-quality vegetable stock
>
>   4 ciabatta or other large crusty rolls
>
>   2 cups (473 mL) chopped romaine lettuce
>
>   4 tablespoons (60 mL) Veganopolis Caesar Dressing (page 79)

1. Preheat the oven to 350°F (180°C). Line a roasting pan with parchment paper.

2. Place the Cheitan Patties in the prepared roasting pan and add the dry spices, rubbing them into each piece with your hands.

3. Add the stock, cover the pan tightly with foil, and roast for about 30 minutes, or until the mixture is heated through and most of the liquid has been absorbed. Keep warm.

4. Cut each roll in half and lightly grill them. In a bowl, mix the chopped romaine with the Cheitan Patties and the Veganopolis Caesar Dressing and mix everything together using a pair of tongs. Divide this mixture among the bottom halves of the rolls and cover them with the top halves. Slice each sandwich diagonally and serve with roasted potatoes, chips, slaw, or whatever you like.

Vegan Chicken Pesto Sandwich

This tasty sandwich is always popular at the restaurant. Use the recipe for Cheitan Patties (page 163) or a store-bought vegan chicken substitute.

YIELD: 6 SANDWICHES

> 6 ciabatta or other large, crusty rolls
>
> 2 pounds (1.1 kg) Cheitan Patties (page 163) or store-bought vegan chicken substitute, cut into 1-inch (2.5-cm) pieces
>
> 2 tablespoons (30 mL) olive oil
>
> 1 small handful fresh spinach leaves
>
> 3 tablespoons (45 mL) Basil Pesto (page 96)
>
> 1 tablespoon (15 mL) Veganopolis Mayo (page 91) or store-bought vegan mayonnaise
>
> 1 large red onion, grilled or thinly sliced, to top

1. Cut the rolls in half and grill the inside surfaces lightly.

2. In a large sauté pan over medium heat, warm the Cheitan Patty pieces in the olive oil until they just begin to brown at the edges, about 6 minutes.

3. In a salad bowl, mix the spinach, Cheitan Patties, pesto, and Veganopolis Mayo.

4. Mix everything together rapidly using a pair of tongs, and divide this mixture among the bottom halves of the rolls.

5. Add the grilled or fresh red onions, if desired, to each sandwich.

6. Replace the tops of the rolls, cut the sandwiches diagonally, and serve.

Cooks' Note

Add sliced tomatoes or melted vegan mozzarella on the sandwiches to rock it up a little, if you like.

Vegan New York Reuben Sandwich

This is the most popular sandwich in the restaurant. We have hardcore New Yorkers who have said that they prefer this vegan Reuben to a "real" one! This works best on a panini grill, but you can use a heavy-bottomed frying pan, a cast-iron skillet, or a griddle instead.

YIELD: 1 SANDWICH

> 3 ounces (84 g) Corned Beef Substitute (page 152), heated
>
> 2 slices vegan white cheese substitute
>
> 2 ounces (57 g) drained sauerkraut
>
> 2 tablespoons (30 mL) Veganopolis Thousand Island Dressing (page 85) or Dijon mustard
>
> 2 slices good-quality dark rye bread
>
> Dill pickle spears, to serve

1. Place the vegan cheese on one slice of the bread and spread the Thousand Island Dressing or Dijon mustard on the other slice.

2. Place the warm Corned Beef Substitute over the vegan cheese. Layer the sauerkraut over the Corned Beef Substitute. Top with the other bread slice.

3. Cook the sandwich on a panini grill until the vegan cheese is completely melted, or cook it in a well-oiled sauté pan over medium heat for about 4 minutes on each side or until the vegan cheese is completely melted. Slice diagonally and serve with dill pickle spears.

The VQB: Vegan Quinoa Burger

These delicious vegan burger patties also work well cut into pieces and placed on top of a salad. They're great on the Vegan Burger Buns (page 239). Quinoa makes these burgers high in protein, easy to digest, and delicious!

YIELD: 6 (3-INCH-DIAMETER [7.5-CM-DIAMETER]) PATTIES

> 3 cups (708 mL) vegetable stock
>
> 2 cups (473 mL) quinoa, rinsed well
>
> 1 cup (226 mL) sweet potato, peeled and finely diced
>
> 1 (12-ounce [336-g]) can chickpeas, rinsed and drained
>
> 2 teaspoons (10 mL) salt, divided
>
> 1½ tablespoons (22 mL) arrowroot powder
>
> 2 teaspoons (10 mL) liquid smoke flavor or dry mesquite powder
>
> ⅓ cup (79 mL) quinoa flour
>
> 1 tablespoon (15 mL) ground turmeric
>
> 1 tablespoon (15 mL) garlic powder
>
> 1 tablespoon (15 mL) onion powder
>
> 1 teaspoon (5 mL) paprika
>
> 2 tablespoons (10 mL) ketchup or barbecue sauce
>
> 2 tablespoons (10 mL) chopped parsley
>
> ⅔ cup (158 mL) chunky or creamy peanut butter
>
> ⅓ cup (79 mL) raw tahini
>
> 4 tablespoons (60 mL) vegetable oil, divided

1. Bring the stock to a boil in a medium saucepan over medium-high heat. Add the quinoa and sweet potato and return to a boil. Reduce to a simmer, cover, and cook until the quinoa is soft and chewy, about 15 minutes. Remove from the heat, drain, and set aside.

2. In another saucepan, heat 2 cups (473 mL) water and add the chickpeas. Bring to a boil and then simmer for 15 minutes. Drain, rinse, and remove any remaining chickpea skins by placing the chickpeas in a large bowl of cold water and letting the skins float to the surface. Discard the skins. Drain the chickpeas again, then add 1 teaspoon (5 mL) of the salt and mash them with a fork just until they begin to break up.

3. Combine the chickpeas and the cooked quinoa and sweet potato mixture in a food processor. Add the arrowroot powder and pulse once or twice.

4. Add the smoke flavor, quinoa flour, turmeric, garlic powder, onion powder, paprika, ketchup or barbecue sauce, parsley, and the remaining 1 teaspoon (5 mL) salt. Pulse 5 or 6 times until the ingredients are combined.

CONTINUED ON PAGE 136

CONTINUED FROM PAGE 135

5. Add the peanut butter, tahini, and 2 tablespoons (30 mL) of the vegetable oil and blend for 1 minute.

6. Scrape the mixture into a bowl and form into 4-inch (10-cm) diameter patties approximately 1 inch (2.5 cm) thick.

7. Line a baking sheet with parchment paper and place the patties on it, and then cover them with another sheet of parchment paper. Refrigerate overnight or freeze for 25 minutes.

8. When ready to bake, preheat the oven to 350°F (180°C). Line a baking sheet with parchment paper.

9. Heat the remaining vegetable oil in a large, heavy skillet over medium heat and brown each patty on both sides. Transfer the patties to the prepared baking sheet and bake them for 25 minutes. Remove them from the oven and serve immediately, or cool completely and use later. The cooked patties may be stored, covered and refrigerated, for 4 days. You may reheat them in a skillet or in the oven.

Variations

Indian-style patties: Add 2 tablespoons (30 mL) madras curry powder, ¼ cup (59 mL) chopped cilantro, and 3 tablespoons (45 mL) chopped roasted cashews to the mixture.

Mushroom patties: Omit the smoke flavor and add 1 cup (226 mL) sautéed diced mushrooms and 3 tablespoons (45 mL) chopped fresh rosemary to the mixture.

Almond Pâté Sandwich

A great cold meal for the summertime, this sandwich is light, delicious, and highly nutritious. It also has a high protein content and is easy to digest.

YIELD: 1 SANDWICH

2 slices whole wheat, white, or rye bread

2 tablespoons (30 mL) Vegan Dijonnaise (page 92)

Fresh spinach or romaine leaves

1 recipe Almond Pâté (page 147)

1 red onion, thinly sliced (optional)

1. Spread the Vegan Dijonnaise on one slice of bread and top with a layer of spinach or romaine, followed by the almond pâté.

2. Add the red onion, if desired. Top with the remaining bread, slice diagonally, and serve.

Veganopolis Recipe Barbecue Sandwich

This sandwich is reminiscent of the popular pulled-pork sandwich. The term barbecue comes from barbacoa, *from the sixteenth century Taino people of the Caribbean. The fresh carrot and cabbage give this sandwich a nice crunch. Serve them on a crusty roll or your favorite bun.*

YIELD: 4 SANDWICHES

> 1 pound (454 g) seitan, sliced thinly, then cut into 1 X 2–inch (2.5 X 5–cm) pieces
>
> 1 cup (236 mL) New Orleans–Style Vegan Barbecue Sauce (page 90)
>
> 4 crusty rolls or burger buns
>
> 2 cups (473 mL) chopped spinach or romaine leaves
>
> 1 cup (236 mL) finely shredded green cabbage
>
> 1 cup (236 mL) julienned carrots

1. Preheat the oven to 350°F (180°C). Line a baking pan with parchment paper.

2. Place the seitan in the prepared pan and pour the barbecue sauce over it. Mix well and cover the pan tightly with foil.

3. Bake until the mixture is hot, about 30 to 40 minutes.

4. Divide the spinach or romaine leaves among the bottom halves of the rolls, and top each with a scoop of the barbecued seitan. Combine the cabbage and carrots and place a few tablespoons of the mixture on top of the seitan. Cover each sandwich with the top slice, cut in half, and serve with Oven-Roasted French Fries (page 219) or plain potato chips and slaw.

Broiled Sesame Ginger Tofu Sandwich

This recipe is a bit of a procedure, but it produces a delicious result that is sure to please your guests. For the best results, allow the tofu to marinate for a few hours or overnight. A generous amount of fresh ginger is essential. This smells like heaven while it broils. The day George created this sandwich at the food cart, everyone was very, very happy.

YIELD: 6 SANDWICHES

¾ cup (177 mL) dark sesame oil

2 bulbs fresh ginger, peeled and sliced into matchsticks

⅛ cup (30 mL) tamari

¼ cup (59 mL) turbinado sugar

2 (1-pound [454-g]) blocks extra-firm tofu, cut horizontally into thirds

2 tablespoons (30 mL) Thai yellow curry paste

1 cup (236 mL) Veganopolis Mayo (page 91) or store-bought vegan mayonnaise

1 cup (236 mL) green pea pods

12 slices crusty bread

1 bunch scallions, trimmed and thinly sliced

2 cups (473 mL) fresh spinach leaves

1. Heat the sesame oil in a large skillet over medium-low heat and add the ginger matchsticks. Sauté until the ginger starts to bubble. Add the tamari and turbinado sugar, and stir until the sugar is completely dissolved. Add water as needed if the mixture is too thick to pour. Set aside.

2. Arrange the sliced tofu in a shallow pan and cover with the marinade. Let stand for a few hours or cover and refrigerate overnight.

3. Combine the yellow curry paste with the Veganopolis Mayo and set aside.

4. Blanch the pea pods in rapidly boiling, heavily salted water for about 3 minutes. Immediately plunge them into ice water to stop the cooking. When the pea pods are cool, slice them diagonally into matchsticks. Set aside.

5. When you are ready to broil the tofu, preheat the broiler and line a baking sheet with parchment paper. Transfer the marinated tofu slices to the prepared baking sheet. Make sure there is plenty of ginger on each tofu slice.

6. Broil until the slices are fully browned, about 6 minutes, then remove the pan from the broiler and flip the tofu. Return to the broiler and brown again, this time for about 4 minutes, taking care not to let the slices burn.

7. To assemble the sandwiches, toast or grill the bread and spread a generous amount of the Thai yellow curry paste on half the slices, followed by the spinach, broiled tofu slices, and pea pod matchsticks. Top with the finely sliced scallions and remaining bread. Slice diagonally and serve.

Veganopolis Democracy Burger

George made this up for the Fourth of July at Veganopolis. We were thinking about democracy, then Ancient Greece, then modern Greece, so the Democracy Burger is Greek-influenced. Some customers wanted us to create a Burger of the Republic, but we thought that idea had already been taken up by many larger businesses. The Democracy Burger became extremely popular overnight.

YIELD: 4 SANDWICHES

> 4 Cheitan Patties (page 163), prepared through Step 9
>
> 4 burger buns
>
> 6 ounces (168 g) Almond Feta (page 146)
>
> 2 cups (473 g) fresh spinach leaves
>
> 2 large ripe tomatoes, sliced
>
> 1 large ripe avocado, peeled and quartered then thinly sliced
>
> Pitted Kalamata olives, halved
>
> 1 large red onion, thinly sliced, grilled if desired

1. Grill or sauté the Cheitan Patties until nicely browned. Lightly grill the buns.

2. Spread a few tablespoons Almond Feta on the top half of each bun. Layer with the spinach, the Cheitan Patty, tomato slices, avocado slices, and a few Kalamata olive halves. Add fresh or grilled red onion slices for a finishing touch. Replace the tops of the buns. Serve and enjoy!

Grilled Marinated Tofu Sandwich

Marinate the tofu overnight for best results. The fresh ginger gives the finished sandwich a little extra flavor. This works best on a grill, but it can also be made on a griddle or in a large, heavy skillet.

YIELD: 3 SANDWICHES

> 2 cups (473 mL) tamari
>
> 2 cups (473 mL) water
>
> 1 cup (236 mL) seasoned rice vinegar
>
> 1 bulb fresh ginger, sliced thinly
>
> 1-pound (454-g) block extra-firm tofu, cut horizontally into thirds
>
> ¼ cup (59 mL) vegetable oil (safflower oil preferred)
>
> 6 slices crusty bread
>
> 1 cup (236 mL) fresh spinach or romaine leaves
>
> 1 large ripe tomato, sliced
>
> 1 large red onion, peeled and sliced
>
> ½ cup (118 mL) Veganopolis Mayo (page 91) or store-bought vegan mayo

1. To prepare the marinade, combine the tamari, water, seasoned rice vinegar, and sliced ginger in a large, shallow container. Place the tofu slices in the marinade, cover, and refrigerate.

2. Grill the tofu on a hot, well-oiled grill, griddle, or heavy skillet. It is important to oil the cooking surface generously using oil that will not smoke at high temperature, such as safflower oil. The tofu tends to stick while cooking, so move it around as it cooks, especially at the beginning of the process.

3. Once the tofu is fully cooked, slice it horizontally in half again. Place the uncooked sides face down on the cooking surface, and grill until well marked and firm.

4. Lightly grill or toast the bread.

5. To assemble the sandwiches, spread the bottom slices with the Veganopolis Mayo and layer with the fresh spinach or romaine, grilled tofu slices, sliced tomato, and onion. Top with the remaining bread and serve.

Variations

Add sliced avocado as the top layer. For a spicier version, blend wasabi powder into the Veganopolis Mayo and use that on the sandwich.

CHAPTER 6

Vegan Proteins

An Introduction to Seitan

Seitan (say-TAHN) is a delightfully chewy, cholesterol-free, high-protein food. It is simple to make and requires only a few ingredients. We have sometimes pondered the sort of place our world might be if seitan became a staple in every kitchen on the planet.

Seitan is made from vital wheat gluten, which is available in many mainstream groceries. Check the bulk section or the baking aisle. Gluten is the protein component of wheat flour and what's left behind when the starch element is removed.

In addition to the vital wheat gluten, seitan requires vegetable stock, a little oil, and seasonings of your choice. It marinates well, stores well, and freezes well. It is easily rehydrated by warming it in a little vegetable stock.

Seitan has many uses. Simmering chunks of it in stock works best for sautés, casseroles, and vegan sausage bits. Form it into patties to make seitan burgers, or form it into a loaf and slice it after cooling for sandwiches. For burger patties and loaves, we have found that adding beans to the recipe allows the chef to create different colors, flavors, and textures.

Kneading the seitan is part of the process, and the longer you knead the dough, the denser and chewier the final result will be. Shorter kneading times produce softer seitan. The moisture content can be adjusted even after finishing the recipe by drying the seitan in a 300°F (150°C) oven for 30 minutes or so.

We first came up with the recipe for Cheerful Chimichurri (page 202) for an important catered event. We served medallions of seitan, which had been marinated overnight and then grilled quickly, with a sauce. A guest approached us after the meal and told us that his meal pleased him more than an expensive dish of filet mignon he had been served the previous night in New York City.

The history of seitan is long, dating back to the seventh century. Chinese Buddhist monasteries left records of the monks making bread with wheat flour. They learned that washing the flour repeatedly in water removed the starch, leaving just the protein. This became a staple of their vegetarian diet, and the technique spread throughout Asia, including Japan, where seitan simmered in a stock flavored with ginger and kombu was developed.

CONTINUED ON PAGE 144

CONTINUED FROM PAGE 143

In Asian markets, you may find a wide variety of gluten-based meat and fish replacements. Some of these are excellent, but use your judgment in selecting products, and read the labels carefully. Some contain egg white or whey as binders.

If you have never made seitan before, by all means try it. The process is simple, and the results can be extraordinary.

City Cinnamon Pecan Rolls (PAGE 110)

Veganopolis Tofu Scramble (PAGE 108)

Rosti Hash (PAGE 109)

Santa Fe–Style Pozole Soup (PAGE 32)

Vegan BLT (PAGE 121)

Roadhouse Vegan Burger (PAGE 155), **with Oven-Roasted French Fries** (PAGE 219)

Old-Fashioned French Lentil Salad (PAGE 71)

Savory Bread Pudding (PAGE 103)

Almond Pâté Sandwich (PAGE 137)

Classic Pot Pie (PAGE 178)

Bouillabaisse with Rouille (PAGE 18)

Veganopolis Caesar Salad (PAGE 60)

Grilled Tofu Salad with Avocado (PAGE 73)

Super Rainbow Oatmeal Cookies (PAGE 246)

Simple Seitan

Here is a quick recipe for seitan chunks that can be used in soups, stews, sandwiches, sautés, and salads. The result is a chewy protein that you can season with your choice of dry spices. Though the finished product is not as firm as our loaf and patty proteins, it will suffice for those uses. This recipe produces a single lump of seitan that is then cut into chunks and boiled. It can then be used immediately in a recipe or stored, in its cooking liquid, in the refrigerator for up to 1 week or tightly sealed and frozen for several months. Be sure to drain most of the liquid before freezing. If your seitan dries out, reconstitute it by warming it in a little broth.

YIELD: 2 POUNDS (1.1 KG)

> 2 cups (473 mL) vital wheat gluten
>
> 2 teaspoons (10 mL) salt
>
> 1 tablespoon (15 mL) onion powder
>
> 2 teaspoons (10 mL) garlic powder
>
> 1 teaspoon (5 ml) white pepper
>
> 5¼ cups (1.2 L) vegetable broth, divided
>
> 2 tablespoons (30 mL) olive, safflower, or canola oil
>
> 1 tablespoon (15 mL) liquid smoke or tamari

1. In a bowl, stir together the vital wheat gluten and dry spices.

2. In a separate bowl, combine 1¼ cups (315 mL) of the vegetable broth, the oil, and the liquid smoke or tamari.

3. Slowly add the liquid ingredients to the dry ingredients, stirring as you go. Stir with a spatula until a stiff dough forms.

4. On a clean surface, with lightly oiled hands, knead the dough firmly for 2 to 3 minutes. Allow the dough to rest for 5 minutes.

5. Knead again 20 to 25 times, and then allow to rest for another 10 minutes.

6. In a saucepan over medium-high heat, heat the remaining 4 cups (.95 L) vegetable broth to a boil.

7. Cut the dough into 2-inch (5-cm) chunks.

8. With a long spoon or tongs, add the dough chunks to the stock and boil for 1 minute.

9. Reduce the heat to a simmer and cook the seitan for 45 minutes to an hour.

10. Remove the seitan from the stock and allow the stock to cool. You may reuse the stock the next time you make seitan. It can be stored in the freezer until then. Your seitan chunks are now ready to be used in a recipe.

Cooks' Note

The longer you knead the dough, the chewier and less spongy the finished seitan will be. You may also reduce the 1¼ cups (310 mL) stock to ¾ cup (177 mL) to produce a slightly denser seitan.

Almond Feta

Almond Feta is great on sandwiches, on salads, or in a vegan moussaka or spanokopita. The almonds will need to be soaked in clean water overnight, then carefully drained and rinsed. This dish keeps for five days in the refrigerator.

YIELD: 2 CUPS (473 ML)

> **2 cups (473 mL) raw, unsalted almonds**
>
> **1 or more cups (236 mL) fermented wheat berry water (see Veganopolis Cashew Ricotta recipe, page 162) or ⅓ cup (79 mL) lemon juice plus ¼ cup (59 mL) water**
>
> **Lemon juice, to taste**
>
> **Salt, to taste**

1. Soak the almonds overnight in fresh, cold water. Drain and rinse them thoroughly under running water until the water runs clear.

2. In batches, run the soaked almonds through a Champion juicer or other juicer with the solid screen in place, or blend in a food processor. As you process the almonds, gradually add the fermented wheat berry water to soften the mixture.

3. When all the almonds are processed, add lemon juice and salt to taste. You should be able to taste a little salt, just as in dairy feta.

Cooks' Note

You may wish to experiment with the addition of other spices to your almond feta. Cracked black pepper, finely sliced chives, lemon zest, and chopped parsley are all possible additions.

Almond Pâté

Loaded with vitamin E, the almond has the highest nutritional value of all the nuts on the planet. This pâté is the perfect addition to a salad. A few scoops on a bed of mesclun, lightly dressed in lemon vinaigrette with sliced ripe tomatoes, would make an elegant brunch dish. It makes a perfect sandwich spread on your favorite bread with lettuce and tomato.

YIELD: 3 CUPS (708 ML)

> **2 cups (473 mL) raw, unsalted almonds, soaked overnight in fresh cold water**
>
> **3 carrots, peeled**
>
> **1 large red onion, peeled and cut into eighths**
>
> **1 cup (236 mL) finely diced celery**
>
> **½ cup (118 mL) finely diced parsley**
>
> **½ cup (118 mL) thinly sliced scallions**
>
> **Juice of 1 lemon, or to taste**
>
> **Salt, to taste**

1. Drain the soaked almonds and rinse them very well under cold running water. Almond skins release a lot of grayish material as they soak, so make sure that you rinse the soaked almonds thoroughly.

2. Using a masticating juicer with the solid screen in place or a food processor, alternately process the almonds, carrots, and red onion. Combine all in a large bowl.

3. Add the celery, parsley, and scallions. Stir to distribute the ingredients evenly through the pâté.

4. Add lemon juice and salt, to taste.

Cooks' Note

The almond pâté can be covered, stored, and refrigerated for up to one week, but it will taste best if used as soon as possible. The color, which comes primarily from the carrots, tends to fade after two or three days. This is a high-protein, mineral- and vitamin-rich dish that is easy to digest and fabulous for people with active lifestyles.

A high-quality masticating juicer is the best tool for making this at home, but the pâté can also be made with a quality food processor.

Almondetta

This creamy almond spread can be used in many recipes. Include on an hors d'oeuvres platter, on sandwiches, in a casserole, in stuffed peppers or stuffed squash, or as a pizza topping during the final ten minutes of baking. The result of this recipe will be firm and moldable.

YIELD: 2¼ CUPS (532 ML)

> 2 cups (473 mL) slivered almonds, soaked in water for 4 hours (or in hot water for 1 hour)
>
> 1 tablespoon (15 mL) olive oil
>
> ⅓ cup (79 mL) plus 2 tablespoons (30 mL) water
>
> 2 tablespoons (30 mL) agar powder
>
> 1 tablespoon (15 mL) lemon juice
>
> 1 tablespoon (15 mL) salt
>
> 1½ (7.5 mL) teaspoons ground white pepper
>
> 2 teaspoons (10 mL) bread crumbs (optional)
>
> 1 pinch cayenne pepper

1. Place all ingredients in a food processor fitted with the S blade. Pulse 3 times, and then blend for 2 minutes or until thick and creamy.

2. Heat the water in a saucepan.

3. Stir in the agar powder and bring to a boil.

4. Reduce the heat and simmer for 2 minutes until thickened.

5. Add the liquid to the almond mixture, blend, and pour into a mold. Chill until firm.

Variation

Stir in 1 tablespoon (15 mL) finely chopped oregano, Italian herbs, cilantro, garlic, shallots, or parsley.

Butter Bean and Walnut Chorizo

This brilliant, soy-free chorizo alternative makes a great filling for tacos and burritos. It can either be formed into a loaf and sliced or used as is.

YIELD: 2½ CUPS (591 ML)

1 (12-ounce [336-g]) can butter beans, drained and rinsed

⅔ cup (158 mL) chopped walnuts or pecans

2 teaspoons (10 mL) cumin

2 teaspoons (10 mL) chili powder

2 teaspoons (10 mL) dried oregano

2 teaspoons (10 mL) whole fennel seed

¼ teaspoon (1.25 mL) cayenne pepper

1 teaspoon (5 mL) freshly ground black pepper

1 tablespoon (15 mL) achiote paste or liquid achiote

2 tablespoons (30 mL) apple cider vinegar

1 tablespoon (15 mL) lime juice

2 teaspoons (10 mL) turbinado sugar

2 teaspoons (10 mL) salt

2 tablespoon (30 mL) canola oil

2 tablespoons (30 mL) water

2 cloves garlic, peeled and crushed or finely minced, divided

¼ cup (59 mL) finely diced onion

2 tablespoons (30 mL) agar powder dissolved in ¼ cup (59 mL) hot water for 5 minutes, optional (use to create a mold loaf)

1 recipe Oven-Roasted Pepitas (recipe follows) (1.25 mL)

1. Preheat the oven to 350°F (180°C). Line a baking sheet with parchment paper.

2. Chop the butter beans roughly or mash them with a fork. Don't purée them; you want to leave some texture.

3. In a bowl, combine the dry spices, achiote paste, vinegar, lime juice, turbinado sugar, salt, and water. Add half of the garlic and stir to combine.

4. Stir the butter beans and nuts into the spice blend. Be sure to coat the beans well.

5. Bake this mixture on the prepared baking sheet for 12 minutes.

6. Heat the canola oil in a sauté pan over low heat. Sauté the onions and remaining garlic for 2 minutes.

CONTINUED ON PAGE 150

CONTINUED FROM PAGE 149

7. Remove the bean, nut, and spice mixture from the oven and scrape it into the sauté pan. Cook everything together for another 5 minutes. (If making a loaf, stir in the agar powder and water mixture at this time.)

8. Remove the pan from the heat and transfer the contents to a clean bowl. After it cools, you can form it into links for frying, or fry it in chunks as is by sautéing it with 2 tablespoons (30 mL) vegetable oil in a sauté pan over medium heat.

To form into a loaf:

1. Line a mini loaf pan with lightly oiled parchment paper. Sprinkle the bottom with ⅓ cup (79 mL) freshly chopped cilantro or oregano.

2. Use a spoon to line the sides of the loaf pan with the chorizo mixture. Then fill with the remaining chorizo and chill in the refrigerator for at least an hour.

3. Remove from the refrigerator and slide a small knife around the edges to loosen the mold. Invert the pan on a plate, tap the bottom, remove the loaf, and garnish with Oven-Roasted Pepitas.

Oven Roasted Pepitas

YIELD: 1 CUP (236 ML)

> 1 cup (236 mL) raw pumpkin seeds (pepitas)
>
> 2 tablespoons (30 mL) canola oil
>
> 1 tablespoon (15 mL) dark chili powder
>
> 1 teaspoon (5 mL) salt

1. Preheat the oven to 350°F (180°C). Line a baking sheet with parchment paper.

2. In a medium bowl, combine the pepitas, oil, chile powder, and salt.

3. Spread the mixture on the cookie sheet and bake for 20 minutes, or until the pepitas are lightly browned and crunchy.

4. Remove the pepitas from the oven and cool to room temperature. They may be stored, unrefrigerated, in a sealed container for several weeks.

Chorizo with Tofu and Walnuts

This vegan chorizo is great in tacos or burritos or as an addition to stews or chili.

YIELD: 2 CUPS (473 ML)

1 pound (454 g) extra-firm tofu

1 tablespoon (15 mL) achiote paste or liquid achiote

1 tablespoon (15 mL) apple cider vinegar

1 tablespoon (15 mL) whole fennel seed

1 tablespoon (15 mL) dried oregano

2½ teaspoons (15 mL) ground cumin

2 teaspoons (10 mL) paprika

2 teaspoons (10 mL) dark chili powder or chipotle powder

2 teaspoons (10 mL) maple syrup or turbinado sugar

1½ teaspoons (7.5 mL) salt

1½ teaspoons (7.5 mL) garlic powder or 2 cloves garlic, peeled and finely minced

¼ teaspoon (1.25 mL) cayenne pepper

⅔ cup (150 mL) chopped walnuts

1. Preheat the oven to 400°F (200°C). Lightly oil a nonstick baking sheet.

2. Over a colander, gently press out the tofu's extra moisture with your hands, keeping your palms flat. Break the tofu into large crumbles.

3. Transfer the tofu crumbles to the prepared baking sheet and bake for 5 minutes.

4. Stir together the achiote, vinegar, dry spices, maple syrup or turbinado sugar, and salt.

5. Place walnuts in a bowl and rub them well with the spice blend. Add the tofu and stir to coat well.

6. Spread the tofu-walnut mixture on the baking sheet and bake for 12 to 15 minutes. The finished mixture should be slightly dry to the touch. For a dryer chorizo, turn the oven off and leave the pan in the oven for another 10 to 15 minutes.

Corned Beef Substitute

Use this for the Vegan New York Reuben Sandwich (page 134).

YIELD: 1½ POUNDS (680 G)

        3 tablespoons (50 mL) olive oil

        8 cloves garlic, peeled

        4 bay leaves

        3 stalks celery, roughly chopped

        2 carrots, roughly chopped

        1 red onion, roughly chopped

        3 tablespoons (45 mL) coarsely ground black pepper

        1 cup (236 mL) red wine vinegar

        1 cup (236 mL) vegetable stock

        1 pound (454 g) Cheitan Patties (page 163) sliced into 1 X 3–inch (2½ X 3½–cm) pieces

1. Preheat the oven to 350°F (180°C). Line a baking pan with parchment paper.

2. In a medium saucepan, heat the olive oil over medium-high heat and then add the garlic, bay leaves, celery, carrots, onion, and pepper. Sauté until the vegetables start to brown, about 10 minutes.

3. Add the red wine vinegar and turn heat to high. Cook until the vinegar is reduced by ⅔.

4. Add the stock and simmer for 5 minutes.

5. Place the sliced Cheitan Patties in the prepared baking pan and pour the vegetable marinade over it. Stir to combine.

6. Cover the pan with foil and bake for 25 to 35 minutes or until heated all the way through. Remove and discard the bay leaves and most of the vegetables. Use immediately, or cool to room temperature and refrigerate in a covered container for up to five days.

Vegan "Bacon" Loaf

Slice, dice, or shred and use in any way you like. Brown slices for breakfast or use browned slices in Vegan Benedict (page 105).

YIELD: 1 (1½-POUND [680-G]) LOAF

½ cup (118 mL) canned kidney beans

½ cup (118 mL) chickpea flour, plus more to dust the kneading surface

4 tablespoons (60 mL) liquid smoke

4 tablespoons (60 mL) maple syrup

2 tablespoons (30 mL) olive oil

1 tablespoon plus 1 teaspoon (20 mL) lemon juice, divided

4 teaspoons (20 mL) salt

2 teaspoons (10 mL) onion powder

2 teaspoons (10 mL) garlic powder

2 teaspoons (10 mL) freshly ground black pepper

2½ cups (591 mL) vital wheat gluten

1½ cups (354 mL) vegetable stock, divided

1. Preheat the oven to 375°F (190°C). Line an 11 × 13–inch (27½ × 32½–cm) baking dish with parchment paper.

2. Rinse the kidney beans well and place in a food processor with the chickpea flour, liquid smoke, maple syrup, oil, 1 tablespoon (15 mL) of the lemon juice, and dry spices. Blend for 30 seconds.

3. Add half of the vital wheat gluten and ½ cup (118 mL) of the stock. Pulse the food processor 6 times, then remove the top and scrape down the sides of the bowl.

4. With the processor running, add the remaining vital wheat gluten and stock and process until a dough forms, about 1 minute. If this has not happened after 1 minute, add water, 1 tablespoon at a time, until the dough forms.

5. Dust a clean surface with chickpea flour and knead the dough for about 3 minutes, at which point it should feel almost dry to the touch. Let it rest for 15 minutes.

6. Mix the remaining stock with the remaining lemon juice. Pour this mixture into the prepared baking dish.

7. Knead the dough another 15 times and form it into a loaf shape. If there are any crevices or seams in the dough, pinch them together until you have a smooth surface all over.

8. Transfer the dough to the baking dish, cover with foil, and bake for 45 minutes.

9. Remove the foil and add ½ cup (118 mL) water. Bake, uncovered, for an additional 15 minutes. Remove from the oven and let cool in the pan. Store in a covered container with whatever broth is left after baking.

Pine Nut Parmesan

This creation is perfect anywhere one would use Parmesan cheese. It even works beautifully on lasagnas or pizzas, browning slightly as it cooks. The flavor is superb.

YIELD: 2 CUPS (473 ML)

> **2 cups (473 mL) pine nuts**
>
> **1 or more cups (236 mL or more) fermented barley water (see Veganopolis Cashew Ricotta recipe, page 162) or 1 cup (236 mL) water and 1 teaspoon (5 mL) apple cider vinegar**
>
> **Juice of 1 lemon**
>
> **Salt, to taste**

1. Soak the pine nuts in cold, fresh water for 3 to 4 hours until soft.

2. In a food processor or blender, blend the nuts until they are well broken up. With the machine still running, gradually add the fermented barley water until you get a consistency similar to tomato paste.

3. Add the lemon juice and salt, enough so that the salty element of the flavor is prominent.

4. Cut pieces of parchment or wax paper to fit your food dehydrator (a razor tool or a very sharp knife will help here) and use them to line each level.

5. Using a thin, flexible rubber spatula, spread the mixture on the dehydrator levels in a thin, even layer and move the dehydrator to an area of your kitchen where it will be out of the way overnight.

6. Dry the mixture thoroughly, about 8 to 12 hours. When the Parmesan is ready, it will crack off the paper into large flakes. You can use it just like that or break it up smaller for recipes that call for grated Parmesan cheese.

Cooks' Note

For this recipe, you can use a food dehydrator. The one we use at the restaurant has 6 trays, which allows us to make about 3 cups (750 mL) in each batch. If you don't have a food dehydrator, you may spread the finished mixture thinly on a baking sheet lined with parchment paper. Bake at 110°F (43°C) (the pilot light on a gas oven may even be sufficient to achieve this temperature) for 3 hours or until the mixture has dried thoroughly.

Roadhouse Vegan Burgers

These big, chewy, moist, spiced-up patties are fit for a grill. With a healthy combination of digestible proteins, they display an array of textures.

YIELD: 6–8 LARGE PATTIES

> 3 cups (708 mL) vital wheat gluten
>
> 1 tablespoon (15 mL) salt
>
> 2 tablespoons (30 mL) garlic powder
>
> 2 teaspoons (10 mL) onion powder
>
> 1½ teaspoons (7.5 mL) freshly ground black pepper
>
> ½ cup black beans, rinsed well
>
> ¼ cup (59 mL) quinoa or chickpea flour
>
> 3 tablespoons (45 mL) olive oil
>
> 1 tablespoon (15 mL) smoky vegan barbecue sauce, or 1 tablespoon (15 mL) ketchup plus 1 tablespoon (15 mL) balsamic vinegar
>
> 2 cups (473 mL) vegetable stock, divided
>
> 2 cups (473 mL) water

1. Preheat the oven to 375°F (190°C). Line an 11 × 13–inch (27½ × 32½–cm) baking dish with parchment paper, or lightly oil the bottom of the dish.

2. In a bowl, blend the vital wheat gluten flour with the salt, onion powder, and pepper. Set aside.

3. In a food processor fitted with an S blade, pulse the black beans, flour, olive oil, and barbecue sauce. Add half the vital wheat gluten mixture and ½ cup (118 mL) of the vegan stock.

4. Blend, adding the remaining vital wheat gluten mixture and another ½ cup (118 mL) of the vegan stock, until a dough forms. If needed, add water, 1 tablespoon (15 mL) at a time, until the dough is not crumbly.

5. Remove the dough from the food processor and transfer to a clean, flat surface. Knead for 3 to 4 minutes until gluten strands begin to form. Add a little more oil to your hands or to the gluten if the dough is very dry.

CONTINUED ON PAGE 156

CONTINUED FROM PAGE 155

6. Form the dough into a log approximately 6 to 7 inches (15 to 17.5 cm) long and 1 inch (2.5 cm) thick.

7. Warm ½ cup (118 mL) of the remaining vegetable stock and transfer it to the baking dish. With clean scissors or your sharpest kitchen knife, slice 1-inch-thick (2.5-cm-thick) rounds from the loaf. Flatten and shape each round into a patty with your palm. Trim around the edges with scissors for a neater edge, if desired, and then place the patties in the baking dish.

8. Cover tightly with foil and bake for 35 minutes. Remove the foil and add the remaining ½ cup (118 mL) vegetable stock and the water. Bake, uncovered, for 12 minutes.

9. Remove from the oven and let cool. If not using immediately, store in a covered container in the refrigerator. When ready to serve, grill on a hot grill or sauté with a little oil in a heavy sauté pan.

Cooks' Note

Serve on spelt burger buns with sautéed greens to make soul burgers. Chop up the patties and sauté them in olive oil with fennel seed, garlic, oregano, and a touch of red chile flakes for vegan Italian sausage. You can also double the batch and freeze the leftovers, vacuum-packed. If they lose moisture, they can be easily reconstituted by heating with a little vegetable stock or water. Chop leftover patties and use them as ground protein for Bolognese sauce, chili, or other dishes.

Seitan and Bean Loaf

When we first sampled this creation, we were amazed by its texture. It is dense enough to slice as thinly as you wish and still moist and palatable. It's also incredibly versatile: Add whole black peppercorns and garlic to turn it into vegan salami, or add fresh herbs and sun-dried tomatoes for an Italian taste. Slice for sandwiches; chop for casseroles or soups; or dice, season, and sauté with herbs for a ground breakfast protein or to use in tacos and burritos. Use it as the protein in Bolognese sauce or your favorite chili.

YIELD: 1 (2-POUND [1.1-KG]) LOAF

1¼ cup (295 mL) vegetable stock, divided, plus more as needed for baking

1 cup (236 mL) canned pinto, black, navy, butter, or kidney beans, drained and rinsed well.

3 tablespoons (45 mL) olive or canola oil

3 tablespoons (45 mL) liquid smoke or balsamic vinegar

2½ cups (591 mL) vital wheat gluten

⅓ cup (79 mL) chickpea or quinoa flour, plus more for the kneading surface

1½ tablespoons (22 mL) dried herbs (such as oregano, rosemary, or an Italian seasoning blend)

1 tablespoon (15 mL) salt

2 teaspoons (10 mL) onion powder

1½ teaspoons (7.5 mL) ground white pepper

1½ teaspoons (7.5 mL) garlic powder

1 teaspoon (5 mL) paprika

1 tablespoon (15 mL) turbinado sugar

1. Preheat the oven to 400°F (200°C). Line an 11 × 13–inch (27½ × 32½–cm) or similar size baking dish with parchment paper. Lightly oil and add ½ cup (118 mL) of the vegetable stock or an equal amount of water.

2. Place the beans, the remaining ¾ cup (177 mL) of the stock, the oil, and the liquid smoke or balsamic vinegar in a food processor fitted with an S blade. Blend for 30 seconds.

3. In a large bowl, stir together the vital wheat gluten and flour. Add the dry spices and turbinado sugar and stir well.

4. Lightly flour a clean, flat surface with chickpea flour.

5. Add the mixture from the food processor to the dry ingredients and blend well. When a dough begins to form, transfer it to the floured surface. Add a little water or oil to your hands to help incorporate all of the dough into a uniform ball. Knead the loaf for 5 to 8 minutes until strands of gluten start to form. Let the dough rest for 10 minutes. Then knead an additional 3 minutes, forming it into a loaf. Pinch to seal any crevices that remain.

CONTINUED ON PAGE 158

CONTINUED FROM PAGE 157

6. Wrap the loaf in parchment paper, then wrap it again in foil and pinch the foil at the top to seal. Place the loaf in the prepared baking dish and bake for 45 minutes.

7. Remove the foil and bake, uncovered, for another 20 minutes, adding more stock or water to the baking dish as needed. Remove from the oven and let cool to room temperature. To store, wrap in plastic wrap or refrigerate in an airtight container with a little vegetable stock.

Variation

Using clean scissors, cut the uncooked loaf into patties and arrange them in the baking dish. Cover the dish with foil and bake for 30 minutes covered and 30 minutes uncovered, replenishing the liquid as needed.

Walnut Tofu Balls or Patties

This dish has a good texture and a high nutritional value, and it makes a great morning protein. Amp up the heat factor by adding chopped jalapeño, chipotle, or serrano chilies. These are stellar alongside biscuits and gravy.

YIELD: 15–18 (1½-INCH [3.5-CM]) BALLS

6 cloves garlic, peeled and crushed

1½ cups (354 mL) quick cooking oats

1 cup (236 mL) chopped or whole raw walnuts or pecans

⅓ cup (79 mL) sunflower seeds or cashews (optional)

1 tablespoon (15 mL) salt

1½ teaspoons (7.5 mL) freshly ground black pepper

2 teaspoons (10 mL) ground sage

2 teaspoons (10 mL) cumin

¼ teaspoon (1.25 mL) cayenne pepper

½ cup (125 mL) dry breadcrumbs

2 tablespoons (30 mL) quinoa flour

1 tablespoon (15 mL) arrowroot powder or cornstarch, blended with ¼ cup (59 mL) warm water

10 ounces (280 g) firm tofu

3 tablespoons (45 mL) vegetable oil, divided

1 tablespoon (15 mL) balsamic vinegar or liquid smoke

2 tablespoons (30 mL) whole fennel seeds

1. Preheat the oven to 375°F (190°C). Line a baking sheet with parchment paper.

2. Combine the garlic, oats, nuts, sunflower seeds or cashews, and dry spices in a food processor. Process until the mixture is chopped medium-fine.

3. Add the breadcrumbs and quinoa flour, and pulse a few times to blend.

4. Add the dissolved arrowroot or cornstarch liquid and blend for 1 minute. Add the tofu and blend while gradually adding 1 tablespoon (15 mL) of the oil and the balsamic vinegar or liquid smoke. Blend just long enough to evenly distribute all the ingredients, then taste the mixture for seasoning and adjust as necessary.

5. Transfer the mixture to a bowl and stir in the fennel seeds.

6. Form the finished mixture into balls, links, or patties and brown them in a sauté pan over medium heat in the remaining 2 tablespoons (30 mL) vegetable oil. Drain on paper towels. Transfer them to the prepared baking sheet and bake 15 minutes, or a little longer if you like them well browned.

7. Serve immediately or cool and store in an airtight container in the refrigerator for later use. These will keep refrigerated for four days.

Zippy's Ground Nut Burgers

This recipe makes a delicious, high-protein, easy-to-make mixture that you can form into burgers or use in tacos, wraps, hors d'oeuvres, shepherd's pie, lasagna, chili, or whatever else you can imagine.

YIELD: 4 (3-INCH [7.5-CM]) PATTIES

¼ cup (59 mL) vegetable stock or water, heated

1 tablespoon (15 mL) arrowroot powder

2 tablespoons (30 mL) flax meal (optional)

⅔ cup (158 mL) raw sunflower seeds

1 cup (226 mL) raw cashews

1½ teaspoons (7.5 mL) salt

1 teaspoon (5 mL) ground white pepper

1 teaspoon (5 mL) paprika

1 teaspoon (5 mL) cumin

2 tablespoons (30 mL) quinoa flour or bread or cracker crumbs

1 tablespoon (15 mL) balsamic vinegar or vegan Worcestershire sauce

¼ cup (50 mL) finely diced onion

2 tablespoons (30 mL) chopped parsley

1 tablespoon (15 mL) olive or canola oil

2 cloves garlic, peeled and crushed

1. Preheat the oven to 375°F (190°C).

2. Line a sheet pan with lightly oiled parchment paper.

3. In a small bowl, combine the hot stock or water, arrowroot powder, and flax meal, if using. Set aside.

4. In a food processor, blend the sunflower seeds until the pieces are about ⅓ of their original size. Add the cashews and pulse again until the pieces are of a consistent size. Add the dry spices, crushed garlic, and olive or canola oil and pulse about 4 times to combine.

5. Add the water or stock mixture, the quinoa flour or crumbs, and the vinegar or vegan Worcestershire sauce and blend for 2 minutes. Transfer the mixture to a bowl and fold in the onion and parsley.

6. Form the mixture into patties or balls, adding a little more quinoa flour if necessary to obtain a workable mixture. Wet your hands and run them over the patties or balls to moisten and seal them, placing the finished ones on the prepared baking sheet as you work.

7. Bake for 12 minutes or until brown on the bottom. Flip them and bake for 5 to 8 more minutes. Remove from the oven and cool for at least 30 minutes. Handle the cooled patties gently.

Variation
Use ground vegan cheddar crackers in place of breadcrumbs.

Veganopolis Cashew Ricotta

This is great in lasagna, spread on a sandwich or crackers, or anywhere you would use ricotta. You will need a good-quality food processor to make this. Your best option is a Champion juicer, available online and in many health food stores. For this recipe, use the Champion with the solid screen in place.

This recipe requires some preparation. The week you want to make it, place 2 inches (5 cm) of winter wheat berries into a sprouting jar with a screw-top lid. Fill the jar with water until the wheat berries are covered by 2 inches (5 cm) and let stand overnight.

In the morning, drain the water. The berries will begin to sprout. Rinse them a few times a day. When they have little tails that are about a quarter of an inch long, submerge them again in a jar with a screw-top lid and fill the jar with water to 1 inch (2.5 cm) above the sprouted berries. Leave the jar out at room temperature and the mixture will begin to ferment. After 24 hours, the water will be ready to use. The water will smell a bit sour as it ferments, but this sourness is what makes the cashew ricotta taste like cheese.

The ancient Celtic people would make this beverage for their children because of its high nutritional value. Later, if left in the jar long enough, the water would begin to turn into beer, and voilà . . . the beginning of Guinness! The fermented wheat berry water can be sealed, stored, and refrigerated for up to a week.

YIELD: 4 CUPS (95 ML)

> 4 cups (95 L) raw, unsalted cashews
>
> 1 or more cups (236 mL or more) fermented wheat berry water
>
> Juice of 1 lemon
>
> Salt, to taste

1. Soak the cashews in water for 4 to 6 hours. Drain and rinse them well in cold running water.

2. Process the cashews through the Champion juicer or in a food processor fitted with the S blade, adding just enough of the fermented wheat berry water to produce a thick, ricotta-like mixture.

3. Season the mixture with the lemon juice and enough salt to bring out the flavors nicely. And there you have it—ricotta without the cow.

Variation

Freshly diced oregano and minced garlic are brilliant if you use the cashew ricotta in vegan lasagna.

Cheitan Patties

This is a breakthrough recipe for patties that have superior flavor and texture. Use as is for burgers, or dice and use in soups, stews, or anything else.

YIELD: 6–8 LARGE PATTIES

1 cup (236 mL) canned white beans

½ cup (118 mL) chickpea flour, plus more for the kneading surface

2½ teaspoons (12.5 mL) salt

2 teaspoons (10 mL) onion powder

1 teaspoon (5 mL) ground turmeric

2 teaspoons (10 mL) garlic powder

2 teaspoons (10 mL) freshly ground black pepper

1 tablespoon (15 mL) plus 1 teaspoon (5 mL) lemon juice, divided

2 tablespoons (30 mL) olive oil

1 tablespoon (15 mL) turbinado sugar

2½ cups (591 mL) vital wheat gluten, divided

2 cups (473 mL) vegetable stock, divided

1. Preheat the oven to 375°F (190°C). Line an 11 × 13–inch (27½ × 32½–cm) baking dish with parchment paper.

2. Rinse the beans well and place them in a food processor with the chickpea flour, the dry spices, 1 tablespoon (15 mL) of the lemon juice, the oil, and the turbinado sugar. Blend for 30 seconds.

3. Add 1 cup (236 mL) of the vital wheat gluten and ½ cup (118 mL) of the stock. Pulse 6 times.

4. With the processor running, add the remaining vital wheat gluten and another ½ cup (118 mL) stock and process until a dough forms, about 1 minute. If this has not happened after 1 minute, add water, a tablespoon at a time, until it does.

5. Next, dust a clean surface with a bit more of the chickpea flour. Transfer the dough to this surface and knead for about 3 minutes, at which point it should feel almost dry to the touch. Let it rest for 15 minutes.

6. Mix ⅔ cup (158 mL) stock with the remaining 1 teaspoon (5 mL) lemon juice and pour the mixture into the prepared dish.

7. Knead the dough another 15 times and form it into a loaf. If there are any crevices or seams in the dough, pinch them together until you have a smooth surface all over.

8. Using a clean pair of large scissors or a very sharp, thin-bladed knife, cut the loaf into 1-inch-thick (2.5-cm-thick) pieces and form the pieces into circular patties about ½ inch (1 cm) thick. You may trim off any excess at this point with your scissors.

CONTINUED ON PAGE 164

CONTINUED FROM PAGE 163

9. Press and stretch the patties until you have formed them into discs about 3 inches (7.5 cm) in diameter. You can cook the excess bits or any remaining dough along with the patties.

10. Place the finished patties in the prepared baking dish and cover it with foil. Bake for 30 minutes. Remove the foil and add ½ cup (118 mL) water. Bake, uncovered, for an additional 20 minutes.

11. Remove from the oven and let cool. Do not remove the patties from the broth.

Cooks' Note

You can store the finished patties and broth in an airtight container in the refrigerator.

To make burger, brown the patties in a sauté pan with a little oil and serve on a bun with sautéed onions, lettuce, tomato, and vegan mayonnaise.

You can also use these patties for Veganopolis Democracy Burgers (page 140), diced in Super Noodle Soup (page 38), or in Paprikash (page 183).

Corned Tofu

Use this as an alternative to Corned Beef Substitute (page 152) if you don't like seitan or don't have time to make it. Extracting as much moisture as possible from the tofu is key. You may skip the freezing step, but the tofu will not absorb as much flavor.

YIELD: 1 POUND (454 G)

1 pound (454 g) water-packed extra-firm tofu, frozen overnight in its container and thawed

2 tablespoons (30 mL) canola oil

2 tablespoons (30 mL) diced shallot or onion

1 bay leaf

1½ teaspoons (7.5 mL) salt

2 tablespoons (30 mL) freshly ground black pepper

1 carrot, diced

1 stalk celery, diced

½ cup (118 mL) red wine vinegar

1 cup (236 mL) vegetable stock

1. Press as much liquid as possible out of the thawed tofu by placing it on a flat, clean plate or other flat surface and placing a heavy object on top.

2. Meanwhile, heat the canola oil in a saucepan over medium heat. Add the onion, bay leaf, salt, pepper, carrot, and celery. Sauté until the celery starts to soften.

3. Add the vinegar and bring to a boil.

4. Cook until the mixture is reduced by ⅓. Add the stock.

5. Cut the tofu block into 4 slices and lay them in a shallow pan. Pour the marinade over the tofu and let stand 1 hour, or cover and refrigerate overnight.

6. Remove from the marinade and brown in a sauté pan or grill the slices on a hot grill. Cut into serving-size portions and use in the Vegan New York Reuben Sandwich (page 134) or anywhere else you like.

Golden Tofu Patties

Golden yellow with a smooth texture, these patties are perfect for Vegan Benedict (page 105).

YIELD: 6 (3-INCH [7.5-CM]) PATTIES

> 1 pound (454 g) extra-firm tofu, well drained and pressed
>
> ⅓ cup (79 mL) canned great northern or cannellini beans, rinsed
>
> 1 tablespoon (15 mL) lemon juice
>
> ⅓ cup (79 mL) chickpea or quinoa flour
>
> 2 tablespoons (30 mL) flax meal
>
> 2 teaspoons (10 mL) ground turmeric
>
> 1½ teaspoons (7.25 mL) onion powder
>
> 1 teaspoon (5 mL) garlic powder
>
> 1 teaspoon (5 mL) salt
>
> 1 tablespoon (15 mL) olive or safflower oil, plus more to sauté
>
> 1 pinch cayenne pepper
>
> 1 tablespoon (15 mL) finely chopped fresh parsley
>
> Salt, to taste

1. Break up the tofu and place it in a food processor along with all the other ingredients. Pulse 6 to 8 times until evenly blended. Do not overpulse, as this will make the patties crumbly and wet.

2. With a small dessert scooper, scoop the mixture to form rounds about 3 inches (7.5 cm) in diameter.

3. Heat a skillet over medium heat and add a few tablespoons olive or safflower oil. Brown the patties until crispy on both sides.

Cooks' Note

You may form these into patties and store them in the refrigerator overnight, which will firm them up a little more.

Variation

Add 2 tablespoons (30 mL) finely sliced sun-dried tomatoes and 2 tablespoons (30 mL) finely sliced fresh basil.

Golden Bean Flax Rounds

A soy-free alternative to Golden Tofu Patties, these patties are every bit as tasty. You can use them for Vegan Benedict (page 105), in an English muffin breakfast sandwich, or with a simple marinara or pesto.

YIELD: 6 (2-INCH [5-CM]) PATTIES

> 1 (12-ounce [336-mL]) can cannellini, navy, or great northern beans, drained and well rinsed
>
> 2 tablespoons (30 mL) chickpea or quinoa flour
>
> 2 teaspoons (10 mL) flax meal (or substitute 2 more teaspoons [10 mL] flour)
>
> 2 teaspoons (10 mL) vegetable oil
>
> 2 teaspoons (10 mL) lemon juice
>
> 1 teaspoon (5 mL) onion powder
>
> 1½ teaspoons (7.5 mL) ground turmeric
>
> 1 teaspoon (5 mL) garlic powder
>
> ½ teaspoon (2.5 mL) salt
>
> ¼ teaspoon (1.25 mL) cayenne pepper
>
> 2 tablespoons (30 mL) finely chopped fresh parsley
>
> 2 teaspoons (10 mL) warm water
>
> 2 tablespoons (30 mL) canola or safflower oil

1. Place all ingredients in a food processor and blend for 30 to 40 seconds or until the mixture begins to form a ball.

2. Scoop into patties about 3 inches (7.5 cm) in diameter and brown on each side in the canola oil in a sauté pan placed over medium heat.

CHAPTER 7

Entrées and Sides

Ecuadorian Yapingachos

The potato originated in South America, where there are more than 2,000 varieties. A more brilliant way of preparing potatoes has yet to come to my attention. Your guests will love you and beg you to make them again soon. Achiote, also known as annato, is a blood-red seed used to color many foods. It has a dark, citrus-pepper flavor, somewhat akin to tamarind. Its coloring power is almost as powerful as that of saffron, so you might want to change into a black tee while you are making these. You can purchase achiote paste from specialty stores. A liquid achiote condiment is also available in many Mexican groceries and is quite easy to use. If you like, you can form the potato patties the day before serving.

YIELD: 18 SMALL (3-INCH [7.5-CM] DIAMETER) PATTIES

For the potatoes:

6 large, starchy potatoes, peeled

Salt, to taste

1 tablespoon (15mL) ground white pepper

¼ cup (59 mL) vegan margarine

½ cup (118 mL) soy or rice beverage

12 ounces (336 g) vegan white cheese substitute, such as block-style soy mozzarella

2 teaspoons (10 mL) achiote paste dissolved in ¼ cup (59 mL) hot water or 2 teaspoons (10 mL) liquid achiote condiment (if you can't find achiote in either form, substitute 2 teaspoons [10 mL] ground turmeric)

1. Bring a large pot of salted water to a boil. Add the potatoes and boil until they are fork tender. Drain the potatoes and transfer them to a large bowl. Mash them well and break up any chunks that may remain. Season with the salt, white pepper, and achiote. The potatoes should turn a golden yellow color.

2. Add the vegan margarine and soy or rice beverage. What you want is a mixture that you can shape with your hands, thicker and drier than North American–style mashed potatoes. Adjust the seasoning to taste. If the potato mixture is too watery, you may add flour to adjust the texture.

3. Using a small circular pastry cutter or a sharp-edged bottle-cap, cut the vegan cheese into 1-inch (2.5-cm) discs about ¾ inch (1.5 cm) thick.

4. Take a small handful of the potato mixture and a cheese disc and form the potato into a small pancake with the cheese disc inside. Make sure the potato mixture completely surrounds the disc. Repeat with the remaining potato mixture and cheese.

CONTINUED ON PAGE 170

CONTINUED FROM PAGE 169

5. Arrange the finished pancakes on a baking sheet or tray lined with parchment paper and chill. At this point, you can stack the patties between sheets of parchment paper in a lidded plastic container and freeze them, tightly sealed, for several weeks.

For the sauce:

3 tablespoons (45 mL) canola oil

1 white onion, peeled and finely diced

2 jalapeño peppers, stems removed, seeded, and finely minced, plus more to taste

2 cups soy or rice beverage

1 teaspoon (5 mL) achiote paste or liquid achiote condiment

1 cup (236 mL) creamy peanut butter

Green jalapeño hot sauce, to taste (optional)

1. Heat the canola oil in a saucepan over medium heat and add the onion and peppers. Cook until the onions are softened.

2. Add the soy or rice beverage and bring to a boil. Add the achiote paste and peanut butter and stir well. If the sauce becomes too thick, add more soy or rice beverage.

3. Season the finished sauce with green jalapeños or green jalapeño hot sauce until it has the flavor you desire. The peanut flavor should dominate, with just a little spice from the peppers.

For serving:

4 tablespoons (60 mL) canola oil

1–2 fresh avocados, peeled, pitted, and sliced, for garnish

½ cup (118 mL) fresh cilantro leaves, for garnish

1. Heat a very large skillet over medium heat and add the canola oil.

2. Sauté the yapingachos on each side until they are golden brown.

3. For each serving, arrange a few yapingachos on a warmed serving plate and top with a dollop of the sauce. Arrange a few cilantro leaves on each yapingacho patty and serve with fresh sliced avocado on the side. Take some hot sauces to the table for those who like it spicy.

Oven-Roasted Potatoes

I'm of Welsh descent, and George is Scotch and Irish, so I guess our love of potatoes is encoded somewhere in our genes. People who tell me they don't like potatoes make me nervous, as if they have some mysterious moral aberration in their nature.

At the restaurant, potatoes of some kind are available all the time. To vary the selection, we have learned to season potatoes in various ways, and the most successful of those variations are listed here.

YIELD: 6 SERVINGS

> 6 medium or 4 large white or red potatoes, unpeeled and cut into bite-size chunks
>
> Salt and pepper, to taste, or one of the seasoning alternatives that follow the recipe
>
> ¼ cup (59 mL) olive oil
>
> ¼ cup (59 mL) canola oil

1. Soak the cut potatoes in cold water for at least 20 minutes or as long as overnight. Line a baking sheet with parchment paper. Drain the potatoes well and lay them on the prepared baking sheet in a single layer.

2. Preheat the oven to 400°F (200°C).

3. Season the potatoes. Combine the two oils and pour them over the potatoes. Toss them with your hands to coat.

4. Roast the potatoes until browned and crisp, about 30 to 45 minutes. Serve as is or with malt vinegar, ketchup, Veganopolis Mayo (page 91), and/or your favorite hot sauce.

Seasoning alternatives:

> Minced garlic, finely chopped fresh rosemary, salt, and freshly ground black pepper
>
> Fresh (chopped) or dried oregano, freshly ground black pepper, salt, and the juice of 2 lemons
>
> 1 tablespoon (15 mL) grated achiote; ½ cup (118 mL) finely minced fresh cilantro; the juice of 2 limes, 1 jalapeño pepper, stemmed, seeded, and very finely diced; and ½ cup (118 mL) of canola oil

Variation

Smashed Potatoes: Roast as in the original recipe, with salt and pepper. Remove the potatoes from the oven and place them in a bowl. Mash them with ¼ cup (59 mL) of thinly sliced chives and a few tablespoons (about 45 mL) vegan margarine.

Red Cabbage with Apple Sauté

I learned to prepare this fantastically flavorful side dish at the Escoffier School in Paris. The humble cabbage is elevated to gourmet status in this simple recipe. This is great alongside Paprikash (page 183).

YIELD: 8 SERVINGS

¼ cup (59 mL) vegan margarine or light olive oil, divided

6 shallots, peeled and finely minced

2 tablespoons (30 mL) fresh grated orange zest

1 tablespoon (15 mL) caraway seeds

¼ cup (59 mL) red wine vinegar

1 head red cabbage, cored and diced

Freshly ground black pepper, to taste

½ cup (118 mL) turbinado sugar, for dredging

1 cup (236 mL) full-flavored red wine, such as pinot noir or any red Burgundy

Salt, to taste

2 Granny Smith apples

1. Melt half the vegan margarine or heat half the olive oil in a large, heavy-bottomed saucepan over medium-high heat. Add the shallots and cook until they soften. Add the orange zest and caraway seeds.

2. Cook for 3 minutes and then deglaze the pan with the red wine vinegar. Allow it to cook down until just a bit of moisture remains in the bottom of the pan.

3. Add the cabbage and a generous grinding of black pepper. Stir well. Cook until the cabbage starts to soften, about 10 minutes, stirring frequently.

4. Add the wine and cook for an additional 15 minutes, until the cabbage is fully cooked. Add salt, to taste.

5. Peel and core the apples and cut each lengthwise into 16 slices. Dredge each slice in the turbinado sugar.

6. Heat the remaining vegan margarine or oil in a separate large sauté pan and sauté the apple slices until they are just golden. Avoid overcooking so that they retain their shape for serving.

7. To serve, mound the red cabbage on a serving platter and arrange the sautéed apple slices on top.

Sacré bleu! C'est magnifique!

Stuffed Baby Pumpkins

You can find baby pumpkins in the market in the late summer. Often used as Halloween decorations, they are absolutely delicious and tender prepared this way. To eat, simply scoop the pumpkin away from the skin and enjoy.

YIELD: 4 SERVINGS

> 4 baby pumpkins, each about 8 inches (20 cm) in diameter
>
> 4 tablespoons (60 mL) olive oil
>
> 2 teaspoons (10 mL) salt
>
> 1 teaspoon (5 mL) white pepper
>
> 1 pod grated or 2 teaspoons (10 mL) ground nutmeg
>
> 8 tablespoons (120 mL) vegan coffee creamer, divided
>
> 4 fresh sage leaves, for seasoning
>
> 4 (1-inch [2.5-cm]) cubes white vegan cheese substitute

1. Preheat the oven to 350°F (180°C). Line a baking sheet with parchment paper.

2. Slice the tops off the pumpkins about ½ inch (1 cm) down from the stem. Reserve the tops. Carefully scrape out all of the seeds and fibrous material from the inside of the pumpkins and discard. Coat the insides and outsides of the pumpkins with the oil, and season the inside surfaces with the salt, white pepper, and nutmeg.

3. Pour 2 tablespoons (30 mL) of the vegan creamer into each pumpkin and place 1 ounce (29.5 mL) white vegan cheese in each pumpkin. Place a few sage leaves on top of the cheese in each pumpkin and replace the pumpkins' tops. Try to find the correct tops for each pumpkin for a secure fit.

4. Place the pumpkins on the prepared baking sheet, and bake for about 45 minutes, or until the outsides start to brown nicely.

5. Check to make sure the insides are tender, and serve.

Achiote Rice

This recipe produces that golden-red Mexican rice characteristic of good Mexican kitchens. Great as a side dish any time, this rice is particularly good with Enchilada Lasagna (page 207).

YIELD: 8 SERVINGS

> 6 cups (1.4 L) vegetable stock
>
> 2 tablespoons (30 mL) achiote paste* or 3 tablespoons (45 mL) achiote condiment**
>
> 2–3 tablespoons olive oil
>
> 1 white onion, peeled and finely diced
>
> 1 teaspoon (5 mL) cumin
>
> 1 teaspoon (5 mL) turmeric
>
> 1 teaspoon (5 mL) dried oregano
>
> 1 teaspoon (5 mL) dark chili powder
>
> 2 cups (473 mL) uncooked basmati or other long-grain white rice
>
> 3 tablespoons (45 mL) finely diced red bell peppers (optional)
>
> 3 tablespoons (45 mL) finely diced green bell peppers (optional)
>
> 3 tablespoons (45 mL) finely diced yellow bell peppers (optional)
>
> Fresh cilantro leaves, for garnish

1. Preheat the oven to 375°F (190°C).

2. Heat the stock and dissolve the achiote paste in it.

3. In a sauté pan, heat the olive oil over medium heat and sauté the onions and diced peppers briefly. Stir in the dry spices. Remove from the heat and set aside.

4. In a deep roasting pan (a large loaf pan works nicely for this), combine the rice with the lightly sautéed vegetables and spices.

5. Pour the stock seasoned with achiote over the rice and stir well.

6. Cover the pan tightly with aluminum foil and bake for 70 minutes.

7. Check the rice. When all the liquid is absorbed and the rice is tender, it's done. Never serve undercooked rice.

8. Fluff up the rice with a fork and serve garnished with fresh cilantro leaves. The rice will stay warm enough to serve for at least 45 minutes after it is cooked, as long as you keep it covered.

*Shave the paste off the block with a sharp knife and dice it very finely. You may need to strain the achiote-seasoned stock into the rice if the achiote has not entirely dissolved into the stock.

**This is a liquid condiment available in many Mexican groceries.

Roasted Stuffed Squash with Almondetta and Spinach

This is a wonderful harvest-time recipe.

YIELD: 4 SERVINGS

2 acorn squash, halved, seeds and fibrous material scooped out

3 tablespoons (45 mL) olive oil, divided

2 shallots, peeled and very finely diced

1 tablespoon (15 mL) dried oregano

⅓ cup (79 mL) diced red bell pepper

2 cloves garlic, peeled and finely minced

¼ teaspoon (1.25 mL) ground nutmeg

½ cup (118 mL) dry breadcrumbs, divided

1 pound (454 g) fresh spinach, chopped

1 cup (236 mL) Almondetta (page 148)

1. Preheat the oven to 375°F (190°C). Line a large baking dish with parchment paper.

2. Use 1 tablespoon (15 mL) of the olive oil to lightly oil the insides of the squash halves and sprinkle with salt and pepper.

3. Arrange the squash halves face up in the prepared baking dish and roast for 45 minutes.

4. Heat the remaining olive oil in a medium skillet over medium heat. Add the diced shallots and sauté until softened.

5. Add the oregano, diced red bell pepper, garlic, nutmeg, and 2 tablespoons (30 mL) of the breadcrumbs. Sauté for a few minutes.

6. Add the chopped spinach. Cook until the spinach is fully wilted and most of the moisture is gone.

7. Stir in the Almondetta. Remove from the heat.

8. When the squash halves are finished roasting, remove the pan from the oven and lower the heat to 350°F (180°C).

9. Divide the spinach mixture among the squash halves, mounding it up a bit on top with a rounded spoon or scoop. Sprinkle the remaining breadcrumbs on top.

10. Bake for 15 minutes or until the breadcrumbs are browned nicely.

11. Remove the stuffed squash halves from the oven, plate, and serve.

Variations

Add dried cranberries, cherries, walnuts, or crumbled Roadhouse Vegan Burgers (page 155).

Ardennes-Style Vegan Scalloped Potatoes

The Ardennes region of France is up north, near the Belgian border. It is where you will find Charleville, the birthplace of poet Arthur Rimbaud. The local insignias often feature a wild boar, as does Gordon's gin. This recipe features juniper berries, as does any gin.

YIELD: 8 SERVINGS

> 6 large potatoes, peeled, sliced ⅛ inch (3 mm) thick, and placed in cold water to cover
>
> 1 recipe Veganopolis Béchamel Sauce (page 89)
>
> Salt, to taste
>
> Freshly ground black pepper, to taste
>
> 12 juniper berries, crushed
>
> 4 tablespoons (60 mL) finely chopped fresh rosemary
>
> 1 Spanish onion, peeled and sliced thinly

1. Preheat the oven to 400°F (200°C). Oil a baking dish.

2. Drain the potato slices and transfer them to a large pot of salted water. Bring the pot to a boil, lower the heat to a simmer, and cover the pot. Let simmer for about 8 minutes, then remove one slice and check it for doneness. It should be flexible but still firm. When the potatoes are done, drain and rinse them in a large colander.

3. Pour the Veganopolis Béchamel Sauce into the baking dish and spread it evenly over the bottom. Arrange a layer of potato slices on top of the sauce. Season the potato slices with salt, pepper, and a pinch of the crushed juniper berries and chopped rosemary. Then arrange a layer of sliced onion over the top. Top with sauce. Continue building the layers this way until you have filled the dish. Finish with sauce and a generous grinding of black pepper.

4. Bake until the top is golden brown, about 45 minutes. Serve immediately.

Ceviche

When our Mayan chef, Santos Cauich, created this recipe for the first time, we gathered around the bowl as if it was a sacred vessel, and our palates lit up like sunrise over the Yucatan.

YIELD: 3 POUNDS (1.4 KG)

> **1 pound (454 g) vegan tuna substitute* or 1 pound (500g) Veganopolis Simple Seitan (page 145), cut into ½-inch (1-cm) cubes**
>
> **2 large ripe tomatoes, finely diced**
>
> **2 jalapeño peppers, stems removed, seeded, and finely diced**
>
> **1 large red onion, peeled and finely diced**
>
> **1 cup (236 mL) finely diced fresh cilantro**
>
> **1 tablespoon (15 mL) toasted ground cumin****
>
> **Juice of 4 fresh limes**
>
> **Salt, to taste**

1. Combine all ingredients in a large bowl and stir.

2. Let sit for at least 30 minutes and stir again. For best results, refrigerate overnight.

*Vegan tuna substitute is available in many Asian groceries. It is usually a soy and mushroom product wrapped in nori. For ceviche, unwrap and discard the nori skin before dicing.

**To toast ground cumin, heat it in a small, heavy (preferably cast iron) frying pan over medium heat. With a fork, scrape the cumin over the hot surface until it darkens, but do not let it blacken. This will only take a few moments. Immediately scrape the ground cumin out of the hot pan and use as desired. It's great in the above recipe or in pico de gallo.

Classic Pot Pie

This recipe was perfected over several years. The crust is especially nice and so absurdly simple that it is a wonder that every cook on earth doesn't do crusts this way. Make the pot pies in ovenproof soup bowls.

YIELD: 6 SMALL OR 4 LARGE POT PIES

For the crust:

> 4 cups (.95 L) white spelt flour
>
> 2 teaspoons (20 mL) salt
>
> 3 teaspoons (30 mL) turbinado sugar
>
> 1½ cups (354 mL) olive or canola oil, placed in the freezer for 30 minutes
>
> ½ cup (118 mL) ice water, or more as needed

1. Mix the dry ingredients in a bowl and make a well in the center.

2. Mix the cold liquid ingredients and pour them into the well. With a flat-blade rubber spatula, drag the flour into the well and rotate the bowl, dragging more flour in as you turn it.

3. Once the dough is partially mixed, switch to your hands and mix everything into uniform dough. If the dough is too moist, add a little more flour. Form it into a ball and let it rest while you prepare the filling.

For the filling:

> ¼ cup (59 mL) canola oil
>
> 1 onion, peeled and diced
>
> 1 teaspoon (5 mL) ground white pepper
>
> 1 teaspoon (5 mL) ground sage
>
> 1 teaspoon (5 mL) dried thyme
>
> 1 teaspoon (5 mL) onion powder
>
> 1 teaspoon (5 mL) garlic powder
>
> 1 cup (236 mL) white spelt flour
>
> 2 cups (473 mL) vegetable stock
>
> 2 cups (473 mL) soy or rice beverage
>
> 2 cups (473 mL) diced potatoes, parboiled*
>
> 2 cups (473 mL) Cheitan Patties (page 163) or other vegan chicken substitute, cut into ½-inch (1-cm) dice
>
> 1 cup (236 mL) diced carrots, parboiled
>
> 1 cup (236 mL) frozen peas, thawed

1. Heat the oil in a large saucepan over medium heat. Add the onions and dry spices and sauté until the onions are softened and the spices are fragrant.

2. Add the flour and whisk to form a roux. Cook the roux for 5 minutes.

3. Add the stock and soy or rice beverage 1 cup (236 mL) at a time, until you achieve a sauce that is thick enough to coat a spoon.

4. Add the potatoes, Cheitan Patties, carrots, and peas and cook together for 10 minutes. At this point, the mixture can be cooled and stored for later use.

To assemble and bake the pot pies:

1. Preheat the oven to 350°F (180°C).

2. Between two pieces of parchment paper, roll a handful of dough into a circle large enough to easily cover one of the ovenproof soup bowls you will use for the pot pies. If needed, sprinkle a little flour over the paper to prevent sticking. Fit the dough circle into the bowl. Repeat with the remaining bowls

3. Fill each bowl with the filling—to about ½ inch (1 cm) below the top edge of the bowl.

4. Roll the remaining dough into circles and place a dough circle on top of each bowl. Press the dough down around the edges of each bowl, and make a few slits in the top surface of each pie with a very sharp knife.

5. Place the bowls on a flat baking sheet and bake until the crust is golden brown and the filling is bubbling hot, about 35 to 40 minutes. Serve immediately.

*Parboil means just what it sounds like: partially boil. Potatoes and carrots need just 6 minutes or so in boiling salted water. They will cook the rest of the way in the sauce and again in the oven. For those of you who aren't averse to using a microwave oven, place the diced potatoes and carrots in a microwave-safe container and fill the container with hot water. Then microwave on high for about 10 minutes. Voilà! Perfectly parboiled vegetables.

Moussaka

I think of moussaka as the Greek version of Italian lasagna, where the pasta layers are replaced with layers of thinly sliced eggplant. One thing is critical for the flavor in this recipe: a Greek tomato sauce made with red wine and a touch of cinnamon. This recipe is fairly involved, but it's well worth the effort.

YIELD 10–12 SERVINGS

For the sauce:

4 tablespoons (60 mL) extra virgin olive oil

6 cloves garlic, peeled and minced

1 red onion, peeled and finely diced

1 tablespoon (15 mL) dried oregano

1 tablespoon (15 mL) freshly ground black pepper

1 teaspoon (5 mL) ground cinnamon

3 tablespoons (45 mL) red wine vinegar

1 cup (236 mL) strongly flavored red wine, such as Burgundy

1 (32-ounce [1.1-kg]) can diced tomatoes or an equal amount of chopped fresh tomatoes

Salt, to taste

1. Heat olive oil in a saucepan over medium heat. Add the garlic, red onion, and dry spices. Sauté until the onions are softened and the mixture is fragrant.

2. Deglaze the pan with the red wine vinegar and cook for about 5 minutes or until the liquid is reduced by ⅔.

3. Add the tomatoes and bring to a simmer. Continue simmering until the tomatoes begin to break up.

4. Blend with an immersion blender or in a food processor. Taste for seasoning and add salt as needed. You should be able to taste just the barest hint of cinnamon. The wine flavor should be distinct. Set the sauce aside while you prepare the moussaka.

For the moussaka:

> 6 baking potatoes, peeled and sliced into ⅛-inch-thick (.25-cm-thick) slices, placed in cold water to cover
>
> 6 large eggplants, peeled and sliced lengthwise into ¼-inch-thick (.5-cm-thick) slices
>
> Salt, to taste
>
> Freshly ground black pepper, to taste
>
> Dried oregano, to taste
>
> 2 pounds (1.1 kg) fresh spinach, stemmed and chopped
>
> 1 teaspoon (5 mL) grated nutmeg
>
> 20 ounces (560 g) Italian style vegan sausage, chopped
>
> 2 tablespoons (30 mL) finely chopped fresh oregano
>
> Sprigs of fresh oregano, for garnish
>
> 2 cups (473 mL) Veganopolis Cashew Ricotta (page 162)

1. Preheat the oven to 400°F (200°C). Line several baking sheets (enough to hold all the eggplant slices in a single layer) and a roasting pan with parchment paper. Oil a lasagna pan.

2. Transfer the potato slices to a pot of salted water and bring to a boil. Reduce the heat to a simmer and cook until the potatoes are just tender but not soft, about 7 minutes. Drain and rinse in cold water to stop the cooking process.

3. Arrange the eggplant slices on the prepared baking sheets and lightly season them with salt, black pepper, and oregano. Roast in the oven until the eggplant just begins to brown, about 20 minutes. Remove from the oven and set aside. Leave the oven on.

4. Place the chopped spinach in the prepared roasting pan and season it with salt and pepper, to taste, and the nutmeg. Cover the pan tightly with foil and roast for about 30 minutes, or until the spinach is completely wilted. Remove the pan from the oven and remove the foil. Lower the oven temperature to 350°F (180°C).

5. Combine the vegan sausage with 1 cup (236 mL) of the tomato sauce and mix well with your hands. Set aside.

6. Stir the chopped fresh oregano into the cashew ricotta and set aside.

7. Place ¾ cup (177 mL) of the tomato sauce in the prepared lasagna pan. Shake the pan to create an even layer of sauce.

8. Place some of the roasted eggplant slices over the sauce layer, overlapping them a little to create one even layer. Top with the vegan sausage and press it in place.

9. Continue with another eggplant layer, then the blanched potato slices.

CONTINUED ON PAGE 182

CONTINUED FROM PAGE 181

10. Grind some black pepper over the potato slices, and then add a thin layer of tomato sauce. Continue with another layer of eggplant slices, then the wilted spinach. Add another layer of eggplant slices, then the cashew ricotta. Finish with a final layer of eggplant slices and cover with more sauce, reserving some sauce for serving. You may find it helpful to cover the entire moussaka with parchment paper and press it down firmly with your hands as you create layers.

11. Using your sharpest knife, carefully cut the moussaka into serving-size pieces. Bake the finished moussaka for 1 hour or until the dish is cooked through and bubbling.

12. To serve, reheat the sauce and spoon a bit of the remaining tomato sauce in a circle on a heated plate and remove a serving-size portion of the moussaka and place it in the circle of sauce. Serve immediately, garnished with a sprig of fresh oregano.

Variation

After building the moussaka layers, scatter vegan Parmesan over the top. Or if you want to get even closer to the moussakas served in Greek restaurants, make the Vegan Béchamel Sauce (page 89) and ladle two cups of it over the tomato sauce on top of your moussaka.

Paprikash

This dish goes great with noodles, rice, or a side of potatoes. It's fantastic with the Red Cabbage with Apple Sauté (page 172).

YIELD: 10–12 SERVINGS

1 cup (226 mL) white spelt flour or other white flour

4 tablespoons (60 mL) paprika

2 teaspoons (10 mL) salt

2 teaspoons (10 mL) ground white pepper

2 teaspoons (10 mL) garlic powder

6 Cheitan Patties (page 163)

8 tablespoons (120 mL) canola oil, divided

1 red onion, peeled and finely diced

4 cloves garlic, peeled and minced

2 cups (473 mL) finely diced roasted pimentos

1 quart (.95 L) rich vegetable stock, heated

Salt, to taste

Fresh chopped parsley, for garnish

1. Combine the flour and dry spices. Dredge the Cheitan Patties in the spiced flour mixture and set aside. Reserve the remaining flour mixture.

2. In a saucepan, heat 4 tablespoons (60 mL) of the canola oil over medium-high heat and whisk in 6 tablespoons (90 mL) of the remaining spiced flour. Cook, whisking constantly, for 5 to 6 minutes. Add the onions, garlic, and pimentos. Cook, whisking frequently, until the onions are softened and the mixture is fragrant.

3. Add the hot stock in 2-cup (473-mL) batches, whisking after each addition, or until you achieve the consistency you desire. Taste for seasoning and add salt as needed. Heat the remaining 4 tablespoons (60 mL) canola oil in a large sauté pan over medium heat and sauté the flour-dredged Cheitan Patties for about 5 minutes on each side.

4. Serve the patties covered with the sauce and garnished with fresh chopped parsley.

Portobello Mushroom Burgers with Caramelized Onions and Horseradish Cream Sauce

The large portobello mushroom works beautifully as a burger patty. It's dressed up here with caramelized onions and horseradish sauce. If you don't like horseradish, mustard, or Veganopolis Mayo, ketchup is also grand with this burger.

YIELD: 4 SERVINGS

> 4 large portobello mushrooms
>
> 4 tablespoons (60 mL) olive oil, divided
>
> Salt, to taste
>
> Freshly ground black pepper, to taste
>
> 2 tablespoons (30 mL) balsamic vinegar
>
> 2 onions, peeled and very thinly sliced
>
> Crusty rolls or burger buns
>
> Horseradish Cream Sauce (recipe follows)
>
> Chopped romaine lettuce, to serve
>
> Sliced tomato, to serve

1. Preheat the oven to 400°F (200°C). Line a baking sheet with parchment paper.

2. Remove the stems from the mushrooms, and, using a very sharp paring knife, carefully cut away the dark gills from the underside of each mushroom. Make a few shallow slashes in the top surface of each mushroom to help them absorb more of the oil and seasonings.

3. Lightly oil the mushrooms with 2 tablespoons (30 mL) of the olive oil and season them generously with salt and pepper. Arrange them on the prepared baking sheet and drizzle the mushrooms with the balsamic vinegar. Roast for 15 to 18 minutes, or until the mushrooms begin to soften and darken a bit. Remove from the oven and set aside.

4. Heat the remaining oil in a large, flat sauté pan over very low heat. Cook, stirring occasionally, for 20 to 40 minutes, until the onions darken appreciably. Season with salt, pepper, and a splash of balsamic vinegar. Remove from the heat and set aside.

5. Grill the rolls or buns and the mushrooms on a grill or in a large, lightly oiled sauté pan. Spread the Horseradish Cream Sauce on the inside surfaces of the rolls or buns. Layer the chopped romaine over the sauce and place the grilled portobello patty on top, followed by the onions and sliced tomatoes.

Horseradish Cream Sauce

> 1 cup (236 mL) Veganopolis Mayo (page 91)
>
> 2 tablespoons (30 mL) prepared horseradish or grated fresh horseradish
>
> Salt, to taste, optional

1. Stir the horseradish into the mayonnaise. Taste for seasoning and add salt as needed.

Puerto Rican–Style Three Bean Stew

This recipe is from one of our best customers, Delia Feliciano, who educated us about the great flavors and recipes of her native Puerto Rico. The recaito *and* alcaparado *turn this simple stew into a feast fit for a holiday celebration.* Recaito *comes out of the blender looking like Christmas and smelling like heaven. Viva Puerto Rico!*

YIELD: 12 SERVINGS

For the recaito:

> 4 cloves fresh garlic, peeled and chopped
>
> 3 roasted red peppers, peeled, seeded, and roughly diced
>
> 1 jalapeño pepper, stemmed, seeded, and roughly diced
>
> 1 white onion, peeled and roughly diced
>
> 1 bunch fresh cilantro, thoroughly washed, dried, and stemmed

1. Combine all the ingredients in a food processor and pulse until combined, but not pureed. You should still be able to see the individual elements finely diced throughout the mixture.

For the alcaparado:

> ½ cup (118 mL) diced roasted red peppers
>
> ½ cup (118 mL) black olives, pitted and halved
>
> ¼ cup (59 mL) capers

1. Combine all ingredients and set aside.

CONTINUED ON PAGE 186

CONTINUED FROM PAGE 185

For the stew:

1 medium-to-large butternut or acorn squash peeled, and cut into 1-inch (2.5-cm) cubes

4 tablespoons (60 mL) olive oil

1 white onion, peeled and diced

1 teaspoon (5 mL) cumin

1 teaspoon (5 mL) dried oregano

1 teaspoon (5 mL) dark chili powder

½ pound (226 g) seitan, cut into ½-inch (1-cm) cubes

½ pound (226 g) vegan chorizo

1 (12-ounce [336-g]) can tomato sauce

½ pound (226 g) dried black beans, soaked overnight, or 1 (12-ounce [336-g]) can black beans

½ pound (226 g) dried chickpeas, soaked overnight, or 1 (12-ounce [336-g]) can chickpeas

Fresh cilantro leaves, for garnish

Salt, to taste

1. Place the squash in a saucepan with enough cold water to cover. Bring to a boil, then reduce the heat to a simmer and cook for 12 minutes. Drain and set aside.

2. In a large, heavy-bottomed pot, heat the olive oil over medium heat. Add the onions and dry spices and sauté until the onions are transparent and the mixture is fragrant.

3. Add the seitan and vegan chorizo and sauté until the mixture is nicely browned.

4. Add the recaito and tomato sauce and cook for about 10 minutes.

5. Drain and rinse the black beans and chickpeas thoroughly. Add them to the pot and add water to cover. Cook until the beans are tender, about 1 hour. If using canned beans, simply cook until they reach serving temperature.

6. Add the squash and the alcaparado. Cook until the squash is fork tender, but not falling apart, about 20 minutes. Taste the stew for seasoning and add salt as necessary. Garnish with fresh cilantro leaves and serve with Achiote Rice (page 174) or some good crusty bread and a green salad.

Soul Shake Black-Eyed Casserole

In this comfort food–style casserole, we use a spice blend influenced by Cajun, soul, and Caribbean cuisines. Keep a large shaker of this tasty spice blend in your pantry and use it in casseroles, soups, tofu scrambles, and roasted potatoes.

YIELD: 6–8 SERVINGS

For the spice blend:

2 teaspoons (10 mL) sea salt

2 teaspoons (10 mL) cumin

1½ teaspoons (12.5 mL) ground white pepper

1½ teaspoons (12.5 mL) smoked paprika

1½ teaspoons (12.5 mL) freshly ground black pepper

1½ teaspoons (12.5 mL) garlic powder

1 teaspoon (5 mL) onion powder

½ teaspoon (2.5 mL) allspice

½ teaspoon (2.5 mL) cayenne pepper

1. Combine all the ingredients and stir or shake to distribute evenly. Store in a shaker or a covered container. Multiply the recipe if you like.

For the casserole:

2 cups (473 mL) quinoa or semolina shells or elbow macaroni

2 tablespoons (30 mL) olive oil

1 cup (236 mL) diced Spanish onion

6 cloves garlic, peeled and finely minced

½ cup (125 mL) diced red bell pepper

1 cup (236 mL) diced celery

1 cup (236 mL) fresh or frozen okra, well rinsed

2 tablespoons (30 mL) cornmeal or quinoa flour

12 ounces (336 g) canned or frozen black-eyed peas

1 (12-ounce [336-g]) can diced tomatoes or fresh equivalent

1 tablespoon (15 mL) flax meal (optional)

2 cups (473 mL) breadcrumbs seasoned

2 tablespoons (30 mL) oregano

Thinly sliced scallions, for garnish

CONTINUED ON PAGE 188

CONTINUED FROM PAGE 187

1. Preheat the oven to 350°F (180°C). Lightly oil a 9 × 13–inch (22½ cm × 32½–cm) baking pan.

2. Bring a pot of salted water to a rapid boil and cook the pasta until al dente. Drain in a colander and rinse under cold running water to stop the cooking process. Set aside.

3. Heat the olive oil in a large sauté pan over medium heat. Add the onions and the spice mixture. Sauté until the onions are soft and transparent.

4. Add the garlic and bell pepper and sauté for about 1 minute, stirring constantly.

5. Add the celery and sauté, stirring, for 2 more minutes.

6. Add the okra, stir a few times, and add the cornmeal or quinoa flour. Sauté for 3 minutes, scraping the bottom of the pan, until the cornmeal or flour is lightly browned but not scorched.

7. Stir in the black-eyed peas.

8. Add the tomatoes, reserving about ¼ cup (59 mL) juice.

9. Add the flax meal, if using, and the reserved tomato juice. Simmer for a few minutes, and then remove from the heat.

10. Combine the breadcrumbs and oregano.

11. To assemble the casserole, place half the cooked pasta in the prepared baking pan, followed by half the sautéed vegetables and black-eyed peas. Follow with the remaining pasta and then the remaining vegetable mixture. Top the casserole with the seasoned breadcrumbs and bake for 30 minutes, or until the breadcrumbs are evenly browned. Remove from the oven, garnish with the sliced scallions, and serve.

Spanakopita Spinach Pie Squares

The only tricky bit about this recipe is working with the phyllo dough. It is important to use fresh phyllo and to work with it quickly, as it dries out easily and then tends to stick together and shred. A good-quality olive oil makes this dish absolutely brilliant.

YIELD: 6 SERVINGS

Zest and juice of 1 lemon

3 tablespoons (45 mL) extra virgin olive oil

1 red onion, peeled and finely diced

1 tablespoon (15 mL) dried oregano

1 tablespoon (15 mL) freshly ground black pepper

3 pounds (1.36 kg) fresh spinach, chopped

2 teaspoons (10 mL) grated nutmeg

Salt, to taste

1 (12-ounce [336-g]) box frozen phyllo dough, defrosted

1 cup (236 mL) extra virgin olive oil, for brushing

1 recipe Almond Feta (page 146)

1. Preheat the oven to 375°F (190°C). Oil a rectangular roasting pan, line it with parchment paper, and oil the paper.

2. Grate or finely chop the lemon zest.

3. In a very large sauté pan, heat the extra virgin olive oil over medium heat. Add the onion and sauté until it is transparent.

4. Add the oregano, black pepper, and lemon zest. Sauté for another minute or two, or until the mixture is fragrant.

5. Add the chopped spinach by handfuls, filling the pan and then waiting for the spinach to cook down between additions if necessary.

6. Add the nutmeg and salt to taste. When the spinach is completely wilted, remove everything from the pan and let it cool down as much as possible. Place in the freezer while you proceed with the recipe.

7. Lay a sheet of phyllo dough in the prepared roasting pan. You may cut or fold the phyllo as needed to make it fit the pan. Working quickly, lay down two more layers. Using a soft, clean pastry brush, completely coat the phyllo with olive oil.

8. Lay down another three layers so that you have six layers in the pan. Brush the top layer with olive oil.

9. Spread the cooled spinach mixture over the top layer of phyllo, pressing it down gently to form an even, flat layer.

CONTINUED ON PAGE 190

CONTINUED FROM PAGE 189

10. Lay down another three layers of phyllo dough and coat the top layer with olive oil.

11. Spread a ½-inch-thick (1-cm-thick) layer of Almond Feta over the dough.

12. Top with three layers of phyllo dough and brush with olive oil.

13. Add another three layers and brush with olive oil. Bake 1 hour, or until the top is evenly browned. Cut into serving-size squares and enjoy!

Stuffed Paisano Roast

YIELD: 8 SERVINGS

For the loaf:

2 pounds (1.1 kg) firm tofu

3 cloves garlic, peeled and crushed

⅓ cup (79 mL) breadcrumbs

⅓ cup (79 mL) vital wheat gluten

¼ cup (59 mL) chickpea or quinoa flour

2 tablespoons (30 mL) julienned fresh basil

1 tablespoon (15 mL) Italian seasoning or dried oregano

1 tablespoon (15 mL) whole fennel seed

1½ teaspoons (7.5 mL) salt

1 teaspoon (5 mL) freshly ground black pepper

⅓ cup (79 mL) vegetable stock, heated

2 tablespoons (30 mL) arrowroot powder or cornstarch

2 tablespoons (30 mL) tomato paste

1½ tablespoons (22 mL) olive oil

1. Crumble the tofu and place in a clean, paper towel–lined colander. Place another clean paper towel on top and press it down to extract as much moisture from the tofu as possible.

2. Combine the garlic, breadcrumbs, vital wheat gluten, flour, fresh basil, and dry spices in a bowl and set aside.

3. In a Pyrex measuring cup, combine the arrowroot powder or cornstarch with the hot vegetable stock and stir to dissolve. Stir in the tomato paste and olive oil.

4. In a bowl, combine the drained, crumbled tofu, the flour mixture, and the arrowroot-thickened liquid. Mix well with a spoon until everything is uniformly combined. Set the mixture aside while you make the stuffing.

CONTINUED ON PAGE 192

CONTINUED FROM PAGE 191

For the filling:

2 large tomatoes, quartered

1 tablespoon (15 mL) olive oil

¼ cup (59 mL) diced red onion

1 cup (236 mL) stemmed mushrooms, cut into ½-inch (1-cm) dice

2 tablespoons white wine or 1 tablespoon (15 mL) water

4 cloves garlic, peeled and thinly sliced

Salt, to taste

Freshly ground black pepper, to taste

1 cup (226 mL) asparagus, cut into 1-inch (2.5-cm) pieces

2 cups (473 mL) croutons

¼ cup (59 mL) vegetable stock, heated

1. Preheat the oven to 400°F (200°C). Lightly oil a baking sheet. Line a loaf pan with parchment paper and lightly oil it.

2. Place the tomato quarters on the prepared baking sheet. Roast for 15 minutes. Remove from the oven and set aside. Lower the oven temperature to 375°F (190°C).

3. Heat the oil in a skillet over medium heat. Add the onion and cook for 2 minutes.

4. Add mushrooms and the white wine or water. Sauté another 2 minutes.

5. Add the garlic, salt, and pepper. Sauté for 2 more minutes, stirring constantly.

6. Add the asparagus and sauté for 2 more minutes.

7. Add the tomatoes, vegetable stock, and croutons. Remove from the heat, cover, and set aside.

To assemble the roast:

1. Press a 1-inch (2.5-cm) layer of the loaf mixture into the bottom of the prepared loaf pan.

2. Place the stuffing mixture in the center of the loaf pan, leaving a 1-inch (2.5-cm) border all the way around. Pack the rest of the loaf mixture around the stuffing and over the top. It will be crumbly at this point, but it will firm up and stick together as it bakes.

3. Cover the top of the roast with parchment paper and then tightly cover the pan with aluminum foil. Bake for 25 minutes. Remove the foil and parchment paper and bake uncovered for another 25 minutes.

4. Remove from oven and allow to set for 10 minutes before inverting it over a serving platter, slicing, and serving. Serve as is or with some hot marinara sauce alongside or ladled over the slices.

Stroganoff

Serve this classic Eastern European–style dish over a bed of fettuccine for a cold winter night's rejuvenation. Brussels sprouts and fresh sliced rye bread make nice sides.

YIELD: 4 SERVINGS

> 1 quart (.95 L) rich vegetable stock, heated
>
> ¼ cup (59 mL) plus 2 tablespoons (30 mL) olive oil, divided
>
> 4 shallots, peeled and finely diced
>
> 1 pound (454 g) stemmed mushroom, halved
>
> 2 tablespoons (30 mL) finely minced fresh rosemary
>
> Salt, to taste
>
> Freshly ground black pepper, to taste
>
> 4 tablespoons (60 mL) white wine vinegar
>
> 1 cup (236 mL) dry white wine
>
> 2 pounds (1.1 kg) seitan, cut into 1-inch (2.5-cm) pieces
>
> ½ cup (118 mL) white spelt flour
>
> 1 cup (236 mL) vegan sour cream substitute
>
> 1 bunch fresh Italian parsley, thoroughly washed and finely chopped
>
> 1 pound (454 g) fettuccine or other broad noodle

1. In a large sauté pan, heat 2 tablespoons (30 mL) of the olive oil over medium-high heat. Add the shallots and cook until soft.

2. Add the mushrooms and rosemary. Sear the mushrooms, seasoning them liberally with salt and freshly ground black pepper.

3. Deglaze the pan with the white wine vinegar, and then add the white wine. Let the wine cook down until it is reduced by half. Transfer the contents of the sauté pan to a bowl and set aside.

CONTINUED ON PAGE 194

CONTINUED FROM PAGE 193

4. To the same pan, add 2 tablespoons (30 mL) more olive oil. Add the seitan pieces and sear them until they are lightly browned. Season the seitan with salt and pepper to taste. Transfer the seared seitan to the bowl with the mushrooms and set aside.

5. In a large, heavy-bottomed saucepan, heat the remaining ¼ cup (59 mL) olive oil. Whisk in the flour and cook for 5 minutes, whisking steadily.

6. Add the stock 1 cup (236 mL) at a time, whisking to incorporate after each addition.

7. Add the vegan sour cream substitute and stir well to combine.

8. Add ½ cup (118 mL) of the parsley and the mushroom and seitan mixture. Simmer for about 10 minutes, stirring frequently. Taste for seasoning and add salt and pepper as needed. If the wine flavor is not strong enough for your liking, add a few more tablespoons of white wine vinegar.

9. Cook the pasta until al dente and drain it.

10. Serve on heated plates by placing about ¼ of the cooked noodles at the center of each plate and a generous portion of the stroganoff on top. Finish with a sprinkling of the chopped parsley and a grinding of freshly ground black pepper.

Squash Mushroom Hazelnut Roast

This makes a great side dish for holiday meals. The complexity of flavors, colors, and textures adds to its appeal.

YIELD: 8 SERVINGS

2 medium acorn or butternut squash, peeled, seeded, and cut into 1-inch (2.5-cm) dice

Salt, to taste

1 tablespoon (15 mL) freshly ground black pepper

5 tablespoons (75 mL) olive oil, divided

2 teaspoons (10 mL) ground nutmeg

2 tablespoons (30 mL) ground sage

1 cup (236 mL) hazelnuts

5 shallots, peeled and very finely diced

4 tablespoons (60 mL) stemmed and finely chopped fresh rosemary

1 pound (454 g) stemmed button or crimini mushrooms

2 tablespoons (30 mL) white wine vinegar

¼ cup (59 mL) dry white wine

1. Preheat the oven to 375°F (190°C). Line a baking sheet with parchment paper. Lightly coating the inside of a large roasting pan with olive oil.

2. Arrange the squash on the prepared baking sheet. Season the squash with salt and pepper, 2 tablespoons (30 mL) of the olive oil, and the nutmeg and sage. Roast it until it has begun to brown slightly on the edges, about 20 minutes.

3. At the same time, toast the hazelnuts, spread in a single layer in a shallow pan, in the oven until they are fragrant and just beginning to turn color. They will burn quickly, so begin checking them often after 10 minutes. Remove them from the oven. When they are cool enough to handle, chop them roughly and set them aside in a bowl.

4. Heat the remaining 3 tablespoons (45 mL) olive oil in a large, heavy-bottomed sauté pan over medium-high heat. Add the shallots and rosemary and cook until the shallots begin to soften.

5. Add the mushrooms and sear them, seasoning the pan with salt and freshly ground black pepper. When the mushrooms begin to soften, deglaze the pan with the vinegar. Let the vinegar cook off, and then deglaze again with the white wine. Allow the wine to cook down by at least ⅔. Remove the pan from the heat.

6. When the squash has finished roasting, transfer it into a large baking pan. Add the sautéed mushrooms and the hazelnuts and stir to combine. Bake, uncovered, for about 15 minutes, or just until everything has come up to serving temperature. Serve immediately.

Veganopolis Mac and Cheese with Green Peas

This recipe is easy to make and very popular with children—and their parents. It stays moist under its breadcrumb crust, so it works well in a buffet setting. Serve with a green salad and/ or fresh fruit, if you like.

YIELD: 8 SERVINGS

1 recipe Vegan Béchamel Sauce (page 89), heated

12 ounces (336 g) shredded or diced American- or cheddar-style vegan cheese substitute

Jalapeño pepper hot sauce or apple cider vinegar, to taste (optional)

1 pound (454 g) penne or small shell-shaped pasta

8 ounces (224 g) frozen green peas, thawed

6 ounces (168 g) breadcrumbs

Salt, to taste

1. Preheat the oven to 400°F (200°C). Oil a roasting pan or ceramic baking dish.

2. Melt the vegan cheese substitute into the Vegan Béchamel. Taste for seasoning and add salt, hot sauce, or apple cider vinegar, as desired. You don't want to make the sauce spicy, but I have found that just a few drops of the hot sauce enhance the overall flavor.

3. Cook the pasta in a pot of salted, boiling water until al dente. Drain.

4. Place the pasta and peas in the prepared roasting pan or baking dish.

5. Pour the sauce over the cooked pasta and peas and stir everything together.

6. Top the dish with the breadcrumbs and bake until they are nicely browned, about 35 to 45 minutes.

Variation

Add a cup of diced tomatoes, diced sautéed zucchini, or other vegetables. Add fresh herbs such as rosemary, parsley, or basil.

Blackened Tofu Étouffée

This recipe reflects an untarnished enthusiasm for the cuisine of New Orleans. The tofu works best if grilled on a very hot grill before being smothered in the dark and fragrant étouffée sauce, but a very hot cast-iron skillet will do the trick. Étouffer is the French verb for "to smother."

YIELD: 6 SERVINGS

For the tofu:

4 tablespoons (60 mL) onion powder

4 tablespoons (60 mL) garlic powder

1 tablespoon (15 mL) paprika

2 teaspoons (10 mL) freshly ground black pepper

2 teaspoons (10 mL) ground white pepper

1 teaspoon (5 mL) cayenne pepper

2 teaspoons (10 mL) dried thyme

2 teaspoons (10 mL) salt

2 teaspoons (10 mL) sugar

2 pounds (1.1 kg) extra-firm tofu, cut into ½-inch-thick (1-cm-thick) slabs

1. Mix the spices together and coat each piece of tofu with the mixture. Set aside while you make the sauce. For an even better result, coat the tofu and refrigerate it overnight.

For the Étouffée Sauce:

1 quart (0.95 L) rich vegetable stock

½ cup (118 mL) canola oil

¾ cup (177 mL) white spelt flour or other white flour

½ cup (118 mL) finely diced onion

½ cup (118 mL) finely diced celery

½ cup (118 mL) finely diced green pepper

1 tablespoon (15 mL) garlic powder

1 teaspoon (5 mL) ground white pepper

1 teaspoon (5 mL) freshly ground black pepper

½ teaspoon (2.5 mL) cayenne pepper

Thinly sliced scallions, for garnish

CONTINUED ON PAGE 198

CONTINUED FROM PAGE 197

1. Preheat an outdoor or indoor grill and oil it generously. In a saucepan over medium-high heat, bring the stock to a simmer.

2. In a separate heavy-bottomed saucepan over high heat, heat the canola oil until it is almost smoking.

3. Using a long-handled whisk, add the flour and cook it until it is very dark brown, like the color of dark rye bread. This will take anywhere from 10 to 20 minutes, depending on how hot your flame is. Take care not to splash this roux on your skin, because it will stick and burn you.

4. Add the onions, celery, and peppers to the darkened roux and stir everything together with a long-handled wooden spoon. Add the dry spices and stir again.

5. Cook for 5 to 7 minutes, or until the onions and peppers start to soften, stirring frequently. The mixture will be quite thick.

6. Add the hot stock 1 cup (236 mL) at a time, stirring and whisking steadily and firmly after each addition, until you achieve a very thick, dark sauce. Taste it for seasoning and add salt as needed.

7. Reduce the heat to low, and simmer while you grill the tofu.

8. Grill the tofu on both sides until it is well done and marked with black grill marks. If you're using an indoor grill, make sure your exhaust fan is on. Alternatively, heat a cast-iron skillet over high heat and add a few tablespoons of canola oil. Sauté the tofu until it is very well done and the outsides are partially blackened. If you wish, slice the tofu pieces diagonally to make more manageable serving pieces.

9. To serve, ladle a circle of the sauce on the center of a warmed plate and then arrange a few slices of the blackened tofu on top of the sauce. Ladle more sauce on top and garnish with the thinly sliced scallions.

Variation

Serve with the rice recipe that accompanies the New Orleans–Style Vegan Red Beans and Rice (page 216).

Broccoli Normandy with Chickpeas

This makes a lovely meal in the summer, when fresh broccoli is abundant. The chickpeas add a healthy protein component. I suppose this dish is associated with Normandy because of this region's reputation for producing some of the best dairy products in France. The béchamel in this version is vegan, of course.

YIELD: 12 SERVINGS

> ½ pound (226 g) dried chickpeas, soaked overnight, or 1 (20-ounce [560-g]) can chickpeas, drained and rinsed
>
> 2 fresh bunches broccoli, cut into florets
>
> 1 recipe Vegan Béchamel Sauce (page 89), heated
>
> 3 tablespoons (45 mL) finely chopped Italian parsley, for garnish
>
> ¾ cup (177 mL) sliced roasted red peppers

1. Preheat the oven to 350°F (180°C). Lightly oil a roasting pan.

2. Boil the chickpeas in salted water until they are tender (for the soaked chickpeas, about 40 minutes; for the canned, about 10 minutes). Remove any skins that float to the surface. Drain, rinse, and set aside.

3. Bring a large pot of salted water to a boil. Add the broccoli florets to the pot and return to a boil.

4. Drain the florets, rinse them in cold water until fully cooled, and set aside.

5. Spread a layer of the Vegan Béchamel Sauce in the bottom of the prepared roasting pan. Add the chickpeas and broccoli florets, and cover with the remaining béchamel.

6. Bake until the béchamel is bubbling and slightly browned on top.

7. Garnish with chopped parsley and red pepper strips and serve.

Cooks' Note

If you like, you may melt some vegan cheddar or blue cheese substitute into the béchamel before using it in this recipe. Another variation is to replace the broccoli florets with cauliflower florets or use a combination of broccoli and cauliflower.

Brussels Sprouts

A big fresh stalk of Brussels sprouts from the farmer's market is really attractive. If you buy some, here's one great way to enjoy them.

YIELD: 4 SERVINGS

18 or more Brussels sprouts, on the stalk

2 tablespoons (30 mL) olive oil

3 shallots, peeled and finely diced

1 cup (236 mL) dry breadcrumbs

Zest and juice of 1 lemon

Salt, to taste

Freshly ground black pepper, to taste

1. Bring a large pot of salted water to a boil.

2. Snap the sprouts off the stalk and remove any loose or discolored outer leaves. Cut the stem end carefully, then insert the tip of a small sharp knife into the stem end and make a cut. Turn the sprout and make another cut crosswise. This will allow the boiling water to penetrate the sprout a little and cook the inside leaves more evenly.

3. Rinse the prepared sprouts in clean water.

4. Plunge the sprouts into the boiling water and let them cook for about 10 to 12 minutes. Remove one and cut it in half. A fully cooked Brussels sprout should be tender inside. Once the sprouts are done, drain them in a large colander.

5. Heat the olive oil in a large sauté pan over medium heat and add the finely diced shallots and the lemon zest. Add the breadcrumbs and sauté until they start to brown.

6. Add the cooked Brussels sprouts and season liberally with salt and pepper to taste. Serve immediately.

Cajun Slow-Cooked Greens

I learned the correct way to cook greens from the people I worked with who were from the south side of Chicago. I also learned about Curtis Mayfield's music and a wealth of other information that serves me to this very day. The major difference between this recipe and the traditional version is the omission of ham or bacon. So put on some good music for a change, and cook some greens. They are plentiful year round, inexpensive, and absolutely the healthiest of health foods.

YIELD: 6 SERVINGS

2 tablespoons (30 mL) olive or canola oil

½ cup (118 mL) finely diced celery

½ cup (118 mL) finely diced onions

½ cup (118 mL) finely diced red or yellow bell peppers

1 tablespoon (15 mL) garlic powder

1 tablespoon (15 mL) onion powder

2 teaspoons (10 mL) ground white pepper

2 teaspoons (10 mL) freshly ground black pepper

½ teaspoon (2.5 mL) cayenne pepper

2 teaspoons (10 mL) ground nutmeg

2 bunches collard or mustard greens or 1 of each, stemmed, if desired, and chopped

1 cup (236 mL) rich vegetable stock

Salt, to taste

Seasoned rice vinegar, to taste

Liquid smoke, to taste (optional)

1. In a large sauté pan, heat the olive or canola oil over medium heat. Add the diced celery, onions, and peppers. Add the dry spices and cook until the onions are softened.

2. Add the chopped greens in big handfuls. You may have to wait for the first panful to cook down a bit before adding the rest. Cook everything together for at least 30 minutes.

3. Taste for seasoning, and add enough salt and seasoned rice vinegar to bring the flavors together. Add a few drops of liquid smoke, if desired.

Cooks' Note

Other leafy greens, such as red or green kale, lacinato kale, dandelion greens, turnip greens, and beet greens, can be substituted or added to the collard or mustard greens.

This is a great dish to serve alongside New Orleans–Style Vegan Red Beans and Rice (page 216), or Blackened Tofu Étouffée (page 197).

Cheerful Chimichurri

Marinades, sauces, and condiments such as this are standard in many Spanish, Basque, and South American kitchens. An Argentine friend of mine says that in his childhood kitchen, the container was constantly replenished with herbs and vinegar and rarely washed out—a bit like the way sourdough bakers use their starters. The flavors blend and mellow over time. If you are cooking for 4, this amount works fine.

YIELD: 2 CUPS (473 ML)

⅔ cup (158 mL) lemon juice

⅓ cup (79 mL) lime juice

¼ (59 mL) cup orange juice

⅔ cup (158 mL) olive oil

¼ cup (59 mL) seasoned rice vinegar

1 cup (236 mL) chopped cilantro

⅓ cup (79 mL) chopped parsley

¼ tablespoon (1.25 mL) raw agave syrup

2 teaspoons (10 mL) finely chopped ginger root

2 teaspoons (10 mL) cumin

2 teaspoons (10 mL) chipotle, ancho, or dark chili powder

1 teaspoon (5 mL) ground white pepper

1½ teaspoons (7.5 mL) salt

1. Combine all the ingredients in a food processor or blender, and blend until well mixed. Pour into a clean container and reserve.

2. Heat the marinade on the stovetop or microwave and serve over seitan or tofu.

Cooks' Note

For an absolutely remarkable dish, serve the Chimichurri with seitan or Cheitan Patties (page 163):

1. Slice 1 pound (454 g) of the protein into 1-inch-thick (2.5-cm-thick), 3-inch-diameter (7.5-cm-diameter) rounds. Marinate the slices overnight in the Chimichurri.

2. Grill on a lightly oiled grill until grill marks appear, or brown in a lightly oiled heavy sauté pan. Serve with additional Chimichurri ladled over the individual seitan rounds.

Grilling is the preferred method here, and the results are amazing. Alternatively, you may bake the marinated seitan or Cheitan Patties in the marinade in a foil-covered pan for 25 minutes at 400°F (200°C). Then remove the foil and bake for an additional 15 minutes.

Variation

You can also use the Chimichurri with crumbled tofu.

1. Slice a block of extra-firm tofu into 1-inch (2.5-cm) slices. Marinate overnight.

2. Remove the tofu from the marinade and break the pieces into large crumbles with a fork.

3. Place the crumbled tofu in a baking pan and pour about ½ cup (118 mL) of the marinade over it. Bake at 350°F (180°C) for 15 minutes covered, plus 10 minutes uncovered. Serve in burritos, tacos, salads, or fajitas or over rice.

Vegan Coq au Vin

This version of the classic French dish is great for a special occasion. A rule of thumb for the gourmet chef: If you would not drink the wine, do not use it in a sauce. I know this goes against the idea of using up cheap wine. But in a dish like this one, the flavor of the sauce is paramount, and one should not risk ruining the dish with poor-quality wine.

YIELD: 4 SERVINGS

  1 baguette, sliced diagonally into ovals about ¼ inch (.25 cm) thick and 4 inches (10 cm) long

  7 tablespoons (105 mL) extra virgin olive oil, divided, plus more to brush the baguette slices

  2 cups (473 mL) red Burgundy or pinot noir

  1 pound (454 g) fresh button mushrooms, stemmed

  Salt, to taste

  Freshly ground black pepper, to taste

  4 tablespoons (60 mL) red wine vinegar, divided

  2 pounds (1.1 kg) Cheitan Patties (page 163) cut into bite-size pieces

  9 tablespoons (135 mL) extra virgin olive oil, divided

  ¼ pound (125 g) vegan Canadian bacon, cut into ¼-inch (.25-cm) dice

  6 tablespoons (90 mL) white spelt flour or other white flour

  1 pound (454 g) white baby onions, peeled

  4 cloves garlic, peeled and minced

  1 quart (.95 L) rich vegetable stock, heated

  1 bunch Italian parsley, washed, dried, and finely minced

1. Preheat the oven to 350°F (180°C).

2. Brush the baguette slices with 3 tablespoons (45 mL) of the olive oil and arrange them on a baking sheet.

3. Bake the baguette slices for about 10 minutes, or until they are crisp and lightly browned. Remove from the oven and set aside.

4. Pour the wine into a small saucepan and bring it to a boil. Ignite it at the surface with a match or lighter. The alcohol will ignite in a bluish flame and burn off. Once the flame dies down, take the pan off the heat and set aside. Use care in this, and make sure you have a good-quality oven mitt with which to manipulate the small saucepan. The alcohol should burn off this quantity of boiling wine in less than 1 minute.

5. Heat 3 tablespoons (45 mL) of the olive oil in a large sauté pan over high heat. Sauté the mushrooms, seasoning liberally with salt and freshly ground black pepper. Once they are well seared, deglaze the pan with 3 tablespoons (45 mL) of the red wine vinegar and set aside.

6. Sauté the Cheitan Patties and vegan Canadian bacon in 2 tablespoons (30 mL) of the olive oil over medium-high heat until nicely browned. Season with salt and pepper to taste and set aside.

7. In a large saucepan, heat the remaining 4 tablespoons (60 mL) olive oil and whisk in the flour. Cook just until the roux begins to bubble.

8. Add the baby onions and cook for 6 to 8 minutes, until the onions begin to soften. Add the minced garlic.

9. Add the heated stock to the roux 2 cups (473 mL) at a time, whisking after each addition to achieve a smooth emulsion. After adding all the stock, add the reserved red wine. Cook the sauce for 10 minutes, stirring constantly. Taste for seasoning. If the red wine flavor is not strong enough for your liking, add the remaining 1 tablespoon (15 mL) red wine vinegar.

10. Add the mushrooms and sautéed Cheitan Patties and bring everything up to serving temperature.

11. Taste for seasoning and add salt as necessary.

12. To serve, mound the finished Coq au Vin on the center of a heated serving plate. Dip 8 or 10 of the toasted baguette slices ½ inch (1 cm) deep into some of the sauce and then into the finely minced parsley. Arrange a few of these dipped baguette slices around the Coq au Vin, garnish the whole plate with more parsley, and serve. A side of rice or fettuccine would be ideal with this.

Et voilà! C'est magnifique!

Easy Vegan Dumplings

These are amazing cooked in soups or stews and just the thing to easily turn an ordinary meal into an extraordinary one. The result is comfort food par excellence!

YIELD: 18–24 DUMPLINGS

2 cups (473 mL) all-purpose flour

4 teaspoons (20 mL) baking powder

1 teaspoon (5 mL) salt

1 teaspoon (5 mL) ground white pepper

1 tablespoon (15 mL) finely minced parsley

2 tablespoons (30 mL) vegan margarine, softened

¾ cup (177 mL) soy or rice beverage

1. Combine the dry ingredients, including the parsley, in a large bowl. Mix in the softened vegan margarine, and then stir in the soy or rice beverage until just blended. Do not overmix; some lumps are okay.

2. Lightly oil 2 soup spoons, and drop spoonfuls of the dumpling mixture into a simmering stew or soup. Cover the pot. Do this just as the stew or soup is finishing up, when the vegetables in the stew are almost done.

3. Cook for about 12 minutes. Serve immediately.

Cooks' Note

Add about 2 tablespoons (30 mL) nutritional yeast for color, flavor, and nutrition.

Enchilada Lasagna

This dish was invented in our kitchen, and it's always a crowd pleaser. Frying the fresh corn tortilla is a little messy, but it's well worth the effort. If you are in a hurry, you can use a canned enchilada sauce, but I recommend making your own, using the recipe on page 99. The layers mimic the red, white, and green of the Mexican flag. You can, of course, alter the recipe and add layers of your choosing. Roasted, peeled, and seeded poblano peppers could be used to good effect.

YIELD: 12 SERVINGS

1 pound (454 g) dried pinto or black beans, soaked overnight

1½ cups (354 mL) plus 4 tablespoons (60 mL) canola oil

1 white onion, peeled and finely diced

4 cloves garlic, peeled and minced

1 teaspoon (5 mL) dried oregano

1 teaspoon (5 mL) ground cumin

1 teaspoon (5 mL) dark chili powder

1 teaspoon (5 mL) salt

Hot sauce, to taste (optional)

2 jalapeño peppers, stemmed, seeded, and finely diced

½ cup (118 mL) finely chopped fresh cilantro

1 recipe Veganopolis Cashew Ricotta (page 162)

2 pounds (1.1 kg) fresh spinach

1 teaspoon (5 mL) grated nutmeg

2 teaspoons (10 mL) ground white pepper

36 fresh corn tortillas

1 recipe Veganopolis Recipe Enchilada Sauce (page 99) or 1 (32-ounce [1.1-kg]) can enchilada sauce

1. Preheat the oven to 400°F (200°C). Line a large roasting pan with parchment paper. Line a baking sheet with parchment paper. Oil a lasagna pan.

2. Drain the beans and rinse them well.

3. In a large saucepan, heat 4 tablespoons (60 mL) of the canola oil over medium heat. Sauté the onions, garlic, and dried spices until the onions are soft.

4. Add the drained beans and stir to combine. Add water to cover by 2 inches (5 cm) and bring to a boil.

5. Lower the heat to a simmer and cook until the beans are quite soft, about 45 minutes to 1 hour. Drain any remaining liquid from the pan and mash the beans with a potato masher or blend them with a stick blender.

CONTINUED ON PAGE 208

CONTINUED FROM PAGE 207

6. Add the salt and your favorite hot sauce to taste, if desired, and set aside.

7. Add the jalapeños and cilantro to the Veganopolis Cashew Ricotta and stir well. Set aside.

8. Place the spinach in the prepared roasting pan. Season the spinach with the grated nutmeg, salt to taste, and the white pepper. Cover the pan tightly with aluminum foil.

9. Roast for about 25 minutes or until the spinach is wilted. Remove the pan from the oven, remove the foil, and set aside.

10. Heat the remaining canola oil in a large frying pan over medium-high heat. Fry the corn tortillas, a few at a time, for about 30 seconds per batch, taking care not to fry them crisp. When they are just softened, use long tongs to pull them from the oil and lay them on the prepared baking sheet, slightly overlapping one another.

11. Ladle a thin layer of enchilada sauce over the tortillas. Lay another sheet of paper over the finished layer to prevent the tortillas from sticking to one another. Continue until you have used up all the tortillas.

12. Ladle a cup of enchilada sauce into the prepared lasagna pan. Shake the pan gently until the sauce covers the bottom evenly.

13. Line the bottom of the pan with the tortillas, slightly overlapping them to achieve a uniform layer.

14. Spread the refried beans across the tortillas, and cover them with another layer of tortillas. Spread the Veganopolis Cashew Ricotta over the tortillas, and cover with another layer of tortillas. Spread the wilted spinach mixture across the tortillas, and cover with another layer of tortillas.

15. Cut the lasagna into serving-size squares. Top with the remaining enchilada sauce.

16. Bake for about 45 minutes, or until the enchilada lasagna is heated through. Remove from oven and garnish with fresh cilantro leaves, if desired. Serve with Achiote Rice (page 174) and perhaps a simple salad.

¡Viva México! (Or Italy, for that matter.)

Cooks' Note

To save time, you may substitute canned refried black or pinto beans. Check the label, as some contain lard.

Holiday Sage Dressing or Stuffing

This dish is simple to prepare and great as part of a holiday meal.

YIELD: 8 SERVINGS

 2 cups (473 mL) vegetable stock

 3 tablespoons (45 mL) olive oil

 4 stalks celery, diced

 1 Spanish onion, peeled and diced

 1 tablespoon (15 mL) dried sage

 2 teaspoons (10 mL) ground white pepper

 1 loaf of bread, any kind or combination, cut into 1-inch (2.5-cm) pieces

 Salt, to taste

1. Heat the stock in a small saucepan.

2. Heat the olive oil in a large sauté pan over medium heat. Add the diced celery, onions, sage, and white pepper.

3. Cook until the onions begin to soften. Add the bread pieces and stir with a wooden spoon.

4. Add as much of the hot stock as you need to moisten but not drown the bread, stirring again.

5. Taste for seasoning and add salt to taste as needed. Serve immediately.

Veganopolis Recipe Lasagna

I like to prepare all of the elements for lasagna the day before I am going to serve it, assembling the finished layers cold and then baking the whole dish to completion. As one might imagine, numberless variations can be produced to good effect. When cooking lasagna noodles, always cook about 15 percent more than you count on for your recipe, because a few always shred or stick. On rare occasions I have found lasagna noodles that do not need to be boiled. I highly recommend this "no-boil" noodle for any lasagna recipe. It takes an entire step out of the process, and the result is fabulous. No more soggy lasagna.

YIELD: 12 SERVINGS

2½ pounds (1.4 kg) fresh spinach, stemmed and chopped

Salt, to taste

1 tablespoon (15 mL) garlic powder

2 teaspoons (10 mL) ground nutmeg

2 cups (473 mL) dried lentils

1 quart (0.95 L) vegetable stock

6 cloves garlic, peeled and crushed

2 tablespoons (30 mL) fennel seeds

1 tablespoon (15 mL) Italian seasoning

1 teaspoon (5 mL) red chili flakes

¼ cup (59 mL) olive oil

3 shallots, peeled and finely diced

2 pounds (1.1 kg) mushrooms, stemmed and thinly sliced

1 tablespoon (15 mL) fresh rosemary, stemmed and finely chopped

Freshly ground black pepper, to taste

2 tablespoons (30 mL) white wine vinegar

¼ cup (59 mL) dry white wine

1 recipe Marinara Sauce (page 100)

24 lasagna noodles, cooked in boiling, salted, and oiled water until al dente; drained; and cooled in cold water, lightly oiled, and set aside

1 recipe Veganopolis Cashew Ricotta (page 162), to which you may add chopped parsley and garlic, if desired

12 slices vegan mozzarella cheese substitute

1. Preheat the oven to 400°F (200°C). Line a large, flat roasting pan with parchment paper. Coat a lasagna pan with olive oil.

2. Place the chopped spinach in the prepared roasting pan. Season the spinach with salt to taste, garlic powder, nutmeg, and black pepper. Toss the mixture with your hands to evenly distribute the seasoning.

3. Cover the pan tightly with foil and steam the spinach in the oven for about 25 minutes or until it is completely wilted. Uncover the pan and set it aside to cool.

4. Meanwhile, cook the lentils in the stock over medium heat until tender, about 40 minutes. Drain them well, using the back of a large spoon to press the excess liquid out of them through a strainer. Season them with crushed garlic, fennel seeds, Italian seasoning, red chili flakes, and salt. Set aside to cool.

5. Heat the olive oil in a large sauté pan over high heat. Add the shallots, cooking them and shaking the pan until they are softened, about 2 minutes.

6. Add the mushrooms and rosemary and sauté, seasoning liberally with salt and freshly ground black pepper.

7. Once the mushrooms begin to sear and soften a bit, deglaze the pan with the vinegar and then the white wine. Taste for seasoning and transfer the sautéed mushrooms from the pan into a bowl or other container. Set aside.

8. Ladle approximately 1 cup (256 mL) of Marinara Sauce into the prepared lasagna pan. Gently shake the pan back and forth to coat the bottom of the pan evenly.

9. Lay a layer of lasagna noodles down in the bottom of the pan and follow with the lentil mixture. Lay down another layer of noodles, followed by the Veganopolis Cashew Ricotta. Lay down another layer of noodles, followed by the spinach. Lay down another layer of noodles, followed by the vegan mozzarella slices. Lay down a last layer of noodles. Finally, ladle a thick layer of Marinara Sauce over all and spread it evenly across the surface.

10. Slice the lasagna into serving-size pieces.

11. Bake the lasagna for about 1½ hours. Remove it from the oven and warm up the remaining Marinara Sauce. To serve, ladle the warmed Marinara Sauce onto large, heated plates, and place a slice of lasagna on each plate. Use a small, flat-bladed stainless spatula to get the first slice out.

Variation

To make White Lasagna follow the same recipe, but substitute Vegan Béchamel Sauce (page 89) to which you have added a good quantity of crushed garlic for the Marinara Sauce. Replace the mushrooms with thinly sliced sautéed leeks. Or make up your own lasagna recipe! Sliced roasted zucchini and/or eggplant can be used to good effect. For an extra-fancy topping, sprinkle a handful of vegan Parmesan over the lasagna before you place it in the oven, and then place a fried basil leaf on each portion before serving.

Lentil Loaf with Mushrooms and Roasted Walnuts

This dish is vegan comfort food at its best, and it's quite economical. Try it with mashed potatoes and gravy alongside.

YIELD: 12 SERVINGS

> 1 pound (454 g) dried lentils
>
> 2 quarts (1.9 L) vegetable stock
>
> 1 pound (454 g) mushrooms, stemmed and quartered
>
> 4 stalks celery, finely diced
>
> 1 red or white onion, peeled and diced
>
> ¼ cup (59 mL) canola oil, divided
>
> 1 tablespoon (15 mL) ground sage
>
> 1 tablespoon (15 mL) garlic powder
>
> 1 tablespoon (15 mL) freshly ground black pepper
>
> 1 tablespoon (15 mL) salt
>
> 2 teaspoons (10 mL) paprika
>
> 6 tablespoons (90 mL) cornstarch dissolved in ¼ cup (59 mL) cold water
>
> ½ cup (118 mL) finely chopped Italian parsley
>
> 1 cup (236 mL) roasted walnuts, roughly chopped
>
> 4 tablespoons (60 mL) vegan Worcestershire sauce

1. Cook the lentils in the stock for about 40 minutes until they begin to soften. Drain the lentils, reserving the stock. Place them in a large bowl and use a potato masher to break them up.

2. Preheat the oven to 350°F (180°C). Oil a loaf pan or roasting pan.

3. In a large sauté pan set over medium-high heat, sauté the mushrooms, celery, and onion in 3 tablespoons (45 mL) of the canola oil until the onion is softened, about 10 minutes.

4. Add the dry spices to the mixture and cook for an additional 5 minutes.

5. Add the cornstarch mixture to the lentils and stir well to combine.

6. Add the sautéed mushrooms and onions to the lentils. Stir in the parsley, walnuts, vegan Worcestershire, and canola oil. Mix everything together.

7. Taste the mixture for seasoning and adjust as needed. This recipe needs a little more salt than other dishes, so taste carefully.

8. Press the mixture into the prepared pan and bake for approximately 1 hour or until the surface is nicely browned.

9. Brush the top with the reserved stock, if you wish, and return the pan to the oven for 10 minutes.

10. Remove the loaf from the oven and let stand for 15 minutes.

11. Slice into serving-size pieces and serve.

Moroccan Vegetable Tagine with Preserved Lemon and Almonds

Moroccan food is unique among African cuisines, having been influenced by centuries of invasions and occupations from all over the Mediterranean region. Most recently, French cooking influenced the cuisine of Morocco, and it is still very much in evidence there, even though Morocco gained its independence from France in 1956. The tagine, a dish of native Berber origin, has survived it all.

YIELD: 10 SERVINGS

2 tablespoons (30 mL) olive oil

2 red onions, peeled and cut into eighths

2 jalapeño peppers, stemmed, seeded, and finely diced

6 cloves garlic, peeled and minced

2 tablespoons (30 mL) paprika

2 teaspoons (10 mL) cumin

2 teaspoons (10 mL) oregano

2 teaspoons (10 mL) thyme

4 large, ripe tomatoes

4 carrots, peeled and cut into 1½-inch (3.5-cm) pieces

4 potatoes, peeled and cut into 1-inch (2.5-cm) cubes

2 turnips, peeled and cut into eighths

4 preserved lemons*, cut into sixths

1 bunch fresh cilantro, ½ cup (118 mL) leaves reserved, the rest chopped

2 cups (473 mL) vegetable stock

2 cups (473 mL) whole roasted unsalted almonds

Salt, to taste

Fresh lemon juice, to taste

*Preserved lemons are sold in jars in many Middle Eastern groceries and other specialty food stores.

1. Preheat the oven to 350°F (180°C).

2. In a very large, oven-safe sauté pan or a stovetop-safe roasting pan, heat the olive oil over medium heat. Add the onions and jalapeño peppers and sauté until the onions begin to soften, about 5 minutes.

3. Add the minced garlic and the dry spices and sauté until the mixture is fragrant.

4. Add the tomatoes, carrots, potatoes, turnips, and preserved lemon pieces. Stir everything together so that the oil and spices coat the vegetables well.

5. Add the chopped cilantro and stir.

6. Add the stock and bring to a boil.

7. Cover the pan with foil and bake for 45 minutes to 1 hour, or until the potatoes and carrots are fork tender.

8. Remove the pan from the oven. Add the roasted almonds and stir everything together.

9. Return the pan to the oven for about 10 minutes. The idea here is to let the roasted almonds remain crunchy among the cooked vegetables. If you want the almonds softer, add them when you add the vegetables.

10. Remove the pan from the oven and adjust the seasoning with salt and fresh lemon juice.

11. Serve with couscous or rice and garnish with the reserved whole cilantro leaves.

Cooks' Note

You may wish to add more protein to this dish. If so, add chickpeas or a pound of vegan chicken when you add the vegetables.

New Orleans–Style Vegan Red Beans and Rice

I love red beans and rice prepared this way. Nourishing and satisfying, for some reason the combination also makes a great hangover food. Spicy but not burn-your-tongue spicy, this recipe will produce enough beans and rice for a party. To serve just a few guests, you may halve the recipe.

YIELD: 12 SERVINGS

For the beans:

1 pound (454 g) dried red kidney beans, soaked in fresh cold water overnight

2½ cups (591 mL) finely chopped celery

2 cups (473 mL) finely chopped onions

2 cups (473 mL) finely chopped green bell peppers

4 bay leaves

2 teaspoons (10 mL) ground white pepper

2 teaspoons (10 mL) dried thyme leaves

2 teaspoons (10 mL) garlic powder

1 teaspoon (5 mL) cayenne pepper

1 teaspoon (5 mL) freshly ground black pepper

1 tablespoon (15 mL) hot sauce

1 pound (454 g) vegan sausage, sliced diagonally into 1-inch (2.5-cm) pieces

2 tablespoons (30 mL) canola oil

4 scallions, thinly sliced, for garnish

2 teaspoons (10 mL) liquid smoke (optional)

1. Drain the soaked beans and rinse them well.

2. In a very large pot, combine all the ingredients except the vegan sausage and scallions. Add fresh water to cover by 4 inches (10 cm).

3. Bring the pot to a boil and skim off any foam that accumulates on top.

4. Reduce the heat to a simmer and cook for about 1 hour and 30 minutes, returning to the pot several times to stir it well and skim off any foam that may appear on top.

5. As the beans approach the end of cooking time, scrape the bottom of the pan often to prevent sticking or scorching. If you accidentally scorch the beans, immediately dump the contents of the pot to a fresh pot and finish cooking them. Anything sticking to the original pot should be discarded. Add water to the pot if necessary during the cooking procedure.

6. When the beans are quite tender and just starting to break up, sauté the vegan sausage in the canola oil in a large sauté pan over medium heat until they are nicely browned and heated through. Add the sausage slices to the beans.

7. Taste the beans for seasoning and add salt, more hot sauce, and liquid smoke as needed.

8. While the beans are cooking, prepare the rice.

For the rice:

> **2 cups (473 mL) long-grain white rice**
>
> **2½ cups (591 mL) vegetable stock**
>
> **2 tablespoons (30 mL) finely chopped celery**
>
> **2 tablespoons (30 mL) finely chopped onions**
>
> **2 tablespoons (30 mL) finely chopped green bell peppers**
>
> **2 tablespoons (30 mL) vegan margarine, melted**
>
> **¼ teaspoon (1.25 mL) garlic powder**
>
> **¼ teaspoon (1.25 mL) salt**
>
> **¼ teaspoon (1.25 mL) ground white pepper**
>
> **¼ teaspoon (1.25 mL) freshly ground black pepper**
>
> **¼ teaspoon (1.25 mL) cayenne pepper**

1. Preheat the oven to 350°F (180°C).

2. In a small roasting pan or a loaf pan, combine all the ingredients and stir well.

3. Cover the pan tightly with aluminum foil and bake for at least 1 hour, until all of the liquid is absorbed and the rice is tender. If the rice is not done after 1 hour, reseal the foil and place the pan back in the oven for another 10 minutes or so.

4. Fluff the rice with a fork before serving.

Orange Sunshine Quick Scalloped Potatoes

The creamy sauce, skillet-boiled potatoes and easy assembly will make this dish a regular in your kitchen. Vegan shortening adds to the creaminess, but you may make this recipe soy-free by substituting safflower, canola, or olive oil.

YIELD: 4 SERVINGS

6–7 medium red potatoes, unpeeled

½ cup (118 mL) finely diced shallot or sweet onion

2 teaspoons (10 mL) salt

4 tablespoon (60 mL) vegan margarine

2 teaspoons (10 mL) annatto or turmeric

2 teaspoons (10 mL) garlic powder or 3 cloves garlic, peeled and minced

1 teaspoon (5 mL) paprika

¼ teaspoon (1.25 mL) nutmeg

5 tablespoons (75 mL) quinoa, spelt, or chickpea flour

½ cup (118 mL) finely minced fresh parsley

2 cups (473 mL) rice beverage, divided

1. Preheat the oven to 375°F (190°C). Half-fill a large bowl with cold water.

2. Slice the unpeeled potatoes in ¼-inch-thick (.5-cm-thick) rounds. Pierce the center of each slice with a small knife. Submerse the potato slices in the cold water for 10 minutes, changing the water. This extracts starch to prevent mushiness. The longer the bath, the less starch will remain.

3. Place the potatoes and 1 teaspoon (5 mL) of the salt in an oven-safe skillet and cover with cold water. Bring to a boil over high heat. Reduce the heat slightly and cook until a fork can penetrate a potato slice with just a little pressure.

4. Drain the potatoes in a colander and rinse with cold water. Set aside.

5. In the same skillet, melt the vegan margarine over medium heat. Add the shallots or sweet onions and all the spices. Cook 2 minutes on medium heat.

6. Add the flour 1 tablespoon (15 mL) at a time, whisking constantly so that it does not scorch. Cook for 2 minutes, whisking constantly.

7. Slowly whisk in 1½ cups (354 mL) of the rice beverage.

8. Add half the parsley. Simmer for 3 minutes before adding the remaining ½ cup (118 mL) rice beverage.

9. Layer potatoes in the skillet and bake for 25 minutes. Brown the top by placing the pan under the broiler for 3 minutes or more. Garnish with the remaining parsley.

Oven-Roasted French Fries

These fries are crisp, delicious, and almost oil-free. They work best in a convection oven, where the hot air cooks them quickly, but will do nicely in a home oven set to 400°F (200°C). The overnight soak is not absolutely critical, but it reduces the starchiness of the potatoes. If you have time, change the water once during the soaking process.

YIELD: 4 SERVINGS

> 4 large baking potatoes, unpeeled
>
> Salt, to taste
>
> Canola oil spray

1. Using your sharpest knife, cut the potatoes into long, thin fingers. (If you have a French fry cutter in your kitchen, use it instead.) Soak the fries in cold, clean water overnight, changing the water in the morning.

2. Preheat the oven to 400°F (200°C). Line a baking sheet with parchment paper.

3. Drain the potatoes very well and place them on the prepared baking sheet. Pat them dry with a paper towel or a fresh, clean kitchen towel.

4. Season the potatoes well with salt and spray them with canola oil spray. (Alternatively, drizzle the potatoes with canola oil and use your hands to toss the potatoes in the oil.)

5. Bake until brown and crisp.

6. Taste the finished potatoes for seasoning and add salt as desired. Serve immediately with ketchup or Roasted Garlic Ketchup (page 94).

Variation

Try these with different seasoning combinations: salt and black pepper; salt, paprika, and white pepper; salt and garam masala (Bengali frites!); salt, garlic powder, and finely minced fresh rosemary. The possibilities are limited only to your spice rack and your imagination.

Spanish-Style Paella

This is one of those crowd-pleasing special-occasion dishes that takes a little time to prepare but is well worth the effort. Many variations are possible, but the basics of olive oil, saffron, garlic, white wine, and a good-quality long-grain rice are de rigueur. The garnish can become a minor work of art, which can be a bit of fun for the chef. Make a lattice pattern with the roasted red pepper strips or go Jackson Pollock and just toss them about.

YIELD: 12 SERVINGS

¾ cup (177 mL) extra virgin olive oil, divided

12 cloves garlic, peeled and minced, divided

4 tablespoons (60 mL) tomato paste

1 bunch Italian parsley, washed, stemmed, and chopped, divided

9 cups (2129 mL) vegetable stock, heated

2 cups (473 mL) sliced vegan sausage

2 cups (473 mL) sliced Cheitan Patties (page 163) or seitan

12 ounces (336 g) mushrooms, stemmed and halved

Salt, to taste

Freshly ground black pepper, to taste

Large pinch saffron

8 shallots, peeled

4 cups (946 mL) white basmati rice or other long-grain white rice

1 cup (236 mL) dry white wine

1 cup (236 mL) canned artichoke hearts, drained

1 cup (236 mL) frozen peas and carrots, thawed

1 cup (236 mL) roasted red peppers, cut in thin fingers

2 lemons, sliced thinly or cut in eighths, for garnish

1. Heat ½ cup (118 mL) of the olive oil in a sauté pan over medium-low heat. Add 2 tablespoons (30 mL) of the minced garlic and sauté. Add 2 tablespoons (30 mL) of the tomato paste, 4 tablespoons (60 mL) of the finely minced parsley, and ½ cup (118 mL) of the stock. Stir together until heated through, about 4 minutes. Remove from the heat.

2. In a bowl, combine the vegan sausage and the Cheitan Patties or seitan. Pour the sautéed mixture over them, and let the proteins marinate while you prepare the rest of the paella.

3. Preheat the oven to 350°F (180°C).

4. Heat 2 tablespoons (30 mL) of the remaining olive oil in a sauté pan over high heat. Add the mushrooms and sear them. Season liberally with salt and black pepper, and set aside.

5. Stir the remaining tomato paste and the saffron into the remaining heated stock.

6. In a large metal roasting pan, heat the remaining olive oil over medium heat. Add the remaining garlic and the shallots and sauté briefly, until the garlic is fragrant but not browned.

7. Stir in the rice and sauté until it becomes a little transparent, about 6 to 8 minutes.

8. Add the white wine and sauté for 2 minutes, stirring constantly.

9. Add stock mixture a few cups at a time, stirring after each addition as the rice absorbs the moisture.

10. Add the artichokes, the sautéed mushrooms, and the marinated proteins to the pan. Cover the pan with foil and place it in the oven.

11. Cook for 30 to 45 minutes, or until all of the liquid is absorbed and the rice is tender and fluffy.

12. Stir in the peas and carrots, replace the aluminum foil, and return the pan to the oven for about 10 minutes or until everything comes up to serving temperature.

13. Remove the pan from the oven and remove the foil. Using a fork, fluff up the rice and give everything a good stir.

14. Garnish with the strips of roasted red pepper and the lemons. Sprinkle the remaining parsley over the entire dish. Take to the table and let your guests help themselves, or prepare individual plates and serve. Fresh steamed asparagus or green beans would make a nice side, along with some good crusty bread and the rest of the white wine.

CHAPTER 8

Baked Goods

Bavarian Rye Bread

This recipe produces a large, very dense loaf with a mild, slightly sweet flavor. This bread is great for the Vegan New York Reuben Sandwich (page 134), simply toasted and served with soup or salad, or cubed for croutons when stale.

YIELD: 1 (2-POUND [1.1-KG]) LOAF

5 teaspoons (25 mL) active dry yeast

4 teaspoons (10 mL) turbinado sugar, divided

½ cup (118 mL) warm (110°F [50°C]) water

3 cups (708 mL) dark rye flour

1⅔ cups (394 mL) unbleached all-purpose flour

3 tablespoons (45 mL) caraway seeds

1 tablespoon (15mL) onion powder

2 teaspoons (10 mL) freshly ground black pepper

2 teaspoons (10 mL) salt

¼ cup (59 mL) vegan shortening

⅔ cup (158 mL) water

¼ cup (59 mL) dark molasses

1. In a nonreactive bowl, dissolve the yeast and 2 teaspoons (10 mL) of the turbinado sugar in the warm water. Stir, then set aside for 10 minutes or until foamy.

2. In a large bowl, combine the rye flour, all-purpose flour, caraway seeds, onion powder, pepper, and salt. Stir with a whisk until blended.

3. In a saucepan over low heat, heat the shortening, the ⅔ cup (158 mL) water, and the dark molasses. Once shortening has melted, remove the pan from the heat and allow to cool to room temperature.

4. Add the yeast mixture to the room-temperature shortening mixture.

5. Slowly stir the wet mixture into the dry mixture until well combined. Switch from a spoon or spatula to your hands when the mixture becomes hard to stir.

6. When the dough forms, move it to a clean, floured surface. Knead for 2 minutes, then cover with a clean towel and let the dough rest for 10 to 12 minutes.

7. Knead the dough vigorously until it is smooth, about 5 minutes.

CONTINUED ON PAGE 224

CONTINUED FROM PAGE 223

8. Place the dough in an oiled bowl, cover, and let rise in a warm place until it doubles in size, about 90 minutes. Rye dough does not have a high gluten content and does not rise as quickly or as high as other doughs.

9. Punch down the dough, cover it again, and let rise for another for 25 to 30 minutes.

10. Preheat the oven to 325°F (160°C).

11. Form the dough into one large loaf or round and place it on a baking sheet. Cover with a clean towel. Let the loaf rest, undisturbed, for 30 minutes.

12. Just before baking, use a sharp knife or razor to create a single long slash about ¼ inch (.5 cm) deep across the top.

13. Place the pan in the oven and bake for 45 minutes. To find out if the loaf is properly cooked, remove it from the oven using an oven mitt, invert it, and tap the bottom. It should sound a bit hollow and should resound to your tap.

Variations

Add any of the following by the cup: chopped walnuts, chopped red onion, dried cherries, or cranberries. Or try 2 tablespoons (30 mL) chopped dill or substitute celery seed for the caraway seed.

Rye Rolls

1. After the dough has finished rising, tear off billiard-ball-sized pieces and, using your palm and fingers, roll them on a clean, unfloured surface until they form spheres.

2. Place the rolls on a baking sheet; cover them with a clean kitchen towel and let them rise, undisturbed, for 30 minutes.

3. Just before baking, slash each roll with a sharp knife or razor, and then bake them for about 25 minutes.

Freckled Flax Crust

This is my favorite crust for quiche, and it is the simplest of recipes. Unbleached white spelt flour is my preferred flour for everything because of its high protein content and low starch content compared to standard wheat flour. It is more expensive than many flours, but more nutritious. Spelt is also genetically different from wheat and has not been commercially, genetically modified, as far as I know. Spelt grain has two outer hulls, while wheat grain has only one. This requires an extra step in hulling the grain before it is ground into flour, but it also better protects the inner nutritive part from environmental contaminants.

The reason slight water and oil adjustments are often necessary in baking is that different brands of flours are milled slightly differently. Flour that has been on the shelf too long loses some of its ability to absorb oil. Another reason I prefer unbleached white spelt to whole-grain flours is that I have found whole grain requires more oil per recipe, and I like to use as little of oils and fats in baking as I can. In Italy, spelt is called farro.

YIELD: 1 DOUBLE PIE CRUST OR 2 SINGLE CRUSTS

> **2 cups (473 mL) unbleached white spelt flour**
>
> **1½ tablespoons (22 mL) flax meal**
>
> **1½ teaspoons (7.5 mL) salt**
>
> **1 teaspoon (5 mL) turbinado sugar**
>
> **¾ cup (177 mL) olive or safflower oil, chilled 15 minutes in the freezer**
>
> **¼ cup (59 mL) ice water**
>
> **2 teaspoons (10 mL) lemon juice (optional)**

1. Preheat the oven to 350°F (180°C). Lightly oil a 9-inch (22.5-cm) pie pan.

2. In a large bowl, stir together the flour, flax meal, salt, and turbinado sugar.

3. Combine the chilled oil, ice water, and lemon juice (if using) and add to the dry ingredients, mixing first with a rubber spatula and then with your hands, until a dough forms.

4. On a lightly floured surface, roll the dough into a circle. Place the pie pan face down on the dough, and trim the dough 1 full inch (2.5 cm) beyond the circumference of the pan.

5. Place the dough over the pie pan and gently press into the bottom and sides. Stretch gently to create a thick layer around the top edge. Trim off any excess dough with a sharp paring knife to make a neat circle. If you wish, use the knife to indent the edge of the crust with small adjacent marks all the way around. This will also help the crust adhere to the top edge of the pie pan. Try to avoid cutting all the way through the dough as you score it.

6. With a fork or knife, make several piercings in the bottom of the crust. This allows steam to escape and prevents the dough from lifting or creating bubbles.

7. Bake the crust until very lightly browned, about 20 to 25 minutes.

8. Remove from the oven and let cool a bit, then proceed with your recipe.

Peanut Butter Cookies

YIELD: 12 LARGE OR 18 SMALL COOKIES

> 3 cups (708 mL) unbleached white spelt flour
>
> 1½ teaspoons (7.5 mL) baking powder
>
> ½ teaspoon (2.5 mL) baking soda
>
> 1 teaspoon (5 mL) salt
>
> 1 teaspoon (5 mL) cinnamon or allspice
>
> 1 cup (236 mL) creamy peanut butter
>
> ½ cup (118 mL) vegan margarine, softened
>
> ¼ cup (59 mL) maple or agave syrup
>
> 1 tablespoon (15 mL) arrowroot powder
>
> 2 teaspoons (10 mL) pure vanilla extract
>
> 2 tablespoons (30 mL) warm water

1. Preheat the oven to 350°F (180°C). Line two baking sheets with parchment paper and lightly oil the paper.

2. In a large bowl, mix the flour, baking powder, baking soda, salt, and cinnamon or allspice.

3. In a separate bowl, combine the peanut butter, margarine, maple or agave syrup, arrowroot, vanilla extract, and warm water. Stir with a spatula until creamy and smooth.

4. Using a hand mixer, slowly blend the dry ingredients into the wet ingredients. If the dough does not come together properly you may need to add a little canola or safflower oil. You may need to work the dough together with your hands.

5. Using a spoon or a 3-ounce (84-g) ice cream scoop, drop scoops of the cookie dough on the prepared sheets. Imprint the tops with a fork for a classic style.

6. Bake for 15 to 18 minutes. Remove from the oven and let cool for 30 minutes before removing them from the sheets and transferring them to a cooling rack. Store in a tightly covered container in a cool place.

Peter Pan Chocolate Roll

YIELD: 6–8 LARGE OR 12 SMALL ROLLS

5 teaspoons (25 mL) active dry yeast

1 teaspoon (5 mL) plus 1⅔ cups (394 mL) turbinado sugar

½ cup (118 mL) warm (110°F [50°C]) water

3⅓ cups (787 mL) unbleached white spelt flour or other white flour

¾ cup (177 mL) unsweetened cocoa powder

2 teaspoons (10 mL) salt

1½ teaspoons (7.5 mL) baking powder

½ teaspoon (2.5 mL) cayenne pepper or 2 teaspoons (10 mL) instant coffee (optional; either will enhance the cocoa flavor)

⅔ cup (158 mL) soy or rice beverage

8 tablespoons (120 mL) vegan shortening or margarine, softened

1 teaspoon (5 mL) apple cider vinegar

2 teaspoons (10 mL) pure vanilla extract

½ cup (118 mL) finely chopped almonds

1 cup (236 mL) vegan chocolate chips, roughly chopped

½ cup (118 mL) sweetened shredded coconut

1. In a small Pyrex bowl combine the yeast, 1 teaspoon (5 mL) of the turbinado sugar, and warm water. Let stand for 10 minutes until the mixture is foamy.

2. In a large mixing bowl, stir together the flour, the remaining 1⅔ cups turbinado sugar, the cocoa powder, salt, baking powder, and cayenne pepper, if using.

3. Blend together the soy or rice beverage, vegan shortening or margarine, apple cider vinegar, vanilla extract, and the instant coffee, if using. Combine the yeast mixture to this mixture.

4. Slowly fold the wet ingredients into the dry ingredients, adding a little flour if very sticky or a little water if the dough is not coming together.

5. Turn the dough onto a clean, floured surface and knead for 2 to 3 minutes.

6. Transfer the dough to a lightly oiled bowl and cover it with a clean kitchen towel. Set the bowl in a warm place and allow it to rise for 1 hour.

7. Punch down the dough, cover it, and allow it to rise for another 30 minutes. You may want to split the dough between two bowls for a slightly shorter rising time.

8. After the second rising, place the dough in the freezer for 10 minutes to firm it up and make it easier to roll out and cut.

CONTINUED ON PAGE 228

CONTINUED FROM PAGE 227

9. Preheat the oven to 350°F (180°C). Line 2 baking sheets with parchment paper and lightly oil the paper.

10. Remove the dough from the freezer and, on a floured surface, roll the dough into a 10 × 12–inch (25 × 30–cm) rectangle about ¼ inch (.5 cm) thick.

11. Slice the dough rectangle in half for large rolls or in thirds for smaller rolls.

12. On a clean, flat surface, sprinkle a light layer of almonds, vegan chocolate chips, and coconut.

13. Lay the dough strips on this surface and sprinkle the tops with more almonds, chocolate chips, and coconut.

14. Slice 1- to 1½-inch (2.5- to 3.5-cm) strips along the dough's width.

15. Roll up a strip neatly, using your fingers to keep as much of the filling inside as you can. Repeat this procedure with each strip until all are rolled, pinching the end of each strip to seal the roll.

16. Place the finished rolls at least 1½ inches (3.5 cm) apart on the prepared baking sheets. Decorate the tops with more almonds, chocolate chips, and coconut.

17. Bake for 25 to 30 minutes, turning the sheets around and switching racks in the oven at the halfway point.

18. The rolls are ready when your finger does not leave an impression when you poke the side. Let cool before serving with vegan ice cream and chocolate sauce or fresh fruit.

Pizza Dough

YIELD: 2 (18-INCH [45-CM]) PIZZAS

1 cup (236 mL) warm (110°F [50°C]) water

1 tablespoon (15 mL) agave syrup or turbinado sugar

2½ teaspoons (12.5 mL) active dry yeast

6 cups (1500 mL) unbleached white spelt flour or other white flour

1 tablespoon (15 mL) salt

⅔ cup (158 mL) olive oil

1. Combine the warm water, agave syrup or turbinado sugar, and yeast. Let stand for 10 minutes until foamy.

2. In a large bowl, mix the flour and the salt. Make a well in the center of the flour.

3. Add the olive oil to the wet mixture and stir.

4. Pour the wet mixture into the well and drag the flour slowly into the well with a rubber spatula as you turn the bowl.

5. Mix the dough with the spatula, turning the bowl as you go. Then switch to your hands, rolling the dough down into the bowl and folding it over on itself as you work. Continue to roll the dough over and press it down, until all the flour in the bowl is incorporated. If the dough is too wet at the end of this process, add a bit more flour until you achieve a consistent texture and moisture throughout. The dough should not stick to your fingers, but it should be soft and easy to form into a ball.

6. Form the dough into a ball. Cover the bowl and set aside in a warm place. (An oven warmed up to 200°F (100°C) and then turned off works well, but any slightly warm, draft-free place in your kitchen is fine.)

7. Let the dough rise for approximately 45 minutes while you prepare your pizza sauce and toppings.

8. Preheat the oven to 500°F (260°C).

9. Punch the dough down and divide into two evenly sized pieces and place them on a floured surface.

10. Form the first piece of dough into a disc and push it outwards from the center to enlarge the circle. Transfer it to a well-oiled pizza pan and finish pressing it out toward the edges to form a flat, even layer. Push the dough against the edges of the pizza pan and fold it over slightly to make the edges of the crust. Repeat with the second piece of dough.

11. Brush the finished, unbaked crusts lightly with olive oil and proceed with your sauce and toppings.

12. Bake your pizzas for 18 to 25 minutes. Commercial pizza ovens are usually set to about 650°F (380°C), so even at 500°F (260°C) your home oven is only just about hot enough. If you haven't cleaned your oven for a while, this high temperature might cause some smoking when you open the door, so please be careful. Check the pizzas after 18 minutes and turn them around a bit in the oven. They should be done within 25 minutes.

Queenly Quinoa Crackers

These crackers are wheat-free and very tasty.

YIELD: ABOUT 30 CRACKERS

1½ cups (354 mL) unbleached white spelt flour

½ cup (118 mL) quinoa flour

½ teaspoon (2.5 mL) baking soda

1 teaspoon (5 mL) baking powder

1 teaspoon (5 mL) onion or garlic powder, or a mix of the two

½ teaspoon (2.5 mL) salt, plus more to taste

½ teaspoon (2.5 mL) white pepper

¼ cup (59 mL) canola or safflower oil

⅓ cup (79 mL) plus 1 tablespoon (15 mL) water

1. Preheat the oven to 350°F (180°C). Line a baking sheet with parchment paper. Lightly oil the paper.

2. In a bowl, combine all the dry ingredients.

3. In a separate bowl, combine the water and oil. Slowly add the liquid mixture to the dry ingredients with a rubber-bladed spatula. Work the dough with your hands until the dough forms a ball.

4. On a floured surface or lightly oiled parchment paper, roll out the dough into a rectangle about ⅛ inch (.25 cm) thick.

5. Cut the dough into a 30-square grid and place the squares on the prepared baking sheet. Pierce each square with the tines of a fork a few times and lightly salt them.

6. Bake for about 12 minutes and then flip the crackers over. Bake for an additional 2 or 3 minutes. Remove the pan from the oven and let cool.

7. Store in an airtight container.

Rye and Caraway English Muffins

Rye lovers will go for this unique flavor anytime.

YIELD: 8–10 MUFFINS

½ cup (118 mL) warm (110°F [50°C]) water

2½ teaspoons (12.5 mL) active dry yeast

½ teaspoon (2.5 mL) turbinado sugar

1½ cups (354 mL) rye flour (dark is preferred)

1½ cups (354 mL) unbleached white spelt flour or unbleached all-purpose flour

3 tablespoons (45 mL) whole caraway seeds

1 teaspoon (5 mL) baking soda

1 teaspoon (5 mL) salt

½ teaspoon (2.5 mL) freshly ground black pepper

1 pinch mustard powder

2 tablespoons (30 mL) vegan shortening

2 tablespoons (30 mL) dark molasses

½ cup (118 mL) soy or rice beverage

1 teaspoon (5 mL) apple cider vinegar

1 teaspoon (5 mL) maple or agave syrup

2 tablespoons (30 mL) corn meal

1. In a glass measuring cup or a nonreactive bowl, combine the warm water, yeast, and turbinado sugar. Set aside for about 10 minutes to proof.

2. In a large mixing bowl, combine the flours, caraway seeds, baking soda, salt, pepper, and mustard powder.

3. In a saucepan, warm the vegan shortening with the molasses, soy or rice beverage, vinegar, and maple or agave syrup. When everything is uniformly combined, set the pan aside and let it cool to 110°F (50°C) or cooler.

4. Add the yeast mixture to the molasses mixture.

5. Gradually add the liquid ingredients to the dry ingredients, working it into a dough.

6. Transfer the dough to a floured surface and knead for approximately 10 minutes or until the dough is uniform and not sticky.

7. Transfer the dough to an oiled bowl and cover it with a damp, clean kitchen towel. Set the bowl in a warm place to let the dough rise for 1½ to 2 hours.

8. Punch down the dough and then allow it to rest for 30 minutes.

CONTINUED ON PAGE 232

CONTINUED FROM PAGE 231

9. On a floured surface, roll the dough out until it is ½ inch (1 cm) thick.

10. Preheat the oven to 250°F (120°C). Lightly oil a baking sheet and line it with parchment paper.

11. Use a cookie cutter or a drinking glass to cut out the muffins. Place them on the prepared baking sheet and let them rise, uncovered, for another 30 minutes.

12. Heat a large, heavy, oven-safe skillet or griddle (preferably cast iron) over medium-low heat and scatter the corn meal evenly across the pan's surface.

13. Place the risen muffins in the skillet and cook for 3 to 5 minutes on each side.

14. Return the skillet-cooked muffins to the baking sheet and bake them for 15 minutes. Remove them from the oven and let cool. These are delicious just sliced and toasted. If you are feeling really creative, try them with horseradish mustard, sliced ham-style seitan, and cornichons.

Variations

Add 2 tablespoons (30 mL) dill weed with the caraway seeds. These make delightful breadcrumbs, toasted and ground in the food processor.

For rye croutons, toss 1 cup (236 mL) cubed muffin in ½ tablespoon (7.5 mL) oil and bake on a baking sheet at 250°F (120°C) for 20 minutes or until dry and crisp. A little onion powder rubbed in with the oil adds flavor. Rye croutons with a spinach salad? Oh yes.

Savory Autumn Squash Rolls

These can be colorful appetizers to serve at a party or just a delicious accompaniment to a cup of warm soup or a salad. Choose a firm squash, such as acorn, and mix and match other ingredients according to your liking or what is currently in your kitchen.

YIELD: 12 (3-INCH [7.5-CM]) ROUND ROLLS

For the dough:

> 1 cup (236 mL) warm (110°F [50°C]) water
>
> 1 teaspoon (5 mL) turbinado sugar
>
> 2½ teaspoons [12.5 mL]) active dry yeast
>
> 3 tablespoons (45 mL) vegan shortening or margarine, softened
>
> 3 cups (708 mL) unbleached white spelt flour
>
> 1 tablespoon (15 mL) chopped fresh parsley
>
> 1½ teaspoons (7.5 mL) salt

1. Combine the water and turbinado sugar in a Pyrex measuring cup and stir in the yeast. When the mixture foams up, stir in the shortening or margarine and set aside for 10 minutes.

2. In a separate large bowl, combine the flour, parsley, and salt.

3. Make a well in the center of the dry ingredients and pour in the liquid ingredients. Drag the dry flour into the center with a rubber-bladed spatula while continuously turning the bowl.

4. Once most of the flour is incorporated, use your hands to knead the dough in the bowl, turning it over as you go until you achieve a uniform texture. Transfer the dough to a clean, floured surface and knead it for 5 minutes or so, adding flour if it becomes too sticky to work with.

5. Place the dough in an oiled bowl and cover it with a clean kitchen towel. Set it in a warm place to rise for 1 hour.

6. Punch the dough down and let it rise again for about 45 minutes.

CONTINUED ON PAGE 234

CONTINUED FROM PAGE 233

For the filling:

2 medium-sized acorn squash

2 tablespoons (30 mL) olive or canola oil

1½ teaspoons (7.5 mL) salt

1 teaspoon (5 mL) ground white pepper

1 teaspoon (5 mL) grated nutmeg

⅓ cup (79 mL) dried cranberries or cherries

¼ cup (59 mL) chopped and toasted walnuts or pecans

2 tablespoons (30 mL) finely diced shallots

1 tablespoon (15 mL) maple syrup

1½ teaspoons (7.5 mL) ground sage

½ teaspoon (2.5 mL) ground cumin

½ teaspoon (2.5 mL) allspice

1. Preheat the oven to 400°F (200°C).

2. Slice the squash in halves. Slice a flat spot on rounded side to keep the squash balanced while it is sliced-side up. Scoop out the fibers and seeds, and then rub a little oil inside each half. Sprinkle with salt, pepper, and a pinch of the nutmeg. Roast for 45 minutes, or until the flesh is soft enough to pierce with a fork.

3. Set the squash aside to cool, and then remove the peel (it should slide off easily).

4. Chop squash flesh into ½-inch (1-cm) chunks and place in a bowl.

5. Add the remaining filling ingredients and mix well.

To assemble and bake the rolls:

1. Preheat the oven to 350°F (180°C). Line a baking sheet with parchment paper and lightly oil the paper.

2. Punch the dough down again and place the bowl in the freezer for 10 minutes. This will make it easier to roll it out.

3. Dust a clean, flat surface with flour and roll the dough out into a rectangle about ½ inch (1 cm) thick. Cover the rectangle evenly with the filling.

4. Cut the rectangle into 1½-inch (3.5-cm) strips along the short edge. Roll each strip up tightly, using your fingers to keep the filling inside, then pinch the dough together at the end and place the individual rolls about 1 inch (2.5 cm) apart on the baking sheet.

5. Bake for about 25 minutes, until the rolls are golden brown.

6. Remove the rolls from the oven and let cool before serving. They can be covered and refrigerated for a few days. Reheat, if possible, before serving.

Variation

For savory Italian pizza rolls, substitute for the squash filling layers of fresh spinach, marinara sauce, cashew ricotta, fresh basil leaves, or any other pizza toppings you like. Use the same layering and rolling technique described in this recipe. A very simple filling, such as extra virgin olive oil with crushed garlic, fresh basil leaves, and freshly ground black pepper, is stellar.

Spelt English Muffins

These are so good that you may want to bake enough for a whole week. They keep nicely in the refrigerator and can be sliced and toasted for breakfast or used as the base for Vegan Benedict (page 105). Leftover muffins make great garlic bread rounds or croutons.

YIELD: 8–10 MUFFINS

2½ teaspoons (12.5 mL) active dry yeast

2 teaspoons (10 mL) plus 1 pinch turbinado sugar

1 cup (236 mL) warm (110°F [50°C]) water

6 cups (1.4 mL) unbleached white spelt flour, divided

1½ teaspoons (7.5 mL) salt

1 teaspoon (5 mL) ground white pepper

1 cup (236 mL) soy or rice beverage

1 teaspoon (5 mL) apple cider vinegar or fresh lemon juice

¼ cup (59 mL) vegan shortening, melted

1. Combine the yeast, a pinch of the turbinado sugar, and the warm water in a cup or small bowl and let stand until foamy for at least 10 minutes.

2. In a large bowl, combine 3 cups (708 mL) of the flour, the salt, and the white pepper.

3. Heat the soy or rice beverage in a saucepan until just warm and add the remaining sugar and the apple cider vinegar or lemon juice.

4. In a large bowl, combine the melted shortening, the soy or rice beverage mixture, the yeast mixture, and the spelt flour mixture. Beat until smooth, and then add the remaining 3 cups (708 mL) flour gradually, mixing thoroughly after each addition with a wooden spoon or plastic spatula.

5. With your hands, work the dough in the bowl until all the ingredients are thoroughly blended. Transfer the dough to a floured surface and knead for 10 minutes.

6. Form the dough into a ball, place it in a lightly oiled bowl, and cover. Let it rise until doubled in bulk, about 45 minutes to 1 hour.

7. Punch the dough down and then roll it out on a floured surface into a rectangle about ½ inch (1 cm) thick. Cut out circles about 6 to 8 inches (15 to 20 cm) in diameter (a 3-inch [7.5 cm] diameter can with both ends cut out works well for cutting the circles) and place the circles on a nonstick surface (such as a baking sheet) in a warm place. Let rise again for about 45 minutes.

8. Preheat the oven to 250°F (120°C). Line a baking sheet with parchment paper.

9. Heat a large, heavy skillet (cast iron works best here) over medium-low and lightly oil it with about 2 teaspoons (10 mL) canola oil. Brown the muffins a few at a time, flipping them once until they are just browned, then transfer them to the prepared baking sheet.

10. Bake the muffins for about 30 minutes. Remove them from the oven and serve, or let them cool completely and store them in the refrigerator or freezer for later use. To toast them, simply slice horizontally in half beforehand.

Variations

Add 2 tablespoons (30 mL) finely chopped fresh rosemary and 1 tablespoon (15 mL) finely diced fresh lemon zest to the flour before making the dough. Or try a Mexican variation by adding 2 tablespoons (30 mL) achiote to warm rice beverage and ½ cup (118 mL) chopped cilantro to the flour.

Sunny O'Day Crackers

Crackers fresh from the oven are something special for your family or guests. They are simple and quick to prepare, needing no yeast or rising time.

YIELD: ABOUT 30 CRACKERS

> 2 cups (473 mL) unbleached white spelt flour
>
> ½ cup (118 mL) chopped raw sunflower seeds
>
> 4 tablespoons (60 mL) quinoa flour (optional)
>
> 1 tablespoon (15 mL) onion powder
>
> 2 teaspoons (10 mL) garlic powder
>
> 2 teaspoons (10 mL) paprika
>
> 2 teaspoons (10 mL) salt, plus more to taste
>
> 1½ teaspoons (7.5 mL) baking soda
>
> 1 teaspoon (5 mL) freshly ground black pepper, plus more to taste
>
> 2 teaspoons (10 mL) turmeric
>
> ⅓ cup (79 mL) water
>
> 3 teaspoons (15 mL) turbinado sugar or 2 teaspoons (10 mL) raw agave syrup
>
> ⅓ cup (79 mL) safflower or olive oil
>
> Vegetable broth powder, to taste (optional)

1. Preheat the oven to 350°F (180°C). Line a baking sheet with parchment paper.

2. In a bowl, combine the first ten ingredients and stir well.

3. In a large measuring cup, combine the remaining ingredients. Slowly add the liquid ingredients to the dry ingredients until you achieve a dough that is flexible but still a little dry. If the dough is sticky, you may add more flour, but try not to add liquid.

4. On a clean surface, knead the dough 10 times and then divide it into 2 parts. Set one half aside.

5. Roll out half of the dough into a large rectangle until you have made the dough as thin as you possibly can without tearing it. Slice in rows, lengthwise then crosswise, to make individual crackers about 2½ inches (6 cm) square.

6. Arrange squares on the prepared baking sheet. Pierce the squares three times each with the tines of a fork. Sprinkle with salt, pepper, or vegetable broth powder. Repeat with the other dough half.

7. Bake for 7 minutes, then flip and bake for another 7 minutes. For crisper crackers, bake 2 to 3 minutes longer.

Vegan Burger Buns or Dinner Rolls

YIELD: 12 (5-INCH [11-CM]) BURGER BUNS OR 16 (3-INCH [5-CM]) DINNER ROLLS

3 tablespoons (45 mL) plus 1 pinch turbinado sugar

½ cup (118 mL) warm (110°F [50°C]) water (to dissolve the yeast)

1½ tablespoons (22 mL) active dry yeast

5 cups (1.3 L) unbleached white spelt flour

2 teaspoons (5 mL) salt

2 cups (473 mL) vegetable stock (preferred) or water

1½ (22 mL) tablespoons onion powder

⅓ cup (59 mL) canola or safflower oil

¼ cup (59 mL) sesame or poppy seeds, to top (optional)

1. In a small bowl or measuring cup, combine the ½ (118 mL) cup warm water with the active dry yeast and a pinch of sugar.

2. In a large, nonreactive bowl, combine the flour, the remaining sugar, and the salt.

3. Combine the yeast mixture with 2 cups (473 mL) of vegetable stock or water and the canola or safflower oil. Stir to blend.

4. Add the liquid ingredients to the dry ingredients and use a wooden spoon or plastic spatula to work them slowly together until a soft dough forms.

5. Transfer the dough to a floured surface and knead for 10 minutes, adding flour in small amounts if necessary to keep the dough from sticking. This dough is softer and moister than what you might be used to.

6. Form the dough into a ball and place it into a lightly oiled bowl. Cover the bowl and set it in a warm place until it has doubled in size, about 1 hour.

7. Preheat the oven to 400°F (200°C). Line two large baking sheets with parchment paper.

8. Punch the dough down and transfer it to a lightly floured surface. Divide the dough into 12 equal portions (or 16, if you want smaller rolls).

9. Roll the first piece of dough into a ball using your hand and the floured surface. Think of your fingers as a spherical grid surrounding the roll as you form it. The very bottom of the dough piece should stick just a little to your surface. Repeat with the remaining dough. Place the finished rolls on the prepared baking sheets. At this point you may top the buns with sesame or poppy seeds and pat them into the surface.

10. Place the sheets in a warm place and let the buns rise again for another 30 to 45 minutes. Bake 12 to 16 minutes or until golden brown. Remove from the oven and serve as is for dinner rolls. Or let them cool completely, slice them in half, and use them as buns for your favorite vegan burger.

Variation

Substitute 1 cup (236 mL) water mixed with 1 cup (236 mL) V-8 or other vegetable juice for the water. This will produce pale orange rolls with a delicate vegetable flavor.

Veganopolis Croutons

What shall we do with the stale bread? (Qu'est ce qu'on fait du pain rassis)?

What shall we do with the stale bread? (Qu'est ce qu'on fait du pain rassis?)

What shall we do with the stale bread? (Qu'est ce qu'on fait du pain rassis?)

Croutons, croutons, croutons! (Croûtons, croûtons, croûtons!)

—Traditional 18th century French pirate cook sea chant, arranged by the author

A low-temperature oven will dry out your croutons thoroughly while they are browning. If you cook them at a high temperature, they may still be moist inside and will not be crisp when you are ready to serve them. Croutons that have lost their crispness can sometimes be brought back to life by drying them out again in a warm oven. If they are not crisp and tasty, don't serve them. The literal English translation of the word baguette *is "wand," and a good French baguette is indeed magic.*

YIELD: 2 CUPS (473 ML)

> 1 day-old baguette, cut into 1-inch (2.5-cm) cubes (pay attention when cutting dry baguette so as not to cut yourself)
>
> Juice of 2 fresh lemons
>
> ⅓ cup (79 mL) olive oil
>
> 1 tablespoon (15 mL) freshly ground black pepper
>
> 3 tablespoons (45 mL) finely chopped fresh parsley
>
> 1 tablespoon (15 mL) spiced roasted garlic pepper or garlic powder
>
> 2 teaspoons (10 mL) salt

1. Preheat the oven to 250°F (120°C). Line a baking sheet with parchment paper.

2. Place the baguette cubes in a large bowl and add the lemon juice, olive oil, black pepper, parsley, garlic pepper or powder, and salt. Mix everything well with your hands.

3. Spread the croutons out on the prepared baking sheet. Bake until golden brown and crisp, about 40 minutes, stirring and turning them over a few times as they bake.

4. Take a few finished croutons out to your guests while they are still warm and offer them as appetizers.

Vegan Pie Crust

Here's a quick vegan crust recipe that works every time. You can also try the Freckled Flax Crust (page 225) for a more visually interesting result.

YIELD: 1 DOUBLE CRUST

> **2 cups (473 mL) unbleached white spelt flour**
>
> **2 teaspoons (10 mL) salt**
>
> **1 teaspoon (5 mL) turbinado sugar**
>
> **¾ cup (178 mL) light olive oil or canola oil, placed in the freezer for 30 minutes**
>
> **¼ cup (59 mL) ice water**

1. In a large bowl, combine the dry ingredients and make a well in the center.

2. Mix the oil and water and pour this mixture into the well.

3. With a flat-blade flexible rubber spatula, drag the flour into the well, rotating the bowl and dragging more flour in as you turn it.

4. Once the dough is partially combined, mix with your hands until you achieve a uniform dough. If the dough is too moist, add a little more flour.

5. Form the dough into a ball and let rest while you prepare the filling.

Double Evil Brownies

Our customers gave these brownies their moniker because they said they couldn't refrain from eating them. They are a good evil, with a deep cocoa flavor and a pound of tofu blended in. The recipe is a tad less sweet than the usual brownie recipe, which lets the rich cocoa shine through. If you prefer brownies to be very sweet, add a few more tablespoons of sugar or perhaps a few tablespoons of agave.

YIELD: 12 BROWNIES

3 cups (708 mL) unbleached white spelt flour

1½ teaspoons (7.5 mL) baking powder

½ teaspoon (2.5 mL) baking soda

1 teaspoon (5 mL) salt

¾ cup (178 mL) unsweetened cocoa powder

10 ounces (280 g) firm tofu, broken into chunks

1¾ cups (420 mL) turbinado sugar

¾ cup (180 mL) canola oil

1 cup (236 mL) rice or soy beverage

1 tablespoon (15 mL) pure vanilla extract

2 tablespoons (30 mL) water

⅔ cup (158 mL) vegan chocolate chips (optional)

⅔ cup (158 mL) chopped walnuts (optional)

⅔ cup (158 mL) shredded coconut (optional)

Confectioners' sugar, for dusting (optional)

1. Preheat oven to 350°F (180°C). Line a 9 × 13–inch (22½ × 32½–cm) baking pan with parchment paper and oil the paper and the sides of the pan.

2. In a bowl, blend the flour, baking powder, baking soda, salt, and cocoa powder until well mixed.

3. In a separate bowl, combine the tofu, turbinado sugar, rice or soy beverage, vanilla extract, and water. Stir to combine.

4. Slowly add the wet ingredients to the dry, blending with a hand mixer until the mixture is smooth.

5. With a rubber spatula, blend in any of the optional ingredients you wish to use.

6. Pour the mixture into the prepared baking pan. If you like, decorate the top with additional chocolate chips, nuts, or whatever strikes your fancy.

7. Bake for 25 minutes and remove from the oven. Test for doneness by inserting a thin blade or toothpick into the center and removing it. If it comes out dry, the brownies are done. If not, return them to the oven and bake for a few more minutes.

8. Let cool and slice into serving size portions. If you like, dust the tops with confectioners' sugar before serving.

KooKoo Snickers Cookies

Our little black cat is named Snicky. When he goes completely nuts, we call him KooKoo Snickers. These cookies are among our favorites.

YIELD: 10 COOKIES

> 3 cups (708 mL) unbleached white spelt flour
>
> 1½ teaspoons (7.5 mL) baking powder
>
> 1 teaspoon (5 mL) baking soda
>
> 1 teaspoon (5 mL) salt
>
> 4 teaspoons (20 mL) ground cinnamon, divided
>
> ½ teaspoon (2.5 mL) ground nutmeg
>
> 12 ounces (336 g) vegan margarine, at room temperature
>
> ⅓ cup (80 mL) canola, safflower, or coconut oil
>
> 1⅔ cups (394 mL) plus 4 tablespoons (60 mL) turbinado sugar, divided
>
> 1 tablespoon (15 mL) maple or agave syrup
>
> 1 tablespoon (15 mL) pure vanilla extract
>
> 2 tablespoons (30 mL) water

1. Preheat oven to 350°F (180°C). Line two baking sheets with parchment paper.

2. In a bowl, combine the flour, baking powder, baking soda, salt, 1 teaspoon (5 mL) of the cinnamon, and the nutmeg and mix well. In a separate large bowl, combine the margarine, the oil, 1⅔ cup (394 mL) of the sugar, the maple or agave syrup, the vanilla extract, and the water with a hand mixer until softened and well blended.

3. Using the hand mixer, add the dry ingredients about ½ cup (118 mL) at a time to the wet ingredients, mixing after each addition, until well combined.

4. Cover the finished dough and chill it in the freezer for 10 minutes.

5. Form the dough into 10 equal-sized balls, and then flatten the balls into discs. Fill a small bowl with water. In a second small bowl, combine the remaining sugar and cinnamon. Dip the top of each cookie in the water, then the cinnamon-sugar mixture. Place the on the prepared baking sheets. If you wish, use the tip of a very sharp knife to score a checkerboard design into the top of each cookie.

6. Bake for 12 minutes and check for doneness by lifting the edge of one cookie from the pan with a small spatula and checking the underside. If the cookie is golden brown and firm, it is done. Bake an additional 4 to 5 minutes, if necessary. Remove the pans from the oven and transfer the cookies to a cool surface.

Lavender Cookies

In fields where lavender is grown, the visual and olfactory sensations are remarkable. Acting on the claim that essential lavender acts as a calming agent on the human nervous system, lorry drivers in a Scottish company were issued bouquets of lavender to place in their cabs. The results seemed to be happier drivers. (In rural Scotland, traffic can become snarled by cars, trucks, and even herds of sheep wandering onto the roads.)

YIELD: 10 COOKIES

1½ cups (354 mL) water

1 cup (236 mL) dried culinary lavender flowers

3 cups (708 mL) unbleached white spelt flour

1½ teaspoons (7.5 mL) baking powder

1 teaspoon (5 mL) baking soda

1 teaspoon (5 mL) salt

12 ounces (336 g) vegan margarine, at room temperature

1⅔ cups (394 mL) turbinado sugar

2 teaspoons (10 mL) pure vanilla extract

2 teaspoons (10 mL) pure lemon oil

1 tablespoon (15 mL) canola, safflower, or coconut oil

1 tablespoon (15 mL) agave syrup

1. In a small saucepan, bring the water to a boil. Remove the pan from the heat and stir in the lavender flowers. Let steep while you prepare the rest of the ingredients.

2. Preheat the oven to 350°F (180°C). Line two baking sheets with parchment paper.

3. In a medium bowl, combine the flour, baking powder, baking soda, and salt. Mix well.

4. In a large bowl, combine the vegan margarine, turbinado sugar, vanilla extract, lemon oil, vegetable oil, and agave syrup.

5. Strain the lavender flowers out of the water. With your fingers, press as much liquid out of them as possible. Add 3 tablespoons (45 mL) of the flowers to the liquid mixture and stir well.

6. Add the dry ingredients to the wet, ½ cup (118 mL) at a time, blending with a hand mixer after each addition until you have incorporated all of the dry ingredients and achieved a cookie dough. Cover and chill the dough in the freezer for 10 minutes.

7. Divide the dough into 10 evenly sized balls, flatten the balls into discs, and place them on the prepared baking sheets.

8. Bake for 12 minutes and check for doneness. The cookies should be just lightly browned around the edges. Remove from the oven and use a spatula to transfer the cookies to a cool surface.

Super Rainbow Oatmeal Cookies

YIELD: 12 COOKIES

1½ cups (354 mL) quick-cooking oats

1½ cups (354 mL) unbleached white spelt flour

1 teaspoon (5 mL) salt

1½ teaspoons (7.5 mL) baking powder

½ teaspoon (2.5 mL) baking soda

1 teaspoon (5 mL) ground cinnamon

½ cup (118 mL) dried currants or raisins

½ cup (118 mL) unsweetened shredded coconut

½ cup (118 mL) vegan margarine, softened

2 tablespoons (30 mL) water

2 teaspoons (10 mL) pure vanilla extract

½ ripe banana

1 cup (236 mL) turbinado sugar

2 tablespoons (30 mL) maple or agave syrup

1. Preheat the oven to 350°F (180°C). Line two baking sheets with parchment paper and lightly oil the paper.

2. In a medium bowl, combine the first 8 ingredients.

3. In a large bowl, use a rubber spatula to combine the remaining ingredients until they are well blended and smooth.

4. Using a hand mixer, slowly blend the dry ingredients into the wet ingredients until they are fully mixed.

5. Using a spoon or a 3-ounce (84-mL) ice cream scooper, scoop the cookie dough onto the prepared baking sheets.

6. Bake for 12 to 15 minutes. Remove the from oven and let cool for 30 minutes before removing from the sheets. Store in a tightly covered container in a cool place.

Orange Cashew Cookies

These got rave reviews the night George invented them.

YIELD: 12 COOKIES

> 3 cups (708 mL) unbleached white spelt flour
>
> 1½ teaspoons (7.5 mL) baking powder
>
> ½ teaspoon (2.5 mL) baking soda
>
> 1 teaspoon (5 mL) salt
>
> ½ cup (118 mL) vegan margarine, softened
>
> 1 cup (236 mL) turbinado sugar
>
> 2 teaspoons (10 mL) pure orange oil
>
> 1 teaspoon (5 mL) pure vanilla extract
>
> 2 tablespoons (30 mL) water
>
> 1 tablespoon (15 mL) maple or agave syrup
>
> ¾ cup (177 mL) toasted unsalted cashew pieces, chopped

1. Preheat the oven to 350°F (180°C). Line two baking sheets with parchment paper and lightly oil the paper.

2. In a medium bowl, combine the flour, baking powder, baking soda, and salt.

3. In a large bowl, use a rubber spatula to combine the margarine, turbinado sugar, orange oil, vanilla extract, water, and maple or agave syrup until they are well blended and smooth.

4. Using a hand mixer, slowly blend the dry ingredients into the wet ingredients until they are fully mixed.

5. Fold ½ cup (118 mL) of the cashew pieces into the dough.

6. Using a spoon or a 3-ounce (84-mL) ice cream scooper, scoop the cookie dough onto the prepared baking sheets. Decorate the top of each cookie with the remaining ¼ cup (59 mL) cashew pieces.

7. Bake for 12 to 15 minutes. Remove the cookies from the oven and let cool for 30 minutes before removing from the sheets. Store in a tightly covered container in a cool place.

Index

Acknowledgments

The authors would like to express their gratitude to everyone who has encouraged them in the completion of this book. We thank our friends and family, our customers from all parts of the planet, and all who share our deep love for this radiant universe we share.

We send special thanks to all the chefs and teachers that we have worked with. We hope that you share our pride and joy in what we are creating for the modern table.

We also give sincere thanks to all the dedicated and tireless people who have worked as staff with us over the years in different kitchens and different environments, many of whom helped us develop as chefs.

A very special thank you goes out to Isabel, Santos, and Jorge for your invaluable work. For Michael VanPelt and Mickey Deagle, we give heartfelt thanks for all of your hard work in helping us to organize ourselves in the digital domain.

To Doug Seibold, Perrin Davis, and the hardworking staff at Agate Publishing, we thank you for believing in our work, for helping us through the twists and turns of the manuscript, and for allowing us the opportunity to get this book to the people. For listening to our ideas, for clarifying our vision, and especially for your patience and tolerance, we are very grateful.

We also give a special thank you to our friend Michael Pocius, whose skill and taste in photography is apparent here.

And to our predecessors in history, who paved the way for modern vegans—from Pythagoras to the present—we raise our eyes in thanks to you, for transmitting the wisdom which lights our way today.

About the Authors

David Stowell and George Black are professional vegan chefs with a twenty-two-year-long commitment to creating accessible, cruelty-free cuisine for all. They operated the popular Veganopolis Cafeteria in Portland, Oregon.